AF538858

CRITICAL RESPONSES TO ANITA DESAI

VOLUME - I

EDITED BY
SHUBHA TIWARI

PUBLISHERS & DISTRIBUTORS (P) LTD

Published by

ATLANTIC

PUBLISHERS & DISTRIBUTORS (P) LTD

7/22, Ansari Road, Darya Ganj,
New Delhi-110002
Phones : +91-11-40775252, 23273880, 23275880, 23280451
Fax : +91-11-23285873
Web : www.atlanticbooks.com
E-mail : orders@atlanticbooks.com

Branch Office
5, Nallathambi Street, Wallajah Road,
Chennai-600002
Phones : +91-44-64611085, 32413319
E-mail : chennai@atlanticbooks.com

Printed in India at Glorious Printers, A-13, D.S.I.D.C., Jhilmil Industrial Area, Delhi-110095

Preface

The meaning of an author changes with the passage of time. Shakespeare with post-colonial bombardment has become a racist and so it is with Lamb. We want to see ourselves in a work of literature. Self-centred approach and its appetite in writers as well as readers are amazingly high. We can lead this to a brilliant psychoanalytical discussion on insatiable self. But we will not do so. Instead, let us go to Anita Desai who has given many of us the satisfaction of readers' catharsis. With changing decades, we have found newer reflections of ourselves and newer meanings of our existence in the novels of this novelist. Without naming, let me make a sweeping comment that many novelists who began with Desai have exhausted by now. Since 1963, when Maya appeared on the scene, the *maya* of Desai's world has kept the readers hooked. So much for the test of time! Maya, Monisha, Nirode, Amla, Bim, Tara, Deven, Sita and others have come closer to us than when they were originally born. Readers have discovered newer bonds with this gallery.

The present collection presents many perspectives on the works of Desai. In the first paper, I have tried to catch the spirit of Desai's works. The totality of the thing has been aimed at even if it is an impossible task. It is my own way of making sense out of this mind-boggling mass of literature. It is an effort to see the creative mind at work. It is also an effort to see what the writer herself might not have seen her instincts, that frame of mind that has shaped these novels. The second paper by Mallikarjun Patil is a comment basically on three novels of Desai, namely, *Cry, the Peacock, Voices in the City,* and *Where Shall We Go This Summer*? The next contribution from O.P. Budholia is on *Journey to Ithaca.* It is an effort at explaining the psychological concerns in this novel. It describes Sophie's actual journey as well as her mental progress. Next comes a paper on *Cry, the Peacock.* It is interesting to note that the first novel of Anita Desai continues to enjoy a prime position for critics and holds their interest. The paper, somewhat circumscribing women's area of happiness, nevertheless, gives insight into heightened sensitivity and thereby intensified, agonized self of the protagonist, Maya. In a mega paper, in the name of feminine sensibility, S.D. Sharma gives or better, invents, curious patterns, keeping CCV (Crisis of Conscience and Values) at the centre. It is, as I said, a mega paper, covering many strayed subjects, of which feminine sensibility in only one. Basavaraj Naikar's paper on marital disharmony makes a good reading. The topic is valid because failed marriages are a repeated thing in Desai's works. In clear-cut prose, we have an equally convincing discussion.

Comparative studies are worth their effort. Anita Desai, in particular, constantly, reminds the reader of other great writers. I myself remember being fixed by the character of Raka and that of Pearl in *The Scarlet Letter* by Nathaniel Hawthorne. S.N. Vikram Raj Urs compares two novels, one by Desai, *Where Shall We Go This Summer?* and Atwood's *Surfacing*. The similarities are striking; however, the dissimilarities are glaring too. Asha Choubey tries to give a feminist perspective to *Fasting, Feasting.* All the female characters and their helplessness have been studied in this paper. Basavaraj Naikar's paper on *Diamond Dust* is important because much work has not been done on Desai's short fiction. We can see that these short stories are miniatures of novels. The same glimpses have been captured in fewer words. Ramesh Kumar Gupta's paper on a housewife's trauma in *Fire on the Mountain* tries to portray Nanda's loneliness and state of extreme subjectivity. J.P. Tripathi's paper on *Fasting, Feasting* focuses on lack of focus in this novel. With widened horizon, what we have in this novel according to Tripathi is more wide and spectacular and less sharp and less pointed. Alienation in *Cry, the Peacock,* a traditional and accepted theme has been discussed by B.D. Pandey. He has tried to go into the reasons of Maya's alienated self. Then comes an important paper by Rajeshwar Mittapalli where he has successfully tried a Freudian exposition of Maya's personality. Maya's condition is indeed an expression of her suppressed urges. I have been personally impressed by Rama Kundu's paper on the dimension of space in Desai's *Fire on the Mountain.* It is with such papers that we can free this author from biased reading. Space, landscape, locale and settings are an integral part of Desai's technique and they have been skilfully handled here. In her paper, Asha Susan Jacob connects the theme of alienation in *Bye-Bye, Blackbird* to Christian theme of original separation when God ousted Adam and Eve from paradise. In her next paper Jacob deals with quest motif in *Journey to Ithaca.* The quest here is multi layered, she points out. Jenni Valjento has taken up the interconnectedness of the personalities of Bim and Tara in *Clear Light of Day.* Hariom Prasad's paper on *Where Shall We Go This Summer?* is a critique on existentialist philosophy as reflected in this Novel. Sita's state of mind is such that she fails to see any sense in life. S.P. Swain's paper on *Cry, the Peacock* depicts the polarized, estranged selves of Gautama and Maya. The argument, as the reader will see, comes very close to what Mittapalli has said earlier. It only strengthens the thesis that Gautama's murder is a kind of wish fulfilment for Maya. The last paper in the first Volume compares the short stories of Anita Desai and a less known writer Margaret Chatterjee. The enthusiasm of the paper writer for Chatterjee and his effort to bring credit and recognition to this author is notable.

Thus, this Volume is a serious effort to see Desai's fiction in new and newer light. I, as editor, feel indebted to Dr K.R. Gupta, Chairman, Atlantic Publishers and Distributors for providing the opportunity to me. The boost in publishing critical material in English and our renewed focus on Indian writers is a tremendous incentive for upcoming critics.

SHUBHA TIWARI

Contents

VOLUME II

1

DIMENSIONS OF ANITA DESAI'S FICTION

SHUBHA TIWARI

In *In Custody*, Anita Desai writes, 'I know your kind of jackals from the so-called universities that are really asylums for failures, trained to feed upon our (creative writers) carcasses' (118). The meaning is clear that professors chew and eat literary productions. Her exasperation may be taken as a response to distortion of literary texts by the cannibalistic instincts of the Professors. So, let us begin with the question, 'Why do we, the teacher-critics, respond to literary texts?' Apart from the very obvious and ordinary reason of getting published, I feel, there is something more in us that prods us on and on to analyze literary works. What is it? The pleasure of understanding the hidden meanings of a literary work is same as the pleasure of understanding life—something that sets us apart from others. It is an assertion of our intellectual selves that prods us on. We, as teacher-critics, want the satisfaction of just one sentence, 'I know,' implying thereby that we know better than others. Desai has questioned the legitimacy of this joy of rationally peeling off a literary work. Even if we grant this joy some validity, stressing the inevitable response mechanism of human beings, their cause and effect existence, what we forget happily is immense burden of responsibilities that this joy brings. Sitting apart, pronouncing judgments is indeed very self-complementary. It is true that we write out of self-love, and self-endorsement, nevertheless, what we write is, sometimes read by others, mostly by students, and researchers. We cannot escape the fact that we are mind-makers, even if in very small measures. The trouble with today's English critical scenario in India is the lack of self-consciousness on the part of the teacher-critic. It also results in lack of adequate efforts. It further results in poor standards. Writing critical pieces for self-satisfaction is perfectly okay. But at the same time, an acute awareness of the role we are performing (if, any) is acutely needed. In this context, the not so complementary comment of Anita Desai can be accepted.

Anita Desai, I feel, is one of the most misread novelists. Her being a woman has worked as a deterrent in her correct and accurate estimation as a novelist. But then, this is nothing new—this keeps happening with so many women in so many fields! The male teacher-critic, while assessing a woman, will not let Desai go out of feminine sensibility. And many (less aware?) female teacher-critics follow suit. Skeptical, cynical of the lesser gender's capabilities, the big brothers, with their circus-watching approach to feminine psyche, have imprisoned this genius in terms of 'female, feminine, feminist' syndrome, foolishly ignoring the fact that whatever is feminine is at once human and universal. Tragically severed from their own feminine impulses, their quiet, resting, accepting selves, they have distorted the vision of this gifted novelist. Such injustice has not been meted out to gifted male novelists like Amitav Ghosh, Vikram Seth, and others; their works have been analyzed in totality. Such is the ghastliness of gender discrimination!

Anita Desai, to my mind, is an astonishingly 'male-female complex' free artist. While our attention rains on Maya, Monisha, Sita, and Nanda, poor Deven, Baumgarter and Mattoe are put aside. *Baumgartner's Bombay* and *In Custody* are focally male-psyche centred novels while *Fasting, Feasting,* and *Journey to Ithaca* mainly concentrate on human aching for the unattainable. The lack of recognition of universality is definitely our failure as teacher-critics and not Desai's. Desai writes on the life of the mind, nothing less, nothing more. And the mind does not have a sex. All human being need love, acceptance, understanding, belonging, success, recognition and satisfying patterns in life. It is the interior locales of the mind, be they normal, neurotic or both have been sketched out for us. Here is a novelist almost totally free from the caging impact of body awareness. Desai lives in her mind and not body. Her labeling, therefore, as a woman/female etc. novelist is an utter failure on the part of teacher-critics.

Here is a thoroughly cultivated human mind, creating a fictional world based on individual, and therefore universal patterns. Here we may emphasize that the terms 'universal' and 'individual' are not antonyms; they are complementary. The individual graduates to the universal and *vice versa*. Moreover, the individual only authenticates the universal and again, *vice versa*. In fact, to accommodate the experiences of a woman, who is basically a human being, within the human centred discourse is one of the most challenging challenges before us. Unfortunately, many of us are failing. This tormenting *objectification, commodification, and itemization* of the female gender aborts the creation of a fruitful, interactive, collaborative, unarmed, relaxed, and accepting intellectual environment.

Anita Desai is exciting on many accounts. Her growth as a novelist is there for all to see. Beginning, as she did, with agonizing psychological traumas, imbedded deep within human psyche, she has travelled to revealing use of locales, animal imagery, human thirst for quest, as also the mundane humdrum of life. Her novels are always in a state of 'becoming'; they never 'become.' It is the process, the journey, the expectation, and the *halfness* that mark her creations. There is never a satisfying end. The journey is never complete. There is no solace, and complete union at the end of her novels. Reconciliation, compromise, helpless resignation may be there but no gratifying or complete experience is offered to the reader. This is our reward, our net gain in reading this novelist. The wanderer in us is provoked. Restlessness is celebrated. Alienation is highlighted. Anita Desai comes very close to present day dilemma of human existence. Critics often compare her alienation theme to 'detached action' as propagated in *Bhagwat Gita*. I beg to differ. While the theory of detached action offers the final cushion that God will look into distribution of rewards, there is no such soothing effect in Desai; no poetic justice, so to say. Her progress has been restricted (from Maya's yearning for conjugal happiness) to Mattoe's longing for self-realization. But that actualization itself never gets truly conveyed to the reader. It is the sweating on the way, the road itself that is stressed. This is the perpetual state of 'becoming' in the novels of Anita Desai. There is joy of emptiness as in the case of Nanda, fulfilment of alienation as it happens with Mattoe and completion of loneliness as it is with Maya. Alienation, in a way, has become a precondition of art. A very contended fellow will not write novels. No longing, no aching, no sorrow, then there is no art as well. The very concept of fulfilment, content, union, merging of selves has been questioned, for example, in Mamapapa phenomenon in *Fasting, Feasting.* The couple is not referred separately. They are one and yet this oneness is ever so nauseating. Anita Desai's vision demands separation of selves, not dissolution. Her apparent spiritual concerns have no conviction. She may choose any topic—immigration (Adi, Dev, Sara, Baumgartner), alienation (Maya), spiritual hunger (Mattoe, Sophie, the Mother), artistic desires (Deven), restricting family routine (Sita, Nanda), parental apathy (Mamapapa), identity formation (Bim, Tara), so on and so forth but the core of the matter always remains the incomplete, yearning, anguished, sour human heart. This frame of mind never leaves Anita Desai. Just as Amitav Ghosh revolves around colonization and related themes, Shashi Deshpande around oppression of the female protagonists, Anita Desai is rooted in pining, panting, and craving. The remarkable thing is that she does not visualize an end or even an aim to this constant, perpetual languishing. It is we, the teacher-critics who are blatantly naming the desires of her protagonists; she herself does not do so. That is to say that if Mamapapa leave apathy, will Uma's lot improve? or if Maya finds reciprocity from Gautama, will her end change? etc. My answer is a definite 'no.' If not for one reason, the characters of Anita Desai will hanker for something else because the creator herself does not conceive any uni-dimensional, solvable predicament. Anita Desai sees this world and its people forever longing for something that cannot be achieved.

For me, the feel that a novelist provides is very important. When we look at all the works of a novelist, we are able to identify the peculiar smell, the unique texture of that novelist's world. Anita Desai's world is made up of seemingly contradictory forces. On one hand, we have deep psychological exposition as is harped upon by so many of us. But at the same time, there is something very raw, primitive and pagan about this world. The best part is Desai's indifference to institutionalized religion. She believes in forces, natural symbols, hidden, dangerous push of Nature but she hardly has any respect for your rituals, and agencies of formal, disciplining so-called religion. This is absolutely adorable about Desai's world. It also creates a fabric where psychological truths are more near untamed Nature rather than the civilized world. Nothing can be more true. With her instinct, Desai has developed a vision where human beings have been conceived as part of the larger organic life; hence the deep significance of locales in her novels. What is Nanda without Kausali hills? or Maya without the wild cry of the peacocks. Again and again we encounter animal imagery in the works of Desai. Civilized world, manicured houses, cramped, urban surroundings, luxury or poverty—any, just any sign of human-made vista is antagonistically inclined for Desai and her characters. The rush, the anxiety, the urgent call of the pagan powers is overpowering; it affects us immediately and intensely. This can be taken as one of the fundamental reasons of the unwavering appeal of this novelist. Although the mystery of literary creations and their worth can never be fully measured but we can always try.

Desai defies definitions. The unexpected, unfulfilling turn of events in her novels has been her speciality right from the beginning. Maya's act of murder is the first example of this trend. Here is a clear cut case of clash between civilized, worldly-wise, practical Gautama and instinctive, unpredictable Maya. The polarities between the two temperaments have further been accentuated by the age difference between the duo. Gautama is a friend of Maya's father. The author does not indulge in value judgments. Here is a case with no prelude, no epilogue, no moralizing—a slice of life, open for dissection. Gautama's job, his affluence, his unfeeling, intellectual family, his boring self-confidence—all enforce the forces that weaken the innate human spirit. On the other hand, Maya's umbilical love for her father, her albino-astrologer fixation, her uneasy reaching out to moon, stars, scary Kathakali dancers—all present a world of nonverbal, true emotions. So many critics type Maya as neurotic, psychopathic etc. indirectly telling us that the breakdown of marriage was due to Maya's incurable condition and not because of Gautama's dreary self. It is forgotten that psychic realities are also realities. In simple terms when unfulfilled desires accumulate unbearably, the cover of normalcy is broken and the subconscious takes charge of the conscious. Utterings, deeds and behaviour of this state are a reflection of the unrealized cravings. Now, anyone can see that the root of this dysfunctional behaviour lies with frustrating life experiences rather than with the patient her/himself. Maya and Gautama's instance is that of irreconcilable incompatibility.

Voices in the City is even more chaotic than *Cry, the Peacock*. The concept is that of conflicting, confusing, muddling sounds of a city. Calcutta is portrayed as a corrupting, contaminating influence. It stands for modern, concrete jungles so far away, and so inimical to elemental life. The filth on the streets has gone onto the minds of the inhabitants. The congestion has jammed the very thinking of its people. Nirode, Monisha, Amla, and Dharma are mimic miniatures of what they could have been. They are the personifications of murdered potentialities. Nature versus so-called culture dimension is too glaring to be missed. But the biggest casualty of the stifling urbanity is the love of parents for their children. 'The old she cannibal' that Nirode's mother is called, she typifies a whole range of upcoming characters from Desai's pen who do not feel unconditional love for their kids. Desai has totally freed her women from the emotional responsibility of motherhood. There is hardly any description about the joy of becoming a mother. Sita is frightened at the prospect of yet another birth. Nanda has no loving memory of her years of performing duties as a mother. Those years are an unpleasant bloat on her memory. Mama in *Fasting, Feasting* is again a mother devoid of motherly softness. Here Anita Desai shows direct affinity with latest trends in sociological research in India. These researchers emphasize that grandiose, larger than life, all pervading mother-consciousness in Indian mind where selfless love, sacrifice, and negation of self are attributed to women is a cunning societal construct to limit and control women. This has been going on for centuries. With this burdening of sickening ideals, the innate self of the woman, which is as pleasure-seeking, as wanton, as selfish, as loving and caring as men, has been over ruled. Ashis Nandy writes, 'The most socially valued attributes of the male [...] are a result of the natural selection imposed upon him by the female's original power to instinctively sense which mate was biologically fitter. This primal dominance arouses in man insecurity, jealousy, and hostility towards women [...] he has been trying to work through this basic hostility by limiting the full possibilities of women through sheer oppression' (35). Thus results the creation of the feminine principle in Nature. By imposing mother role in an idealized form on Indian women, the society has decidedly trapped her true self. The importance of conjugality has been sidelined by ubiquitous mother matrix. For the women, to go to Nandy again, the challenge is nothing less than redefinition of herself. The first task that faces her is to devise means of de-emphasising some aspects of her role [...] so that she may widen her identity [...] in India it may involve transcending the partial identity imposed by motherhood [...] (42-43).

Anita Desai has freed her women from this burden. And this is no small task to liberate the mind to such an extent where centuries of cultural conditioning fall apart and do not have any hold on the novelist's mind. Anita Desai conceives women as primal creatures, busy in pursuing their own motivations. This is highly unsettling for a society, which does not have any mechanism to deal with, accept or live with all aspects of womanhood. This nature versus culture paradigm can be successfully extended to all works Desai with construction of binaries on man-woman, colonizer-colonized, slave-master, city-jungle, East-West etc. patterns. The only unexpected factor in this concept is Desai's position as an author. While in *Cry, the Peacock*, Maya is the primitive, inner force, in *Journey to Ithaca*, Matteo takes this role. Gautama is suffocating agent in one, in the other it is Sophie. Whosoever may take whatever role, but the thought is very much there, in tact. After all these novels and short stories, we may say that Desai is with the psychical energy. But again this can be contested because Desai, as I said earlier, defies definitions. Sita does not identify with pristine island as she thought she had. Sophie fails to love sophisticated Italy which again, she thought she loved. The maze is baffling—what will give content ultimately is not certain because the creator herself is not sure. It can also be argued that Sita fails with the island because she does not know it. Had she known and experienced the thrust, she would have succeeded. Similarly, in her mortification in India, Sophie had built romantic and therefore false notions of cultured Italy and so she flopped. The debate continues.

In *Bye-Bye, Blackbird,* the concerns get more civilization bound. England and India are two phases or better, two faces of human condition. Surprisingly what we thought was more civilized is all the more discriminative, ugly and conservative. India, however is no solution either. Many of us emphasize that Adit and Sara come back to India and ignore the fact that Dev stays back. Adit's return gives us the recognition that our land is the real one and after the mirage, here lies the 'nirvana.' Whether this assertion is genuine or not is debatable. In a brilliant movie *Disha* in which the protagonists were enacted by Raghubir Yadav and Nana Patekar, two labourers move to Mumbai from a village in search of bread. The puritan Nana hates Mumbai, remains knotted to his native place, and dreams of returning to green fields and fresh air once again. Raghubir Yadav is more relaxed. He enjoys Mumbai as much as he can, even its cheaper side. In the end the one who hated the cosmopolitan, is forced to stay there because his *family* (wife, to be particular) has adjusted to his absence. Raghubir Yadav, however, after happily enjoying, graduating to adulthood, laughingly returns to the countryside. So it happens in this novel. The erratic patterns of life are such that reverse racist Dev stays *back* and the one with English wife comes *back*. Both are *back*. This staying back and coming back are strange things. It has several connotations. It implies time movement backward and forward. It denotes places. It also indicates coming and going away from one's own self, the true self. From all the three angles, the message that the novel gives is confusing. A frustrated Adit moves to England, marries an English girl, suffers humiliation, receives a friend, undergoes a headlong change in perceptions, stores all the complexes regarding colonizer-colonized mania and at last returns to the land that frustrated his efforts in the first place. The movement, as we can see, is not at all linear; it is circular, and in every possibility, Adit is bound to remain a dissatisfied outcaste in India—a strange specimen with a *firangi* wife.

Sara and Dev, with their respective uprooting, and estrangement present no different prospect. The old feeling of the picaroon, the wanderer, the searcher and the seeker returns. Desai is in her elements. The element of hungering for the unattainable is pointed up.

Where Shall We Go This Summer? is one of the most outright Desai novel and Sita an equally typical Desai heroine. There is lavishness around. She is materially luxurious. The husband has no apparent drawback; the children are equally normal, assertive, rebellious as according to their age. Things would have been perfect for Sita but for her itching within. A traditionally settled woman in every respect, Sita is psychologically outraged. She is a sleepless, unsteady, and worried soul. She is pregnant. She does not want to give birth to the child in the unreal world of Mumbai. The island where her father used to be the overshadowing figure in her childhood temporarily symbolizes for her the real world. As expected the *real* world shatters her hopes. The father comes very close to being revealed as incestuous as also tricky and manipulating. The island and its people are no innocent, *cho chweet* dolls. Children are not a source of delight or pride for this dissatisfied woman. She returns to Mumbai in a resigned, tired, and defeated way. Mumbai or island, peace or anxiety, father or husband, children or island people, memories or realities—everything is unsettlingly disastrous for Sita. A doomed Desai protagonist, Sita's quest is also doomed to go on forever and ever.

Fire on the Mountain is a special novel because of the unusual child character, Raka. While Nanda and her story with all its poignancy stand for the Desai phenomena of unfulfilling experiences, Raka is a natural entity. While in Nanda, the tension between her desired state and circumstances of life allow her no peace of mind, Raka, as a child is not even aware of the duties that life demands. Her effortless rejection of her grandmother, Nanda shows the carefree nature of wild existence. As I wrote elsewhere, 'Her (Raka's) quiet house on the ridge of the mountain adopts and accepts her in a most natural manner. She belongs to this place which is full of wild beauty. Hills, rivers, the peculiar hilltop, stony hillside, grass or bushes of Spanish broom, insects, leaves—all accept her in a unique way. Raka knows the forest. She knows many secret shortcuts within the jungle. She wants to inhale the grace of the jungle all alone. This is one joy she cannot share with anyone. She simply loves solitude. The description is such that one feels that the relationship between Raka and Nature is that of a worshipper and her most private idol. Her grandmother had planned to ignore her, but the way in which Raka ignores her grandmother proves that she is not going through any deliberate course of action. It is her temperament to be alone. For her the forest is more real than human beings. She ignored her so calmly, so totally that it made Nanda Kaul breathless. She eyed the child 'with apprehension now, wondering at this total rejection, so natural, instinctive and effortless' (170). The self-sufficiency of Nature and also of those who are one with her, the corrupting influence of human company, the joys of solitude, the dialogue of a human being with herself, the essential state of being are some of the dimensions that Desai adds to her vision of life in this novel.

Clear Light of Day marks a change in Desai's style of writing. I see this novel primarily as an effort by Bim and Tara at identity formation. Forced spinsterhood is nothing new to our society. The responsibility of rearing younger siblings after the death of parents falling on the eldest daughter is not a very novel idea for a novel. What is to be noted is the process of introspection on Bim's part, her analysis of her role, her efforts to attune herself to her younger sister Tara, and her partial success. The role of the family and inter-connectivity of selves has been clearly established.

In Custody describes the efforts of a young teacher in a college, Deven to accomplish closeness with art and literature. But neither the seeker nor the sought are what they were thought to be or what they ought to be. This is very much a social novel and the urgent call of Nature has been kept at bay. Deven shows that peculiar Indian teacher psychology that makes them tragic caricatures. The teachers, more than members of any other profession nurture the sense of injured merit. They feel that they deserve something better. This is truer of teachers of higher education. On one hand they miss the halo that was once part of this profession; on the other hand, they want the material luxuries that come with other professions, especially, bureaucracy. Deven too is disgusted at his progress in life. We can describe him as a victim of circumstances as well as his own mind. The sudden push that comes to his life when he is asked to interview Nur, a famous Urdu poet soon plunges into disappointment as Nur is nowhere near Deven's idea of a poet. Deven finds that the world of Nur is that of greed, jealousy, and promiscuity. The poet and the man are poles apart. It indicates the hypocrisy of intellectual exercises.

In *Baumgartner's Bombay,* Desai depicts human nature quite at a low. That, she does not have much faith in human goodness is clear from her earlier works, but this one perhaps touches the lowest. Race, caste, blood, country, language, and religion are tools of discrimination, hatred, and savagery. Baumgarter is an outcaste of outcastes, a double outcaste. He is a Jew in Germany and a German Jew in India. A failure from all sides, Baumgartner questions the development of human consciousness. We might have covered the twentieth century; our sensibilities are as brutal as that of early man. Only the means and mechanism of brutality have changed.

Fasting, Feasting strikes one as a major statement on Desai's part. East and West are juxtaposed. Fasting reflects Eastern conditions and feasting connotes Western habits. Through dietary symbols the author has evoked has effectively portrayed the spirit of two different parts of the world. Fasting, starving, lacking in means, depriving oneself of pleasures or getting them denied by others, negating self and its demands—these methods, which, are so common in India evoke repulsion. On the other hand, feasting, overeating, enjoying physical and material life, leading an unrestricted life, and uncovering flesh—these Western motifs do not bring peace and bliss. The idea of feasting has been clearly separated from sumptuousness. The barrenness of mind is compensated by gluttony. Of the two pointers, it is difficult to say that which one is fouler. The choice between Milanie's pool of vomit and Uma's hysteria caused by deprivation is no choice at all. We as readers can take these statements to be warning bells for cultures of extreme.

Journey to Ithaca is supposed to be a big leap on Desai's part as a novelist. Since spiritual lust is the motif, people think that there is great advancement. However, if we look closely, the attitude and intention of the author is the same as in her earlier novels. It is very interesting to watch how an individual is ever a captive of her attitudes and intentions. Deven's search for intellectual interaction and recognition or that of Maya for reciprocity is no different from Mattoe's search for meaning in life. Mattoe wants an alternative definition of this world, its inhabitants and of his own self.

The crisis that Desai presents is that of the whole human race. It is the difference between 'is' and 'ought.' We may supposedly define 'is' but the 'ought' part always evades clarification. What a character in a novel thinks is the situation and whatever vague solution s/he envisages are forever incomplete and as discouraging as the problem itself. That, in my opinion, is the key to literary creations in general and this author in particular. We are endlessly baffled at our own flimsy, temporary, and unstable state. Whatever we thought was substantial, we find to be evaporating. We build our lives on pillars of money, morality, reputation, recognition, reciprocity, power, pleasure, future planning and so on and so forth, only to find in the process their sheer failure and deceit. If this were philosophy, what would be practical wisdom? To my mind, Anita Desai, along with other thinking minds questions our hopeless certainty at our imagined knowledge of worldly wisdom, our false notion of self-assurance, our false joy in unproductive routine of life, in short, our state of being.

REFERENCES

1. Desai Anita. *In Custody.* London: William Heinemann, 1984.
2. Nandy, Ashis. *At the Edge of Psychology.* New Delhi: OUP, 1980.
3. Tiwari, Shubha. 'Nathaniel Hawthorne's Pearl and Anita Desai's Raka: A Comparison' in Bala and Pabby ed. *The Fiction of Anita Desai,* Delhi: Khosla Publishing House, 2002.

2

Anita Desai

MALLIKARJUN PATIL

In the line of Ruth Prawer Jhabvala, Kamala Markandaya and Nargis Dalal, Anita Desai shines as one of the great novelists India has ever produced. From 1950 onwards, India has produced many brilliant male and female novelists. Like the male trio which includes Raj Rao, R.K. Narayan and Mulk Raj Anand, great women novelists are Markandaya, Jhabvala, Dalal, Desai, Attia Hosain, Shakuntala Shrinagesh, Santha Rama Rao, Nayantara Sahgal, Vimala Raina and others. But Jhabvala, Markandaya, Dalal and Desai are of outstanding calibre and distinction.

Anita Desai is a remarkable woman novelist. She began her literary career quite early at the age of 26 and wrote many novels even amidst her house-wifery. Born at Mussoorie in 1937 of a German mother and a Bengali father, and brought up in the capital city of India at the time of the influx of Punjabi culture, Anita Desai had her education in Delhi. Later she married a Gujarati gentleman and she has four children.

Like all other Indian English novelists, Desai is a prolific writer. Like Jhabvala, she is a novelist as well as a short story writer. Her novels offer a satirical view of social change in post-Independence India, with a strong sense of waste, limitation, failure and frustration. Some of Desai's novels are *Cry, the Peacock* (1963), *Voices in the City* (1965), *Bye-Bye, Blackbird* (1971), *Where Shall We Go This Summer?* (1975), *Fire on the Mountain* (1977) and *Clear Light of Day* (1980). Her gentlest short stories are collected and published in *Games at Twilight* (1978). She has also written works for children including *The Village by the Sea* (1982). There is no doubt that with these works Anita Desai has made significant contributions to India English fiction.

Anita Desai, like Jhabvala and others, does not go beyond the line of her sphere. Prema Nandakumar says, "She has in her fiction sensibility adhered to the *Lakshman-rekha* culture and created her own distinctive imaginative world" (174). Her range of themes, as in Jane Austin's, is limited to the domestic affairs, kitchens, gardens, beaches and the like. According to K.R. Srinivasa Iyengar, "The explosions in Mrs Desai's novels occur only within narrow domestic walls. Always, always, it is the intolerable grapple with thoughts, feelings and emotions" (464) Desai began writing quite early. She says, "I studied in Delhi and started writing at the age of seven. My first stories were published when I was in college" (Nandakumar: 175). Her first novel *Cry, the Peacock,* took the literary world by surprise. It was acclaimed as "a poetry-novel" and as "a first novel of unusual distinction." Her novels which are a poetic display of harmonious presentation of form and substance. Her artistic, lively portraitures and beautiful family environs are surely the signs of her genuine talent. Mr B. Ramachandra Rao states, "The sense of form which is late to develop is the sign of the maturity of a literature, and the novels of Mr Desai are a happy example of the fusion of form with content, of structure with texture."

Anita Desai's first novel *Cry, the Peacock,* appeared in her flowery-poetic-language and with her mastery of domestic themes. The heroine of the novel Maya is a young woman. She is married to Gautam, a detached and indifferent man. The novel presents the characteristic contrasts between the two. However, Desai does not give more details about the persona of them, the sketches enable us to draw the differences that persist between the ill-matched couple. Besides, the descriptions indicate that Maya is immature wild and insane. What makes her wild might be the strongest doubt in reader's mind. She is a weak and erring woman. Whenever she wants anything she is to be provided with it immediately, lest she can bring any disaster on anybody inside or outside the family. This is what happens here. She is fond of dance and beautiful things. She wants to go to the South to see *Bharat*

Natyam. When Gautam asks her to wait for some time as a dance-entourage is to come to Delhi, and it would be convenient for them to watch it, she looses her temper. With this and other incidents, the *Saitana* within her makes her a dangerous figure:

> A Demonic creature, the fierce dance, it was the mad demon of Kathakali ballets, masked with heavy skirts swirling, feet stamping, eyes shooting beams of fire (31).

Music, like dance, is sinister to her. So dance, music, Nataraj image and the priest's presence terrify her. As fear becomes her obsession, Maya is less and less able to act with senses. These things represent her private hell. She herself states, "Torture, guilt, dread, imprisonment, these were the four walls of my private hell, without that no one could survive in long. Death was certain" (117). The forces of evil and superstition, the sinister appeal of music and dance, her husband's indifference and detachment create her a 'sinister future.' According to B. Ramachandra Rao, "The evil is picturesquely fascinating" (Rao: 19).

The novel is full of images like Nataraj who looks to Maya as if saying her act of killing her husband is not an unfavourable thing. The 'cry of the peacock' too gives her the idea of life and death. While the image of train-coming convince her of the fact that the world is not a 'pure delight and secure spot':

> Somewhere his train rushed crazily through this same night, screaming as it came to the green signal at a remote level crossing and, without slowing, sped on, leaving the small signalman waving a pointless flag, lonely and sad at the door of his whitewashed nut in the middle of the desert that was so cold at night. The train had woken up his dog, and the night was rent in two by its long howl, filled with mourning for the pitiless, bitter world where men found no security, no response (56).

The novel has three parts, the first part just gives a background about the death of Toto. In the second part, which consists of 17 chapters, we see the bewildering story of Maya. In the final part, the novelist's authorial comment is given. The language is poetic, full of images and fascination. So it is a "well-made" novel.

Voices in the City, Anita Desai's second novel failed to catch the readers. It is not as appealing a novel as the first one. However, it presents the troubled voices of a big city. It does not sound very striking. So K.R. Srinivasa Iyengar dismisses it as a minor novel of Desai.

The novel unfolds the story of Nirode, Monisha and Amla—all from an upper class society. Nirode has no financial problems or burdens. So is Amla, while Monisha is married to Jiban, a man of well-to-do family. What perturbs them is their dislike for Calcutta, the dirty city. The sordidness, the brutality and the sheer dreariness of the physical world are the unwanted things. Desai's characters of this novel rebel against the dirty or ugly physical reality which is also hidden in materialism. It never appeals to their sensitivity. In this sense, the outward dirtiness which is enshrined in the dirty buildings, ugly gutters, street hawkers, beggars and the narrow and filthy roads is personified here. It is rather repulsive. In fact, Calcutta plays an important role as a dirty character against which these voices are raised.

Nirode, the brother of Monisha and Amla feels the pressure of this great city. He is rather afraid and is threatened by the deserted look of it:

> On all sides the city pressed down, alight, aglow, and stirring with its own marsh-bred, monster life that, like an ogre, kept one eye open through sleep and waking [...] the city was as much atmosphere as odour, as much a haunting ghost of the past as a frenzied passage towards early death (41-42).

It seems, he is morally afraid of the city of the odours of 'open gutters' and 'tuberose garlands.' Monisha's reaction is similar. She feels trapped in her husband's house. 'There is no escape from it,' she cries. The city, to her, has two faces; its devilish look and its hapless, vacant one:

> Has this city a conscience at all, this Calcutta that holds its head between its knees and grins toothlessly up at me from beneath a bottom black with the dirt than it sits on? (117).

To Amla, the youngest, the city appears like a monster. She asks Nirode, 'this city, this city of yours, it conspires against all who wish to enjoy it, doesn't it?' (153). The descriptions show the sordidness, spiritual disintegration, menaces, that threaten the integrity of the individuals. The monsoon rains make the city look like a symbol of dissolution. So the city is called 'a black, dead devil' (110), 'a poisoned city' and the like. Here is yet another passage that vividly symbolises the evil forces of the city:

> Calcutta, Calcutta, like the rattle of the reckless train; Calcutta, Calcutta—the very pulse beat in its people's veined wrists. The streets were slaughtered sheep hung beside bright tinsel tassels to adorn oiled black braids, and a syphilitic beggar with his entire syphilitic family came rolling down on barrows, like the survivors of an atomic blast, then paused to let a procession of beautifully laundered Bengalis in white carrying their marigold-decked Durga [...] Kali—on their shoulders down the Ganges, amidst drums and fevered chanting (42).

The very names of goddesses Durga and Kali, as Nataraj in *Cry, the Peacock,* sound tragic. Nirode says they are goddesses of death or ruinage. It also points the paradoxes that exist within the city.

The language, imageries and diction of the novel are plain and simple as usual, however. The story of this novel is not a striking one. Therefore, K.R.S. Iyengar and B. Ramachandra Rao opine that the novel is a failure. The latter remarks that the novel is not interesting and vivid.

Anita Desai's next novel *Bye-Bye, Blackbird* depicts the lives of some Indian immigrants in England. Many Indians live in England. They are engaged in many sorts of business. Some of them are coolies; many are musicians and other professionals. Dev and Adit Sen are two Indians residing in England. Adit has married Sarah, an English woman. In spite of this encounter, the narration of the novel is somewhat weak and unimpressive. All characters both English and Indian, male and female are pale; they appear like puppets, fragile and dull. B. Ramachandra Rao says, "Mrs Desai's forte—her uncanny ability to probe into the minds and hearts of her characters, both major and minor—is missing in this book" (Rao: 47-48).

Where Shall We Go This Summer? is fairly a successful novel. Unlike the earlier one, it is not prosaic and dull. The novel portrays the life of the Sita which is similar to Maya of *Cry, the Peacock.* The protagonist is a woman of aggressive and unadjusting character. She is married to Raman. Though Raman and Sita remind us Rama and Sita of the *Ramayana,* they are ironical names. They are mentally separated beings under a same shelter. If Raman and his family members go eastward, Sita opts for the West. If the former eats food, what she could eat is uncertain. She is reserved and emotionally active. She does not like the members of the family bossing over her. Instead she dominates over, including of her husband. Her smoking and ill-behaviour makes the society dislike her. As a result, she remains lonely and in solitude. When her husband advises her how to become a conformist, she hates him. She not even affectionate towards her own children.

In order to be happy, she goes to Manori, an island her father created for peaceful life. She is overwhelmed by her memory of childhood spent there. But she does not find the beauty, peace and grace in Manori now. Hence, she comes back home and tries to adjust with her husband. Her life in the family displays her tragedy because of her *bad faith*. She tells many things about authentic life, but she herself does not understand others and cannot lead a peaceful and productive co-existence. B. Ramachandra Rao says, "The tragedy in *Where Shall We Go This Summer* arises out of the inability of the characters to connect the prose and the passion in their lives. They have lived only in fragments" (Rao: 60).

Where Shall We Go This Summer and Anita Desai's next novel *Clear Light of Day* (1980) are portratures of Indian women who rebel against the tradition-bound old mode of life in the light of the Western liberty. In transforming her experience in the form of art, Desai uses visual details and an impressionistic style in an attempt to convey a sense of meaning underlying everyday behaviour and objects.

In spite of her achievements, Anita Desai has her own limitations. Like, R.P. Jhabvala and Manohar Malgonkar, she writes only about the upper class urban people. The range of her themes is also restricted to domestic problems—women's city life and men's psychological crisis. She does not depict the pain of poverty or suffering. Besides, Anita Desai excludes what is much authentically Indian. For example, her novel *Bye-Bye, Blackbird* does not represent what is truly Indian or native.

However, Desai is excellent in depicting the inner furies of women and their rising tone for emancipation and empowerment. She also pays much attention to form and technique in writing.

B. Ramachandra Rao is truly acceptable when he says, "Each novel of Mrs Desai is a masterpiece of technical skill" (Rao: 62). To her characterization is as equally important as plot-construction or story-telling. In this way, we find her novels acquire the depth, the 'dimension' and attraction. Therefore, K.R. Srinivasa Iyengar calls her an 'original talent' and admires her skills in both inventing and narrating the stories.

REFERENCES

1. Prema Nandakumar, *Sombre the Shadows and Sudden the Lights: A Study of Anita Desai's Novels*, qt. in *Perspectives on Indian Fiction in English*, ed. by M.K. Naik, Abhinav Publishers, Delhi, 1985.
2. K.R. Srinivasa Iyengar, *Indian Writing in English*, Sterling Publishers, Delhi, IV, edition.
3. B. Ramachandra Rao, *Mrs Anita Desai*, Kalyani Publishers, Delhi, 1977, Main Jacket.

3

Journey Beyond the Senses: An Analysis of Anita Desai's *Journey to Ithaca*

O.P. BUDHOLIA

Anita Desai as a novelist occupies a distinct and distinctive place in the realm of contemporary Indian English fiction. She is a trend-setting novelist for laying bare the inner recesses and the existential trauma of human beings. She makes known to us the unconscious motifs of human psyche, the problem of human relationships, the protagonist's quest for identity almost in all her novels from *Cry, the Peacock* to *Fasting, Feasting,* but her *Journey to Ithaca* (1995) makes some defining and deciding movements in her structural and visionary perspectives. The entire structural scheme, being divided into four well balanced chapters, is patterned skilfully on a new device of *Prologue* and *Epilogue.* The seeds for higher human values have already been sown by her in *Clear Light of Day* and in *Baumgartner's Bombay*; but they sprout to full swing in *Journey to Ithaca.*

The inclusion of *Prologue* helps her disclose the inner human motives for higher values of life. In *Prologue,* the early life of Matteo, the hero of the novel, is made very clear to the readers. To a philosophic child like Matteo, the school was like a "theorem set within a larger theorem" (17). So, this mathematical precision created in him a failure as a student at his early age. The readers are informed through *Prologue* that the school life "baffled him like the geometry and algebra" (18). Whenever, he was inquired of his activities in the school, his answers to questions appeared sullen and monosyllabic. In *Epilogue*, knowledge of Matteo's journey to India, his marriage with Sophie and the role of his parents in nurturing their children—Giacoma and Isabel after his departure from Italy to India is passed on to readers. The anxiety of Matteo's parents brings forth two main aspects of Matteo's life: his withdrawal from the school and the appointment of Fabian as a teacher for his further studies. Fabian acquaints him with Hermann Hesse's *Journey to the East* which kindles in him a curiosity towards the philosophy of *Vedanta*. Another remarkable incident lies in his marriage with Sophie who "was a journalist" (30). After this marriage, both Sophie and Matteo left for India.

Chapter first of this novel reveals Sophie and Matteo's departure from Italy to India, apparent contradictions in their East-West encounters, their experiences of *Kumbh Mela* at Allahabad, their arrival at an ashram in Bihar and their aversion towards the activities of the ashram. Both Sophie and Matteo had "a design, a pattern, to their wanderings" (35). An analogical matrix in the psychic depth of Matteo becomes perceptible when he begins to learn Sanskrit here. Sophie, on the other hand, feels suffocated and always complains to Matteo against the unsavoury atmosphere of the ashram.

Chapter second brings into being yet another challenge to Matteo. Till now, Sophie is pregnant and she wishes to leave this place for another one on a mountain of the Himalayan regions for her safe delivery. On the advice of the doctor, both Sophie and Matteo come to an ashram at Himalayan region. This ashram is run by a beautiful young woman who is known as the Mother. But Sophie suspects the spiritual authority of the Mother: "It sounds as if she gets up on a stage and hypnotises you all like a magician" (102). Sophie with her womanly emotions becomes jealous of the Mother and regards her "a monster spider who had spun this web to catch these silly flies (127). The jealousy of a woman makes her enquire all about the past of the Mother. Her inquisitiveness leads her to discover her arrival in India as a dancer, "looking for a rich somebody to pick her up" (131). Like Sita in *Where Shall We Go This Summer*, Sophie becomes rebellious against the forced decision of her husband. With her future anxieties of a mother, she leaves the company of her husband and comes back to Italy to her parents. In Italy, she tries to fill the absence of Matteo in the company of another gentleman, Paolo whom she meets in a party. He also finds this mature woman quite fascinating. But Sophie still experiences the overpowering effect of the Matteo-consciousness on her: "Her life with Matteo had spoilt her life with a man like Paolo; it was no longer possible" (155). Anita Desai thus upholds sanctity of relations between husband and wife. Chapter third gives a new turn to the story, as it reveals Sophie's ceaseless efforts for discovering the past of Laila. She inquires about her from the doctor and finds the secrets how she became the mother from Laila, the dancer. A daughter of Alma and Hameed, Laila rebels against the traditional code of Muslim religion and leaves her home in search of her spiritual existence. Like Maggie Tulliver in *The Mill on the Floss*, she is a rebel against social norms and craves for self-identity.

At the Al Azhar University, her yearning for freedom is perceptible when she addresses her fellow students "better to go to prison than live as slaves" (172). Laila as a revolutionary student becomes a source of affliction to Alma and Hameed. Even at seventeen, she is determined to break off the traditional custom which snares her like the coil of a serpent. Her stay at Paris and her rebellious thoughts upset her aunt Francoise and uncle Bertrand. When her uncle asks her to eat the meat, she refuses and confesses: "I am a vegetarian. No one will make me eat the flesh of slaughtered animals" (185). In Paris, instead of purchasing Islamic books, she purchases the books of the Oriental philosophy. Above all, as luck would have it, she meets a troupe of Krishna Leela and joins this troupe for learning the Oriental art of dance. Now, she learns the classical art of dance from Krishnaji, but the art of dance does not bind her for long and she gives it up for realizing the higher vision of God. Chapter fourth describes 'Sophie's arrival in Bombay to Krishnaji's house in order to know the past life of Laila.' Sophie recognizes Krishnaji, because she has seen him as a young dancer in Paris, Venice and Laussane. As he listens to the name of Laila, he revives his past and confesses his relations with her as a "father" and as a "teacher." The diary episode in this chapter becomes the real source of Laila's journey to the East and her meeting with Swami Premanandji.

There are three characters who strive in search of the higher vision of human life: Laila, Sophie and Matteo. Apparently, Matteo has shown some seeds of *Adhyatma* in his early life. He questions his teacher Fabian as a boy about an esoteric experience. He thinks over the relationships between the body and the spirit thus: "It seemed that in time, all substance from one image could flow in to the other and only one would remain: Leo He must grow, I must disappear" (24). The growth of "He" becomes suggestive of his divine attributes and the disappearance of "I" symbolizes the extinction of his ego. Matteo as a seeker after truth thinks of unveiling the mystery of life and death. Both husband and wife thus arrive at Bombay in an ashram. But Sophie lacks the faith of Matteo and as a young wife, she is always in search of her existence as a woman with her husband. The novelist propounds the domestic and social vision through Sophie and Matteo—the psychological realism of a young couple. After Sophie gets pregnant, their arrival in an ashram in Himalayan region brings some new reflections. This ashram thus represents the true interests of the devotee irrespective of his caste and creed. Working on the universal norms of life, Desai follows the secular image of India by making Laila confess about the presence of God in the heart of man. Laila as mother also refuses to accept any kind of formalism for the realization of ultimate truth. The Mother as a Muslim girl does not hesitate to be initiated by a Hindu saint. She remarks about the futility of all religions thus:

> This is no church, my friends, this in no temple or mosque or Vihara. We have no religion. Religion? Like the black crows up in the tree caw-caw-caw, scolding, scolding! But, do they crow at us now? No, they are silent! We have silenced them [...]. Religion makes one ashamed, makes one guilty, makes one fearful. The Master has told you not to feel guilty, not to feel ashamed, not to be afraid (98).

The image of "the black crow" in the above passage brings forth the hollowness and emptiness of all religions. The sound of the crow—"caw, caw, caw" is linked with the meaningless sound of different religions which have nothing to do with the absolute reality. When there comes a protest against Laila's

Muslim identity in the ashram, the Master shifts this ashram to another place in the Himalayan region. He gives an example of Kabir who was himself a Muslim, but led his entire life "in the holy city of Benares and he wrote songs of Rama" (134). Matteo as such comes to the right place, now, for his regeneration as a *sadhaka*.

The Mother thus exemplifies an ideal life of high attributes while teaching her disciples: "You must know I mean honey made from spiritual nectar, to nourish your souls. All organizations are useless, Matteo, useless and dry and empty, if they do not contain the nectar of the spirit. I want it to be rich, rich, rich with this nectar" (118).

The "nectar" here symbolizes the essence of life. Matteo works on the advice of the Mother as *sadhaka* with all patience. The western ideology for work is analysed ("work is work and should bear fruits," 125) with reference to Indian hypothesis of "niskama karma." Here is Matteo who confesses the higher and nobler vision of "niskama karma" in the teachings of the Mother before his wife, Sophie: "She teaches us to work without desiring the fruit from that work. Isn't that a higher way of life" (125). In this ashram, love is regarded as the nucleus for God realization. Matteo too acknowledges his sacred love towards the Mother:

> Matteo: Sophie, my love for her isn't the love one feels for a beautiful or glamourous or intriguing woman, a legend, as you say. You must see that! There is a difference between sacred and profane love. Listen, in her presence I feel I am more alive than I am in the presence of any other living creature [...]. When I leave her, I feel I am falling, down, down in to darkness. No, not darkness but greyness, flatness, emptiness (141).

The constant jealousy of a woman in Sophie makes her depart from India to Italy, but the Matteo-consciousness so overpowers her that she arrives in India again. She discovers now the past life of Laila as student, as a rebel in the Al Azhar University, as a dancer and as seeker of a spiritual Guru in Swami Premanandji. Evidently, the deeper plan of the novelist is to envisage the varied groups of human relationships for a common pursuit of *Adhyatma*. As a novelist,

Desai does not spare even a character like Laila for the instinctual and impulsive flights of human mind. Here is an example for two apparent contradictions in Laila's mind: psychic aberrations and a self-confidence to overcome them:

> Faces leered at me, smiling:/ Are we not fine enough for you? From somewhere strength came to me/ And I repelled them,/ Knowing it better to die/ Fighting Evil/ Than to live without His Grace (301).

Sophie is thus satisfied with her inquiry about the Mother and comes back to the ashram. She is stunned to see the ashram deserted by the spiritual journey of the Mother. Sophie perceives the higher position of Matteo as a seeker after truth in the guidance of the mother: "The urgency to see Matteo, to tell and reveal, had so overtaken her, she had not thought that for Matteo too, the wheel had turned" (303). The "Wheel" image gives the metamorphosis of Matteo as a regenerated man. Sophie thinks and burns with the fire of spiritual thoughts. She finally determines to follow the ideas of Matteo as a seeker. When she says to Diya "I'll have to," and adds "what else" (305). She now intends for completing an inner journey of consciousness like Matteo for esoteric experiences. Thus, Desai through her visionary perspectives achieves a great success in this novel by outlining the higher values of human love, humanism, realism, mysticism and a unified code for the universal vision of brotherhood.

As a novelist Desai succeeds in revealing the subtle and intense expositions of human psyche first in *Clear Light of Day*, in *In Custody* and then in *Baumgartner's Bombay*. *Baumgartner's Bombay* brings in to being the emotional states of a European Jew who explores the basic question of identity as an Indian citizen. This novel prepares the foreground for *Journey to Ithaca* by revealing a super-sensitive mental state of the protagonist. The central issue in *Journey to Ithaca* is not the search for identity of existence, but a "Search for truth, ultimate reality, beauty, joy, ecstasy or whatever form truth has" (4).

The three characters, Laila Sophie and Matteo come to India as the seekers of truth. As a young wife with the West-oriented approach to life, Sophie desires to fulfil the dream of her womanhood but this is not possible in an unruly and stuffy arranged life of the ashram. She feels neglected among the other pilgrims in the ashram: "She scrambled to her feet and returned to eat some bread from the night before and drink a tumbler of tea given her, and even smoked a cigarette furtively behind a hut [...]. Feeling both guilty and grateful to be excluded" (53-54).

The smoking of cigarette "furtively" becomes symbolic of two things: first she breaks the code of the ashram; and secondly, she relieves herself momentarily from her tense nervous system due to an inferiority complex as an ashramite. Again, the smoking of Sophie brings froth the apparent contradictions of her mind: the guilt and gratefulness. She feels guilty, for she smokes furtively as an ashramite and feels grateful as she does not like to develop any association and reconciliation with any of the pilgrims in the ashram. As an expatriate, she experiences the dilemma of her identity. The sense of belongingness so vexes and overpowers her that she questions her husband: "Couldn't we stay in our own country? To die there?" (57). Disenchanted as a ashramite, even the very mention of the word "ashram" baffles her so much so that she longs for her home. Weeping like a child she cries, "I want to go home" (89).

Matteo is yet another important character who aspires to accomplish a higher existence in life. As a devotee, he finds solace when he is blessed by the presence of divine Mother. During his illness in an ashram of Bihar, the doctor attending to him suggests that "Matteo doesn't need a doctor, he needs a *guru*" (147). Matteo and Sophie have a basic difference in their respective approach to life: Matteo represents all that comes from the heart, while Sophie represents all that comes from the mind. Imbued with saintly attributes, Matteo acknowledges the grace and blessings of the Mother thus: "Her presence heightens and illuminates the experience of living as no one else's does [...]. When she appears, everything comes to life, it flowers, it brightens" (110). Thus, the Mother as container and repository of all powers and energy creates a spiritual awareness in Matteo.

The third character who becomes rebellious like other heroines of Anita Desai for her spiritual quest is Laila. Spending her childhood in Alexandria, she is educated in Paris and Venice and finally comes to India for her spiritual emancipation. Laila as a Muslim girl revolts against her parental religion, and endures the panics of life in her search for godhead, first in Paris and then in India. As a dancer, she fails, but as a seeker after truth, she succeeds in fulfilling the final goal of her life. There are two women who revolt in this novel against their surroundings: Sophie and Laila. Sophie longs for worldly freedom while Laila aspires for spiritual freedom. As a rebellious daughter of Alma and Hameed, she exhibits "an amber of curiosity." Since her early childhood, her curious nature makes her give up "all orthodox religions" (110).

As the novelist analyses the psychic depth of the characters, her language tends to be situational and contextual. For example, the conversation between Sophie and Matteo becomes a good piece of symbolic and psychological language. Matteo as a seeker after truth finds two kinds of paths while reading the story of *Katha upanishad*: the path of joy and path of pleasure. The linguistic meaning of these two words for Sophie is more or less the same. She seems awe-stricken when Matteo distinguishes the linguistic properties of these two words:

> Sophie's lips felt dry, and she spoke through those dry lips hoarsely, "I can't understand what you mean. The path of pleasure, the path of joy. To me, they are the same, they are not the separate. But I see that you are saying I am the fool, the one who takes the path of pleasure and that you are the wise one (295).

Sophie expresses her contempt towards other people in the ashram through non-verbal language. She does not like to give up her European identity among the ashramites in India. So, she does not try to understand the mystical yet the false language of the people at the ashram. She excludes herself from the environment of the ashram due to the "lack of the language" (34). She rather tries to understand the language of birds and animals through their gestures, and motions, but ignores willingly to understand the language of people at the ashram. Here is an example by which Sophie comprehends the language of the animals through sound:

> The pai dogs that barked in the village and in other villages, plaintively or aggressively, pleasingly or even conversationally as though addressing each other over great distance in the dark, were more comprehensible to her: she listened to their dialogues with greater understanding and sympathy. Once, she was certain she heard a pack of jackals howling, as eerily as wolves and this roused the dogs to frenzy: she felt their fear in her own veins (53).

The phrases "jackals howling" as "eerily as wolves" and the "dogs to frenzy" are indicative of Sophie's mental turmoil. The fear in her conscious mind creates the fear in her unconscious mind. The animal image haunts her like a psychosis patient. She thus becomes nightmarish and sees her new-born babe as a snake.

Sometimes, Anita Desai like a linguist distinguishes between native and non-native variety of English. Sophie as an ashramite does not understand the regional pronunciation of English. Even Matteo hears a woman, speaking the typical regional variety of English:

> She was speaking very slowly and clearly, enunciating each word very precisely. Almost as if it were lesson in elocution, but it took Matteo sometime to make out that she spoke in English, for her voice and accent sounded so Indian in its pronunciation of "ds" and "ts" rolled "rs" and *heavy emphasis on the first syllable* (74).

The different images used in this novel make the language of the writer symbolic and suggestive. The images like "the gravelled path," "dust-filmed glass," "a velvet tassel," "a cream-flecked smile" prepare the foreground for narrative pattern. Again, Sophie uses the image of "a monster spider" for the Mother and for her spinning web to catch "these silly flies." The images like "breast like a sword" and "an invisible crevice" are functional, for they reveal the hidden and interior regions which are beyond the purview of any written language.

Anita Desai in *Journey to Ithaca* has thus united varied groups of people from different parts of the world in order to present cosmic vision of human life. The novel transcends the barriers of caste and creed. The incomplete journey of Hugo in *Baumgartner's Bombay* for his spiritual quest comes to its completion in *Journey to Ithaca*. The chief protagonist of this novel, Laila, defies social code and comes above the narrow round of caste, creed and a particular religion for attaining the higher vision of human life. The novelist thus professes the universal validity that all religions of the world come to a single stream, representing the religion of humanity. In this novel, Desai also raises a question of universal confirming: how to bring *bhava parivartan* (spiritual change) in man. The novel thus ends with a hope for mankind's regeneration through self-analysing process.

REFERENCE

Anita Desai, *Journey to Ithaca* (London: A Minerva Paperback, 1996).

4

Woman's Striving for a Meaningful Life in Anita Desai's *Cry, the Peacock*

VINOD KUMAR MAHESHWARI

Mostly, the novel *Cry, the Peacock* has been written through the stream of consciousness method with very little conversational episodes. Maya, the heroine of the novel, records the memory of her life with her father, and with her husband Gautam and his family. Being a sensitive daughter of a well-to-do father, her impressions are impulses-borne, reacting to human reality and environment according to her likes and dislikes. The novel is essentially a dream-stuff of the doom-haunted Maya. There is also an element of tragic pathos in her expressions, varying from one moment to another according to her anxiety-ridden moods. Thus, there is dreaminess in what she expresses and to what she reacts.

In Shakespeare's *The Tempest* (1611), one gets aware of the dreaminess of life: '[...] We are such stuff/ As dreams are made off, and our little life/ Is rounded with a sleep' (161). Prospero spoke these words out of his mellowed wisdom. In *Cry, the Peacock*, the anxiety-ridden heroine, Maya also intones herself in dreaminess with the only difference that she is helpless and is haunted by the impending doom.

Even as there may be minor shortcomings here and there in the structure of the novel, the portrayal of Maya is projected in a sympathetic vein. Maya needs the benefit of sympathy and understanding from readers. Her life is shadowed by the three-fold effect of death; doom and destiny. Even as, her mind is at times highly chaotic and anxiety-ridden, she does not lose her discriminating sense. In this way, one is able to appreciate her womanly impulses. In assessing Maya's agonising struggle to wrestle within herself for a meaningful life, Virginia Woolfe's suggestion has been very helpful:

> The greater part of any library is nothing but the record of (noticeable) fleeting moments in the lives of men, women and other creatures. Every literature, as it grows old, has its rubbish-heap, the records of vanished moments and forgotten lives told in faltering and feeble accents that have perished. But if you give yourself up to the delight of rubbish-reading, you will be surprised, indeed you will be overcome, by the relics of human life that have been cast out to moulder. It may be one letter—but what a vision it gives! It may be a few sentences—but what vistas they suggest!

In the cultural firmament of India which is undergoing vast changes now one finds that there are good, bad, monstrous and erratic specimens of women—ranging from film-actresses, models, house-wives to the fallen sisters of Gandhiji. In this background, a woman like Maya occupies a unique place. Being sensitive and having spent her childhood in comfortable conditions of parental care, it was expected that her marital life should be wholesome and happy; but, it could not come about, mainly, on account of her extra-sensitiveness, and also on account of the death of her pet dog, Toto with whom she had come to establish motherly circuit. Besides, it is equally reasonable to say that had she not gone with her *ayah* to an astrologer with albino eyes, she would not have been doom haunted for this gnome-like astrologer had prophesied to Maya in her girlhood an unnatural death four years after marriage to either husband or wife. Suddenly, she undergoes a hallucinatory experience of 'remembrance of things of the past' and gets terrified and panic-ridden. This is an important component of female psyche (*The Hindustan Times*). Maya was conscious of this sinister impact on her mind: It is vividly expressed. The allusion is to astrologer:

> A persistent sense of some disaster I had known, and forgotten, or perhaps never known, only, at one time, feared, and now rediscovered. [...] Not merely a foreboding, but a distant apprehension of a presence. Like an under-current beneath the throbbing of drums, a foreign odour

> amidst the scent of lemon blossoms, a struggle of despair that continued beyond the sleep of death. [...] I searched the stars, unhappily, fearsomely even. [...] It was as though I were faced with an important message in a language I could not read. Thinking now of Toto (the dead pet dog), then of a growing desire to call Gautama, and ultimately of whatever I knew of the constellations, I sifted through the hieroglyphs. It was a language I had once known. [...] God! God! I cried, and sat up in terror. There was no clash and clamour after that. I was aware of a great, dead silence in which my eyes opened to a vision that appeared through the curtains of the years, one by one falling back till I saw again that shadow. A black and evil shadow. Its name was not that of a demon in a Kathakali dance drama, nor was it one of the limpid appellations of the moon. It was, I remembered it now, Fate (27-28).

It is the unbearable turmoil in a haunted woman who suffers more than a man in a similar condition. It is primarily because women are more emotional than men. While men can counterbalance the emotional surge by reason women find it well-nigh impossible to tame the uncontrollable emotions on the strength of their psychic resources. And when the surge of emotions has to pass under the shadow of an ominous prophecy, then, a woman like Maya is left with no other alternative but to heave a maddening sigh—oh God! oh God!, as in the above extract; and now to continue with the same, one finds:

> He had been large or small? I cannot remember, but his eyes I do: they were pale, opaque, and gave him an appearance of morbidity, as though he had lived, like a sluggish white worm, indoors always, in his dark room at the temple gates, where the central lingam was painted a bright, vicious red as though plunged in sacrificial blood, and light burned in a single lamp from which oil spilled into a large, spreading pool. Just as his shadow spread and spread, a stain edging towards me who stood, clutching my ayah's hand, in paralysed terror and even fiercer fascination, my toes curling away from the oil, from his shadow. 'Not only here, but in your horoscope

> also,' he said, tapping the long chart the *ayah* had had made for me, 'and there, on your forehead too,' he smiled, and laying down the paper, he raised his hand, a plump, oiled hand with dyed nails, bringing it close to my face so that I felt as though a bat were caught in the same room with me, and shrank involuntarily (28-29).

Maya, the frightened woman, recapitulates the shadowy presence of the albino-eyed astrologer. She is terrified of him and feels the repulsiveness. Had Maya been a woman given to heightened sexuality she would have allowed herself to become a victim of the old astrologer. This is how the uneducated and ignorant women cater to the whims and fancies of the 'religious-minded' people like the astrologer, from whom Maya shrank back in terror. From the novel, one can make out that Maya was not an orthodox Hindu. All the same she was acquainted with Hindu philosophy and mythology. Above all, she had a sense of dignity and a silent belief in her womanly grace. It is true that in spite of her being caught in the web of mischievous circumstances she tries to recapitulate feelingly her affectionate relationship with her father. In contrast, the atmosphere at her father-in-law's house was more social and political than being personal and familial, to which a married woman like Maya would be more responsive. However, the fate had not granted Maya this fulfilment of womanly need. It contributed a great deal in making Maya encased within herself. What is known as the meaninglessness in life is essentially a product of the impersonal tone of family life. In her married life, Maya could get everything possible within the parameters of formal dignity from her husband, Gautam, and also from her other relatives at the father-in-law's house; but she failed to get an adequate balmy response to her distracted mind at her in-law's place. Precisely, in her moments of temporary relief from her doom-haunted distractions she could remember with gratitude her father's affection in her pre-marital stage. This difference in the attitude of her father and that of her husband and other relatives at her-in-law's place would be touched upon shortly hereafter.

In the meanwhile, as one tries to analyse her response to the evil-minded astrologer in the underlined portion of the extract, cited above, one has a feeling that Maya was extremely sensitive. She started twitching with horror at the approaching sight of the astrologer as if he was an image of obscenity from whom her toes started curling away. It implies Maya's instinctive repulsion against the perverted astrologer exuding the stench of oil and fruitless passions within him. Maya's instantaneous reaction to his presence is a sign of her purity and sensitiveness, which in explicit term means Maya's struggle to be her own self. It is a sign of the grit of human character to resist the external pressures of circumstances in getting tainted. So long as one remains unpolluted in mind, he or she would not go adrift in the chaotic sea of confusion. In Latin, it has been stated that when the demonic agencies want to destroy man, they first pervert his mind. When the perversion starts, there is no end to human perdition. Human beings then are displaced from their true moorings when they lose the track of true values and clarity of vision.

It goes to the credit of Maya that she maintained her womanly equilibrium even when the demonic astrologer tried to browbeat Maya by his heroic posturings, sometimes showing himself as the messenger of Lord Krishna:

> He chuckled, gnomishly. 'Now we can go back to our very important conversation,' he said. 'Of course, you are still so young, so very young'—flicking the fold of his robe over his loins, flicking it—'there is still so much time. Or have arrangements already been made—for a marriage?' 'No!' I shouted. 'I will never marry,' and at the same time the *ayah* screamed, 'Give me that horoscope you have made—lies, all lies. Give it to me so we can leave now.' And he raised his hands, rolled his eyes, crying, 'Calm yourselves! Calm yourselves! But we were in a frenzy now—I rushed to the door, the *ayah* seized the scroll.' He grew perturbed, peremptory. 'Sit down,' he said, sternly, in a voice of steel. 'Listen to me, woman,' he snapped, like a whip. For there is only a chance, a faint possibility that her life should take this path. The sign is there. The stars prophesy it. But we are in the hands of God, and here his voice dropped, softened, began to quiver with emotion. 'God guides us all. He may guide you onto another path, if you pray for it to

> be so, offer sacrifices in order that it may be so! He had a rosary [...].' 'God guides you, child,' he murmured, close to my ear, and chanted a prayer opening his eyes wide and rolling them so that the iris formed white circles that gleamed around the pale pupils. 'Four years after your marriage, so the stars prophesy, and the space between your eyes, the mark there supports this prophesy. I have warned you, performed my duty. Be wary, child, be wary and fear God. Worship Him, make sacrifices. Pray. Do we not know, all of us here, the story of Prahlad? Of how Krishna saved him again, and again, countless times, through love and mercy? (31-32)

The astrologer, or the magician as Maya called him, played roguish tactics to insinuate himself as the saviour of this woman, before her marriage with Gautam. It was a traumatic experience for Maya to have suffered the evil presence of 'this fearsome magician.' She heaved a sigh of relief when 'he ushered us out, flicking the garment that slipped about his hips, flicking it as a lizard flicks its tongue at a petrified victim, and then hastily drew back into the shadows before a stray of light could strike him with its purifying glare of whiteness (32).

In Gandhian thought, to acquiesce with the evil, is a form of capitulation before it; and as Maya all along remained at a distance from the fearsome, manipulating magician (astrologer), she showed her mettle as a graceful and respectable woman. If a woman surrenders herself before a wily character, she compromises with the essential dignity of her womanhood. Oscar Wilde has a point when he says that in the face of the hostile force from outside, the truth of one's being is revealed only at the subjective level. It is in this context Maya's ceaseless effort to defend her womanhood needs to be lauded.

But, as they say, the human destiny is inscrutable and that its decree just cannot be evaded. Through one's conscious striving one may try to alter its course; but a human being is bound to fail. Somehow, at a particular time, the hour of reckoning came about Gautam's death to befall in strange sequence of events. It was no fault of Maya nor of anybody else; the end of Gautam came so suddenly without anybody's conscious guessing. Maya was already deluged with ill-starred, haunting images.

As far as Maya was concerned, her husband Gautam's practice of entering into his own thoughts exclusively without any note of communication was disorienting to her. This made her fidgety; and her feelings in an abridged form are here quoted to show how she suffered in loneliness:

> Poor Gautama. Not to be able to notice the odour of limes, not to hear the melancholy voice singing somewhere behind the plantains, not to have time to count the stars as they came out one by one—poor Gautama, my poor, poor husband. 'They practise the scales every evening.' I told him, feeling so sorry for his lack of knowledge, his inability to take interest, for it was this that made him a grey shadow stalking, [...] stumbling a little clumsily, a little lost in a world so full of very real things. 'And I have never heard them play another thing.'

'Slow, are they?' he murmured, stamping out one cigarette after having lit another with it. This dancing jet of light at the end of the little white cylinder seemed the only thing about him that was alive, a fine antennae with which he kept in touch with the world, however shakily. [...] 'Listen,' I said, stopping at a sound. 'Do you hear that? It's an owl!'

He stopped because my interruption held him, but he merely shook his head and paced on, a somnambulist's figure in opium white. [...] But when Gautama held his silence too long, detached himself too completely into his exclusive mind. I drew him out again, finding it unbearable to lost touch of him. 'You are so very silent again.'

He was startled at my touch and voice. "Am I? Am I?" he said, "and threw his cigarette over the parapet in repentance" (206-07).

Maya's husband was a smoker; and so by this habit of smoking, Gautam had carved a niche exclusively for himself in the home where his wife also lived. Like Gautam, she dwelt in her own world of make-believe. What is known as *Svabhava* in Sanskrit and Hindi determined the direction of the pattern of their existence. Even as husband and wife, they sailed in their own ships of destiny. It does not mean that they had some animus, subtle or conscious between them. It was nothing like this. Both of them go through a sublimatory process of life in which the ritual of blood ceremony played a negligible role. Gautam was a busy, prosperous, middle-aged lawyer; and necessarily, he had to deal with the country's complicated laws, and the socio-economic ideas associated with them.

The sublimatory parameters also hold true for Maya, who was extremely sensitive, educated having been brought up with care and understanding of her father whom she remembers with gratitude; so a few lines may be cited to show that Maya was more spiritually indebted to her father than anybody else including her gentle husband. The way she off and on spoke of her father's kindly acts shows that her father had an elevated sense of life and wisdom; and that Maya as daughter was grateful to him. In Shakespeare's view, thanklessness is the worst form of sin as has been fittingly expressed by King Lear to his thankless daughter, Goneril:

> How sharper than a serpent's tooth it is
> To have a thankless child! Away! away! (110-11)

Maya stood on a different plank altogether. She had a positive approach towards human life and its values. One can have faith in a meaningful life only when one defends the values underlying human existence. Maya affirms her existence with womanly dignity. As a sensitive woman, she could see through the sinister game of the astrologer and castigate him for his slobbering conduct towards Maya and her *ayah* when they had gone to him in days long back. Here, it may be borne in mind that as this is the 'stream-of-consciousness' novel, in which every happening of the past passes through the discriminating sieve of Maya's mind and one gets to know the true worth of her character as a woman. She is conscious of her womanly dignity and susceptibility. She weighs different values of life; and stands on the side of humanity and true morality. There is no hesitation as far as this is concerned. In this way she is life-affirmative. As a married woman, her motherly instincts remain unfulfilled; and so she saw in her pet dog, Toto—a transferred love-object. Since love is an overwhelmingly powerful element of life in women, it must get instinctual outlet. As the novel begins, the scavenging arrangements are being made to carry away Maya's pet dog; and then, she begins to cry—a sign of her motherly attachment for the dead pet dog.

She bore within herself the finer elements of life—love, devotion, gentleness, sensuous contact with the world around herself and hated with elemental feeling the gnomic presence of the magician-astrologer when she recalled her encounter with this highly degenerated character in the company of her *ayah*. It is to the credit of Maya that she could maintain her girlish innocence even as a married woman. She intoned her sense of devotion to her affectionate father in a tragic vein: 'No one, no one else,' I sobbed into my pillow as Gautam went into the bathroom, 'loves me as my father does.' The curtain fell behind him, in tragic folds. He did not hear me—'the tap was running. The vacuum into which I spoke made me more frantic, and yet he was not really meant to hear' (46).

From this extract, it is apparent that Maya, after her marriage with Gautam, missed her elemental life of childhood. It was the affection-filled love she got from her father. Maya, the affection-filled girl was observant enough to note the pattern her father's life just 'as the streams in a Moghul garden flow musically through channels of carved marble and sandstone, so his thought, his life flow, broken into small, exquisite patterns by the carving, played upon by altering nuances of light and shade, but never overstepping their limitations, never breaking their bounds, always moving onwards with the same graceful cadence' (45). The delicately poised Maya avidly fond of affection and love found herself in a comparatively arid atmosphere after marriage. 'In Gautama's family one did not speak of love, far less of affection. One spoke—they spoke—of discussions in parliament, of cases of bribery and corruption revealed in government, of newspaper editors accused of libel, and the trials that followed, of trade pacts made with countries across the seas, of political treaties with those across the mountains, of distant revolutions, of rice scarcity and grain harvests [...]. They had innumerable subjects to speak on, and they spoke incessantly' (46). It was a painful realisation for her to find: 'Poor Gautam, poor near

Gautam who was so intense and yet had never lived, and never would' (208). All this made Maya disenchanted with her married life. So the fatal hour of reckoning came at the parapet edge of the roof when in the presence of the affection-starved Maya, the husband fell precipitously down. Thus, one can say that Maya's struggle for a meaningful life is a part of the sublimatory drama in rare specimens of womankind enacted all over the world in one form or another. One has to feel for their tragic ordeal! It is a fine story of a woman as Virginia Woolfe would also say.

NOTES AND REFERENCES

1. Anita Desai, *Cry, the Peacock* (Delhi: Orient Paperbacks, 1980).
2. William Shakespeare, *The Tempest* (London: Collins Publishers, 1974).
3. Virginia Woolfe in her famous essay, *How should one read a book.*
4. A front-page news feature in *The Hindustan Times,* March 12, 2001 reports women in Jammu under psychological stress of nightmarish terror-owing to the presence of foreign terrorists in J.K.
5. William Shakespeare, *King Lear* (London: Collins Publishers, 1974).

5

Anita Desai's Fiction: Portrayal of Feminine Sensibility

S.D. SHARMA

In an interview with Atma Ram, Anita Desai admitted, "Of course I do write of the contemporary scene and therefore the characters must contain the modern sensibility" (24-25). And, in fact, in all her major novels, Anita Desai has dealt with the feminine sensibility more emphatically than the description of the man and his exploits. Consequently, Desai's *Cry, the Peacock, Voices in the City, Where Shall We Go This Summer? Fire on the Mountain, Clear Light of Day* and *Custody*—all are replete with a powerful description of feminine sensibility. Not only this, even in her short stories, the central theme is certainly the theme of feminine sensibility.

Cry, the Peacock is a tale of Maya's love for Gautam, her husband. Deeply devoted and affectionate in nature, over sensitive in mental proclivities, Maya requires a love partner who can sympathize commensurably with her sensibilities. But the tragedy begins in her life because her husband Gautam does not possess those wide-ranging sympathies.

In *Voices in the City,* Monisha is endowed with higher sensibilities, which is self-evident when she is attuned to music in the conference hall. "I wander in this labyrinth at will and blessedly we never touch, merely remain in mystic communion with each other. I am willing to follow till I die" (123). In *Bye-Bye, Blackbird,* there is a powerful encounter of the East and the West. Whereas fascination for England has been presented through Adit and Dev, that for India through Sarah, Emma Moffit and Christine Longford.

Disenchantment with England is particularly epitomized through Adit and Dev. However, throughout the novel, it is the feminine sensibility that dominates more than the other thematic strains.

Where Shall We Go This Summer? is again a very powerful novel delineating feminine sensibility. Despite the fact that this delineation is chiefly expressed through the projection of one single theme, *i.e.*, the crisis of conscience and values, Sita, the female protagonist in the novel, dominates the entire theme of the novel. Anita's *Fire on the Mountain* symbolises feminine sensibility in a heightened way. Nanda Kaul, the protagonist in the novel, symbolises the heightened feminine sensibility.

Anita's *Games at Twilight*—a collection of short stories, is also a skilled record of the likes, dislikes, vanities, prejudices, loyalties, eccentricities and jealousies of feminine nature in particular. It is, of course, refreshing and enlightening to have a peep into the thematic structure of such short stories as 'Private Tuition,' 'Studies in the Park,' 'Surface Texture,' 'Sale,' 'Pineapple,' 'The Accompanist' and 'A Devoted Son' in order to comprehend Desai's feminine sensibility *vis-a-vis* her fictional achievements.

For ages, the human experience has been synonymous only with the masculine experience. Female experience has been rather ignored, what Michael Foucault calls 'discontinuity' or 'rupture' in history. Alex Comfort is also of the view that in order to have "the ideology of the whole human being" (170), the female experience must also be given an equal importance. Carl Jung considers a woman the prime mover of the psychic activity which transcends the limit of consciousness. But it is a sad commentary on the existing affairs of events that female experiences have been either dubbed as inconsequential or ignored absolutely, which is certainly a prejudiced view. Latest advances in psycholinguistics and social linguistics have revealed many startling facts. Female sex is as powerful, to be precise, as the male sex in the domain of romantics and syntax. As such, female semantics and syntax has a distinct category of its own and the feminine sensibility is also a distinct category of its own having very distinct differences with those of male sensibility.

Anita Desai's novels offer us a rewarding study not only in the domain of socio-psychological activities but also in semiotics and syntax. Her novels, synoptically speaking, offer a view of the long-smothered wail of a lacerated psyche of a female. They, of course, tell us the harrowing tale of blunted human relationships. The fate of Maya, Monisha, Sita and Nanda Kaul remind us of Mr and Mrs Ramsay in Virginia Woolf's *To the Lighthouse*. Maya in *Cry, the Peacock* is married to an older man, a detached, solar, industrious lawyer, who is unable to recognize and understand the female sensibility. The following passage in the novel is a telling predicament of the likes of Maya and the total disregard for their existence:

> How little he know my suffering, or of how to comfort me [...]. Telling me to go to sleep while he worked at his papers, he did not give another thought to me. To either the soft willing body, or the lonely wanting mind that waited near his bed.

Monisha in *Voices in the City* is a psychic case. Her relationship with her husband is characterized only by loneliness and lack of proper understanding. Whereas her husband is a pseudomoralist, a rotund, minute-minded and 'limited' official, always given to the habit of quoting from Burke, Wordsworth, Gandhi and Tagore, she herself gets bored of him. Ultimately she develops an incurable claustrophobia and commits suicide.

Anita Desai's novels have been interpreted in a number of ways. Some have interpreted them from the standpoint of social criticism, whereas others from that of economic and cultural crisis. Some have traced linguistic inventiveness in them, whereas others find psycho-moral delineations. A perfect artist as Anita is, her novels naturally offer a wide variety of social, cultural and psychological interpretations. However, here our main concern is to show feminine sensibilities and other related issues connected to them and to digress from this main theme will certainly prove preposterous.

Hence in this domain the following issues have largely been treated in Anita's novels:

(a) love, marriage, divorce;
(b) social taboos and inhibitions;

(c) cruelty and violence towards the female sex;
(d) problem of rehabilitation after divorce;
(e) extent of liberty and freedom to the female sex;
(f) recognition to the female sex; and
(g) crisis of conscience and values.

If a deeper analysis of Anita's novels is made from the standpoint of feminine sensibility, completely ignoring the he-man approach and the connected concepts attached thereto, then we shall arrive at a stage where all the issues listed above may appear to be related directly or indirectly to the last one, *i.e.*, crisis of conscience and values. In a mathematical way, the semiotics of the entire problems may be summarized in the following way:

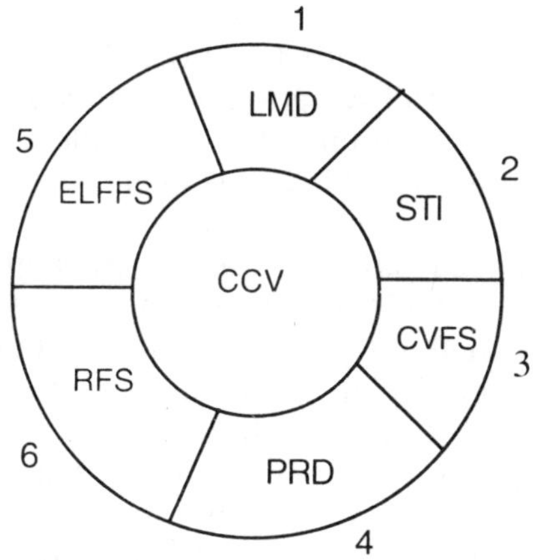

Wherein

1. LMD stands for love, marriage and divorce;
2. STI for social taboos and inhibitions;
3. CVFS for cruelty and violence towards the female sex;
4. PRD for problem of rehabilitation after divorce;
5. ELFFS for extent of liberty and freedom to the female sex;
6. RFS for recognition to the female sex; and
7. CCV crisis of conscience and values.

Out of the above semiotic circles, the pivotal is the CCV. Of all the six possible semiotic circles, which almost complete

Anita's novels from the point of view of feminine sensibility, the circle of CCV is the only one to which all other circle get connected. So what is prudent on the part of a wise reader is to have the key of CCV and then try to understand other circles, which are automatically revealed one after another.

But for this, first of all, *Where Shall We Go This Summer*? has to be analysed in detail, for, the CCV semiotic circle is absolutely complete in this novel. And once Anita's novels are analysed from this angle, it is also worthwhile to understand her shorter fiction by applying the principle of the CCV semiotic principle.

As a matter of fact, Anita Desai has raised a question of crisis of conscience and values (CCV) of universal importance in her novel named *Where Shall We Go This Summer*? If we delete *This Summer* from the title, the perennial question remains—where shall we go? The confusion, as is obtaining today, is worse confounded; for the citadel of conscience and values has almost crumbled or is likely to crumble. The brute forces of money, corruption, machines, automations, skepticism and violence have resulted in despair, maladjustment, divorce, rape, illicit sex, melancholy and frequent emotional and psychological breakdowns. Nobody feels secure: even mothers feel scared of giving birth to their children, not to talk of providing security to the children already wanting in nutrition and prosperity. As I once wrote, "Skepticism surreptitiously increased due to extreme paucity of faith;" for, "man ceases, to have faith even in his own self." Luxurious life purchased through the power of money renders every one fragile in matters of righteous conduct. Sita, Anita's protagonist, is greatly confused not finding a fit society where she can breathe calmly and where she can give birth to her child. In a fit of anger and despondency she utters with a baffled conscience:

> Beginning to pace up the down, up and down, she would strain to catch the precise language of this invisible unquiet, "Where shall we go this Summer?" The words, appearing out of nowhere, worried her and plagued her. "Nowhere, nowhere," she made an effort to control herself and quietly reply. "I'll keep you safe inside. We'll go nowhere." Soothing herself, reassuring herself, she silenced the doubts and walked more slowly till there

entered into her mind again those wavering, disconnected liners she could not place or capture:

Even the slumberous egg, as it labours under the shell. Patiently to divide and sub-divide (82).

Crisis of conscience and values (CCV) leads to a gradual decline in loss of faith, which obviously means a total collapse of culture and civilization (see *Perspectives on Creativity*). A civilization based on magnificent multi-storeyed buildings, perverted vision, sycophancy, cajoling with murder, infanticide, incest, theft and galore robbery practised by frauds, mountebanks, meaninglessness, is no better than a prison. Sita hates such a civilization of the metros, such a culture of the haves, "where there is no mental peace, no emotional richness" (see *Longinus on the Sublime*). Raman, Menaka and Karan love a city of flats and alleys, but Sita is extremely bored of it. Like Moses and Miriam, she prefers Manori to a metro; a birdsong to a pop and zaz music. In fact, she has inherited from her father a genuine love for natural objects; for, nature is a magic for her. A few incidents have been incorporated by Anita Desai to demonstrate how a sensitive soul like Sita may feel ill at ease in the city culture of Bombay. One very strange incident is "an exceptionally cruel drama that had aroused the crow world outside and made them churn the air, joyously screeching, then abash with rapacious claws and breaks at something that lay struggling in a mound of rust on the ledge that jutted out below their balcony" (see notes, 10). It is indeed, a black drama, a cruel drama as that of human beings voracious for power and pelf quite unmindful of their true selves in such a cruel city culture. Sita does not find any qualms of conscience left even in her husband, Raman, not to talk of her other neighbours. Even her own children—Menaka and Karan—appear to her as two machine procreation wholly bereft of conscience and finer feelings.

A very significant question closely related to the crisis of conscience and values (CCV) as raised in the novel, is the question of human survival, of noble existence and of dignified adjustment in the society, and in the married life. Whether one should try to face the odds and buffets of life "with total submission and surrender to what exists" (see *Semantics and Syntax*), to what one's fate dictates one to endure or whether one should construct one's future. Sita's survival, her existence, her adjustment are symbolical of the entire humanity. Her rebellious mood is indicative of thousands of sensitive souls who do not find peace in distrusting environs and corruption spawned by material advancements of all sorts. Her problem of maladjustment is symptomatic of hundred of thousands of Sitas, Ramans, Deedars, Rekhas, Jivans, Moses, Miriams, Menakas, and Karans. But they all adjust except Sita. Is it a difference of temperament? Is it a problem of ego or sublimation to higher issues in life? To a great extent, it is certainly the vision, the outlook that presents before us conscience, values, spectacles whereby to live, to exist, to survive. Sita clearly specifies for herself that life is a constant struggle and the fiercer the struggle, the clearer, the more lasting will be the existence, the survival. Self-improvement, preservation is most human, but this will occur with our faith in our Creator. This is precisely the evolution of man taking place under the kind and benevolent superintendence of God. This is the kind of evolution of man, the golden mean hitherto preached by the seers and saints of all mankind for a noble survival. The instinct to endure challenges of life with a spirit of self-abnegation and commiseration is exactly the stoic instinct which asks Sita to synthesise between what is and what it ought to be. Her assertion is quite conspicuous:

> Life is a challenge to one's instinct for self-improvement. As soon as you have grasped one rung, reach for the next [...] followed often, by a murmur of approval if not a roar of assent (65: see Notes, 12).

But endurance without faith will not bear fruit:

> "No," came the soft, bubbling reply, made effervescent with something like laughter. "No student of chemistry can believe that [...]. But what have these islanders seen? Nothing. Where they have been? Nowhere? Their faith has never been shaken. And do you deny the therapeutic value of faith? They believe gold is the best thing on earth—best because most valuable. So why not add a little to these powers with which I treat their boils and tumours? They believe it does them good and then it really does (59: see Notes, 13).

Emotional maturity is very necessary for leading a life of conscience and values (CCV). It is also equally essential for proper adjustment in the society. Whenever Sita commiserates with Raman for his problems in the factory, she feels fully adjusted; her emotional maturity guides her to be a co-sharer of her husband's misfortunes and discomfitures. In a mood of self-introspection. She ruminates, "His (Raman's) boys at home must have worried him, while he was at work in the factory which was not without its problems either [...]. He looked worn, much older than his years. Nor could he stay here, resting, as she was doing" (133). But in moments of frequent emotional breakdowns, Sita fails to respond to love and affection of her husband. She treats, in such moods of despondency and melancholy, emotional and affectionate reassurances, so frequently needed to sweeten life, as false promises and displays of weak brains: "It simply does not exist for her and should not make to exist. So she did not speak any words of love or reassurance to him. She looked away" (41).

The existing gulf between the old and the young: the looming hiatus between the experienced and the inexperienced, apparently looking like a generation gap, is partly because of psychological differences between the two ages and largely because of a crisis of values and conscience (CCV). Deedar is an incarnate of all those values which make life truly sublime. In his self-abnegating national devotion, in his commiseration with the downtrodden, he certainly stands apart from Menaka and Karan, who represent younger generation brought up in a metro culture with their well-beleaguered fads and caprices. Here arises the question of a crisis of conscience and values. Sita inherits from her father all that which enriches a life with higher values: Menaka inherits from her father (Raman) fall that which makes life rational but bereft of all noble values. For the one, art is much preferable to science, for the other, science is more valuable than art.

Crisis of conscience is deepened all the more with frequent emotional and psychological breakdowns. Mistrust is spawned in an atmosphere surcharged with lust for power and material comforts. Where shall we go in such a state of confusion? What shall we achieve by becoming rich with broken, maladjusted hearts? How long shall we survive with bombs and nuclear weapons in our hands? How shall the coming posterity remain alive with the sword of Damocles of total devastation hanging on its head? We have no compunction of conscience, no qualms of it left within us to ponder over a bit on this very vital issue. We are busy in spreading the vicious dragnets of material civilization founded on very weak basis of mistrust, maladjustment, greed and lust. Sita feels utterly confused at the very prospect of such a degenerating civilization almost coming to naught:

> She folded her hands over it, frightened, certain now that civilization had been created by the godlike efforts of the few, in the face of a constant, timeless war of destruction that had begun with time and was now roaring around her, battering her and her fish-foetus so that survival seemed hopeless. How could civilization survive, how could the child? How could she hold them whole and pure and unimpeached in the midst of this bloodshed. They would surely be wounded, fall and die (37).

The theme of crisis of conscience and values (CCV) is not a sporadic, a passing reference but a recurrent, a pervading strain in all Anita Desai's monumental works. *Voices in the City* is a tale of struggle by men and women of Calcutta for higher life of conscience and values. Nirode, the protagonist, aspires for a life full of values. In fact, he solicits Dharma's friendship for "something unique, astonishing, valuable" (44). Monisha, another major character in the same novel, is enthralled by music and aesthetics. The recital of sitar transports her to a higher region of ecstasy and placid happiness. "I wander in this labyrinth at will and, blessedly, we never touch, merely remain in mystic communion with each other. I am willing to follow till I die" (123). Maya, the heroine of *Cry, the Peacock* is a love-sick and love-impoverished heart, who demands her rightful love from Gautama, "I live my life for you [...] you are untouched [...] you shall never help me. It is all true one of us will win, the other must lose" (114).

Adit and Dev, Sarah, Emma Moffit and Christine Langford are the chief exponents of the East-West concord and discord in *Bye-Bye, Blackbird*. In Emma's opinion wise and wonderful people like Swami Binodananda of Hampstead should come and lecture to "us lesser beings, us little ones, and help us to expand, to set our sights on farther, on Eastern horizons" (48). Emma and Sarah together are in love with everything Indian—the Himalayan flowers, the bandits of Rajasthan, the henna pattern on the palms of ladies, the perfumes of attars, monsoons and famines, items of food and music of Bismillah Khan and Ravi Shankar. It is so because they have an urge to move towards the higher side of life.

Ila Das in *Fire On The Mountains* tries to rise to the higher planes of life notwithstanding her glaring pitfalls; for, "her screeching, horrid, anti-social sound was such as no human being should have possessed as it sent shivers down the spines [...]" (118). In *Clear Light of Day,* Bim has many qualms of conscience and a woman who cherishes values as dearer than anything else. Even the slightest occurrences hurt her deeply. Raja's departure from Hyderabad to lead a life of his own is less pricking to her sensitive soul than his (Raja's) letter directing her (Bim) to retain Hyder Ali's house after his demise: "You may continue to have it at the same rent, I shall never think of raising it or of selling the house as long as you and Baba need it" (27). In *The Village By The Sea,* Hari and Lila's struggle for survival is a moral, righteous struggle, which "seemed to tell Lila to be calm and happy and all would be well" (9).

Devan in, *In Custody,* loves poetry and art. He is enamoured of Nur and wants to be transported to a world of ecstasy and placid happiness through the path of values. Good men are really inspiring to him and he, therefore, aspires for a contact with Nur: "Another realm it would surely be if his god dwelt there, the domain of poetry, beauty and illumination. He mounted [...] casting away the meanness and dross of his past experience" (40).

Weltschmerz is just "the opposite of crisis of conscience and values" (see Johnson's *Preface to Shakespeare*): it connotes "a universal sympathy for those who are suffering," (see, *Makers of Criticism*) who are wanting in money and means. Anita Desai's life-breath appears to dwell in Weltschmerz: for, the spectacle of suffering among human beings, animals, moths, insects and lower animated world magnificently and magnetically draws her mind and heart. A sensitive soul, as Desai is; a woman of conscience and values as she is, the very sight of human sorrow lacerates her heart as deeply as that of the insects snapping under the pull of the beak of a sparrow or any small bird. Though often, Weltschmerz provides her cosmic vision a tinge of deterministic pessimism as in most of her earlier novels such as *Cry, the Peacock* and *Voices in the City*, yet her sombre vision does remain unimpaired by a deep sense of helplessness as in Hardy's case. Her moral and psychological propensities are more with George Eliot's than with Jane Austen's, Emile Bronte's and Maria Edgeworth's. In fact, she endeavours to view life with the spectacles of "a True Greek," (see, *Aristotle's Poetics*) that is, steady and as a whole, not fragmented and punctured. After all, she delights to see human conscience intact and human life whole and untainted, despite all odds and discomfitures.

Anita's shorter fiction is rich in the semiotic CCV circle: for, it offers more than her novels to the readers so far as the domain of feminine sensibilities is concerned, chiefly grounded on the CCV. Nanda Kaul in *Fire On The Mountain* conducts herself in a way that reminds one of the possibility of spiritual evolution of human beings; of the likely extinction of bestiality in human beings; and of course, of the emerging potential that may deter a human being from indulging in whatever is subversive of the divine scheme of things. Anita Desai quotes a few lines from Gerard Manley Hopkins in reference to what Nanda intuitively and instinctively feels to attain or, at the best, what she genuinely struggles to be on a moral plane:

> I have desired to go
> Where springs not fail,
> To fields where flies no sharp and sided hail,
> And a few lilies below.
> And I have asked to be
> Where no storms come,
> Where the green swell is in the havens dumb,
> And out of the swing of the sea (58).

The same strain of moral questioning; of spiritual struggle; of righteous conduct or the semiotic CCV circle is copiously woven into the basic texture of her short stories, notwithstanding the fact that the approach adopted by Anita Desai here is that of a psychologist, of a writer who is keen to draw a psychograph of her characters by exploring their true psyche rather doggedly. The life situations offered in her short stories are doubtless less significant; the thematic strain, too, rather scanty; the action not episodical either, nevertheless the type of exploration of mind and heart rendered possible is, of course, a remarkable artistic feat.

Before attempting at a detailed thematic classification of her short stories, let us know it clearly that she is adept in creating an atmosphere through the use of words and of the mechanism of setting, that even apparently ordinary looking events become live with the feelings the writer really wants to create. In this respect, she deserves a befitting comparison with Thomas Love Peacock, George Eliot, Thomas Hardy and George Meredith. On her diction, there is a palpable impact of scientific spirit with which she uses terse and technical words and expressions so that the effect of the created atmosphere is a finished one. Wherever she delineates a situation with external aids, she appears to adopt a scientific and technical style, which is thoroughly permeated with brevity, clarity, simplicity, technical presentation and utility. Her diction changes from one passage to another in accordance with the changing moods and caprices of her characters. This method of psychological delineation is not entirely a new device employed by Anita, but the fact remains that the precision with which she does it is certainly a unique achievement. If her novels are psychological studies on a macro level, her short stories are certainly on a micro one. If Sita, the protagonist in *Where Shall We Go This Summer*? is a psychological study on a big scale, Pat in *Scholar and Gypsy* (a famous short story), is a psychograph on a micro plane. Raman *versus* David, Karan *versus* Ravi, Monisha *versus* Mrs Amul Bosu are very many psychosomatic character portrayals on macro *versus* micro levels.

Though it is always hazardous to embark upon any scheme of thematic classification of Anita Desai's short stories: for, it is just limiting the sphere of her imaginative world, yet for an easier comprehension and better artistic appraisal, this sort of attempt is worth doing. As a matter of fact, some of her short stories spell out the theme of temperamental differences, some wordily outlooks, some psychological insights, some miserable social plights, some pessimistic philosophies and some just sentimental outbursts. Nonetheless, all revolve round the semiotic circle of CCV. Whereas *Scholar and Gypsy* is a micro study of temperamental differences between David, the husband, and Pat, the wife: *Sale* is the study of the miserable plight of a talented artist, whose paintings never sell. If *The Accompanist* is the micro study of devotion of Mr Misra, the Tanpura Player to master Ustad Rahim Khan, the famous musician, then *Pigeons at Daybreak* tells the tale of Mr Amul Bose as a valetudinarian, an asthma patient, who feigns to feel ill even when at ease. *Games at Twilight* is the study of a child's psychology: for, Ravi does something childlike but also something which is certainly the domain of adults. His philosophical attitude resembles Harish's. Likewise *Surface Textures* studies the psychology of a man who suffers from low spirits of evasiveness and pusillanimity; who is an escapist and a shirker of responsibility. Another short story named *Pineapple Cake* is the portrayal of the pessimistic mood of Victor, on the one side, and the ironic and worldly behaviour of Mrs Fernandez, on the other. *Private Tuition* gives an insight into the teacher psychology of Mr Bose, who does some ridiculous acts in the presence of his pupils. *A Devoted Son* studies the attitudinal contrast between the father and his son. Dr Rakesh, the son, thinks quite differently of old age from what his father does. *The Farewell Party* is a study of the sentimentality of the Ramans. Synoptically, the semiotic circle of CCV dominates the basic texture of Anita shorter fiction.

The plot of her short stories is rather sleek, but it does not lack in coherence, symmetry and organic quality, though there are deviations here and there because of the CCV. *Games at Twilight* centres itself round Raghu and Ravi and other children, who usually play the game of hide and seek at twilight. On day, the children are busy playing the game. Raghu seeks others who are hiding themselves in secret places. Ravi hides himself in a corner of a garage, wherefrom through a crack he slides into shed. There Ravi is frightened to see very strange things—crawling moths and uncanny insects which are trying to eat one another. Raghu vaingloriously tries to find Ravi, who is still watching the drama of struggle among the lesser species. Ravi is thrilled at bit, but at the same time, he is frightened also. Nevertheless, he feels he is securely placed and positioned. Ravi whistles and whacks his stick in despair. Raghu now touches the den so that he may emerge to be the football Champion, which Raghu actually is at present. He does so with a sense of triumph. But while Ravi is doing all this, that is, struggling to touch the den and cherishing the hope to replace Raghu as football Champion, other children cease to take any interest in the game of hide and seek. Moreover, it is now the twilight time and the pall of darkness deepens all-around. The children are now playing a different game, not taking any notice of what Ravi has just done. His hope of the football Championship is dished to the ground. He then ruminates over the petty and Punny actions of his own race—the children. He also develops a sense of helplessness over his insignificant position, he has now been destined to hold. He also treats his victory as inconsequential: for, nobody is now interested in him. The child psychology of Ravi has, thus, deftly been drawn along with that of Raghu and other children. The plot is, therefore, trivial, yet the presentation is wholly surcharged with a psychological delineation of the children, particularly of Ravi and Raghu. Seeing moths and insects, Ravi develops a conspicuous strain of philosophy, and a "terrible sense of his insignificance," (8) which is both appealing and also in tune with Anita Desai's general outlook on life and world.

Scholar and Gypsy is a short story of temperamental contrasts. It centres round an American couple named David and Pat, who have come to India to explore her mystery. David is certainly a scholar, whose interest in sociology entitles him to fame. Pat has entirely a different temperament and attitude from David's: for, she is interested only in visiting other countries. In a way, she is a globe tooter. She, in fact, comes of an American farmer family and loves to be free, unfettered and unchained by bonds of any sort. The environs of Delhi and Bombay appear to her as suffocating, teasing and nauseating. On their arrival in India, David finds Bombay an enchanting city, which Pat disapproves. On the contrary, she feels bored of "the wild jungles of the city of

Bombay" (112). Even the climate of Delhi is suffocating to her, though she assures David that she will somehow tolerate it. "I must" she confides in David, "pull myself together," (112) which she betrays later. Finding both Bombay and Delhi boring and nauseatic, she naturally recollects "the lost home, for apple trees and cows, for red barns and swallows—all that was innocent and sweet and lost, lost, lost" (112-13). Tired of life in India, she joins the hippies being sermonized by an Indian preacher who masquerades to cure "these seekers of *nirvan* and bliss" (132) by administering *bhang* (131) and who often ridicules them more than "meditating or discoursing on theology" (132).

In Delhi, Pat meets a number of people. She develops a sense of antipathy towards the people living in Delhi. Though educated only upto high school, she considers herself to be far superior to the well-educated Indians. For some time, she associates herself with the social activities of Mrs Sharma, who is a social worker herself of longstanding. Pat does not find social work congenial to her temperament and, as such, she gives it up in despair. Pat's Indian ladies appear to her as terrifying and provocating as a red rag to a bull. Earlier, when she was in Bombay, she was given a party by the Gidwanis. Mrs Gidwani is very courteous to Pat at the party, but her obesity drives Pat almost nauseatic. For her physical charm is more tempting than the simplicity of her heart. Pat fails to reciprocate the generous feelings of Mr Gidwani, because of her wrong notions of virtue and vice, of moral and immoral.

In disgust, she goes to Manali in Kullu Valley (Himachal Pradesh) in order to feel happy. The natural beauty, the flora and fauna of this place provide happiness to her. She does a lot of shopping in the Tibetan quarters of Manali Bazaar, where she encounters many hippies roaming to and for. She likes them, their way of life. David regards his wife as a woman of blurred outlook. They enter into heated discussion on religion, hippies, Buddhists etc. at this juncture. David ultimately fails to prevail upon his wife Pat and there ensues an exchange of heated arguments. Pat and David are now separated from each other.

Disgusted and broken-hearted David returns to his country all alone. Pat joins hippies in search of spiritual solace and finally plans to be a Buddhist monk. With high hopes to get *nirvan*, she joins the Nasogi commune of hippies and tries to justify her stand to become a Buddhist monk. She also finds fault with her husband for unnecessarily impeding her religious and spiritual quest. Precisely, this short story deals with the problem of adjustment where there is a lot of difference between the temperaments of husband and wife; where the husband is a scholar with a broader vision of life and the wife an incorrigible wanderer with a blurred vision of life, of good and bad, of virtue and vice.

The semiotic CCV circle comes to the fore in *Pigeons at Daybreak, Pineapple Cake, A Devoted Son* and in *The Farewell Party*. *Pigeons at Daybreak* is a story of the valetudinarian psychology of Amul Bose. A valetudinarian is one who walks even while sleeping. Amul Bose has been suffering from the ailment of asthma for long. His wife, Otima Basu, is highly devoted and sincere. Amul Bose is a type of asthma patient who has some real but many imagined problems. Otima has to attend to all real and imagined problems of her husband in addition to all her tiring daily domestic chores. A very committed and obedient lady as Otima is, she never harbours any grudge or any complaint against her husband. On receiving the information that there would be an electric breakdown the whole night, Amul Bose's problems naturally multiply. Otima does not grudge. She tends him well and when her husband's breathing problem increases, she carries him to the roof-top, where Amul Bose is scared of his quarrelsome neighbour. Throughout the night, Otima massages Amul's body and there is some cool breeze also. This brings Amul some respite. Pigeons fly at the daybreak, and the flight of the pigeons also brings a temporary respite for Amul:

> Then, with a swirl and flutter of feathers, a flock of pigeons hurled upwards and spread out against the dome of the sky—opalescent, sunlit, like small pearls [...]. Then they disappeared into the soft, deep blue of the morning (190).

In fact, Otima knows the psychology of her husband well. Even the slightest occasion enhances her husband's problems to the extent that Otima finds it extremely difficult to deal with these weak moments of her husband: "She knew how rapidly he would advance from imagined breathlessness into the first frightening stage of a full-blown attack of asthma" (102). Precisely, this short story is a psychological story dealing with the imagined problems of an asthmatic patient like Amul Bose. This story also tells how a patient's wife like Otima tends her husband well. Pigeons figure in the story as emblems of peace and liberation. At the time of daybreak, the pigeons like other birds flutter in the air feeling free, liberated and happy. Amul usually sleeps at the daybreak getting a temporary respite from the night's suffocating air and physical groaning. Dwelling upon a very common-place life situation, Anita has raised a very serious question of an honourable existence being buffeted by such a predicament as that of Otima's.

Pineapple Cake, another memorable short story by Anita Desai, is replete with a pathetic touch in the end. What one does and what one is, that is, the chasm between words and actions, is the key-stone of this story. It is based on the child psychology, which is usually highly sensitive and delicate. Victor is the child who is given assurances a number of times to get a pineapple cake by his mother named Mrs Fernandez, who is wordily-wise. She has an ostrich-like appetite and her deeds do not tally with her promises. Victor does not feel assured of her mother ever providing him the pineapple cake. Carmen Maria, who hails from Goa and de Millo, who hails from Bombay are to marry and their wedding ceremony is to be performed in the Church, where Mrs Fernandez will also join the marriage. Victor insists on accompanying her mother to the Church. Mrs Fernandez agrees to carry Victor to the Church and provide him the pineapple cake on the condition of Victor behaves properly there. But at the time of wedding, a gentleman dies, which shocks Victor, who is a child of very sensitive temperament. Instead of enjoying the pineapple cake, which is served at the time of wedding, Victor ruminates over the death of the gentleman. To him, the pineapple cake appears as if it were a corpse. He does not eat the pineapple cake, but his mother eats a lot. She is not at all sorry for the death of a man. Victor finds his mother's conduct at the party quite inconsistent with her utterances.

A Devoted Son is the short story of attitudinal clashes between a doctor son and his retired, aged father. Rakesh is a doctor who by dint of hard work gets brilliant success in his medical profession. He rises to the rank of Director and now runs his own clinic in his father's house. His father is a retired assistant to a kerosene dealer. Rakesh is a very devoted son and obeys his parents more than ordinary sons and daughters. He takes utmost care of his father after the death of his mother. He is keen to see his father healthy and wishes him a long life. With this end in view, he prescribes many medicines, pills and powders to be used regularly by his father. Fried and spicy foods, sweets and irregular diets are completely restricted so that his father may keep fit. But the father is impatient to continue his old food habits. He prefers tasty dishes to simple ones. And when this is checked, he complains of his son's callous behaviour to his neighbour Bhatia. He also complains of his being starved. He prefers death to such restricted diet. In a word, here arises the clash of attitudes. Rakesh is guided by a very rational approach of a doctor whereas his father by a sentimental one of an aged, retired man, for whom the great pleasure on the earth seems to be that of eating. Even a young devoted son and a very competent doctor like Rakesh is suspected by his aged father of tyranny and maltreatment.

The Farewell Party is a story of emotions, sentiments and human relations. Though artistically a powerful portrayal of human emotions, yet its plot is extremely weak. Third person universal observing pattern of narration which we find in this short story, does not, in fact, make it a complete and perfect story in all respects. The slender theme is gradually threaded around human passions and emotions. The Raman family is the centre of discussion by the neighbours. The guests who arrive profusely congratulate Mr Raman on his getting promotion in the Indian Mercantile Company, which deals in the manufacture of cigarettes. The Raman family is known for their altruistic activities and their commiseration with the suffering people in the neighbourhood has become fairly proverbial. The farewell party is, therefore, arranged by the Ramans, and the guests and the neighbours are sumptuously entertained. All praise the Ramans. One after the other, the whole gathering becomes emotional; few of them highly sentimental and maudlin. Some start even weeping for the Ramans would not be seen by them in their neighbourhood after their transfer. Moreover, Mrs Raman is a lady of extrovert temperament. Her associations with her neighbours are quite deep and long-lasting. All this leads to an atmosphere in the farewell party surcharged with emotions and sentimentality. There was about it exactly that kind of sentimental euphoria that is generated at a ship-board party, the one given on the last night before the end of the voyage" (94).

Thus the above shorter fiction of Anita Desai has a predominant delineation of the feminine sensibility and that, too, firmly grounded on the semiotic circle of CCV. *The Accompanist, In Custody, Surface Textures, Private Tuition, Sale* and *Studies in the Park,* may further be analysed under the overall impact of CCV.

The Accompanist deals with the life of those characters who feel happy to pursue the path of virtue and commitment. Devotion appears to be the key-note of this story and aspiration to be an elevated soul seems to be the underlying idea. Mr Misra and Ustad Rahim Khan are two major characters around whom the whole story revolves. Mr Misra is a devoted fellow. He is a Tanpura player to his master Ustad Rahim Khan, a noted musician. Mr Misra is now thirty years of age. He had come to his master just as a boy of fifteen years. As a boy, Mr Misra gets a lot of elementary knowledge of music as well as training from his own father, who himself was a musical instrument maker. Mr Misra remains a life-long accompanist to his master. He admires his master very profoundly. He has unbounded love for his master and does not see any blemish in him (master) as a true and obedient pupil strictly in the traditional sense of the teacher-taught relationship.

In her monumental novel named *In Custody,* Anita Desai has dwelt upon the similar theme of relationship between a poet and his admirer. Devan is the idolater and Nur is the idol, as Mr Misra is the idolater and his master is the idol. Devan has high aspirations for being transported and elevated with his contact with Nur: "Another realm it would surely be if his god dwelt there, the domain of poetry, beauty and illumination. He mounted [...] casting away the meanness and dross of his past existence [...]" (40). Devan, though a University Professor, finds his life monotonous because as an intellectual, he peels off a creative work (like that of Nur's) of its real substance. Imtiaz Begum's observation about the intellectuals of the Devan tribe is certainly far-reaching and raises a separate issue as to the exact relationship between a critic and an artist: "I know your kind jackals from the so-called universities that are really asylums for failures, trained to feed upon our carcasses" (118). Mr Misra does not doubt at all the aesthetic excellence in his master's music, so Devan is perfectly enamoured of Nur's poetry and creativity. Ustad Rahim Khan thinks that creativity is the key-stone of music. Nur considers poetic inspiration just to be a component of creative process. The views both of Ustad Rahim Khan and of Nur perfectly tally with P.B. Shelley's on this count:

> Like a poet hidden
> In the light of thought,
> Singing hymns unbidden,
> Till the world is wrought
> To sympathy with hopes and fears it needed not
>
> (Palgrave: 275)

But the bitter note on university teachers by Nur, the creative artist, is conspicuously missing in *The Accompanist*: for, Mr Misra never finds his master Ustad Rahim Khan wanting in any respect. Nur's denunciation of a critic *vis-a-vis* a creative artist is noteworthy: "Do you think a poet can be grounded between stones, and bled, in order to produce poetry for you? You think you can switch on that mincing machine, and I will instantly produce for you a length of raw, minced meat that you can carry off to your professors to eat" (156). However, *The Accompanist* gives the germinal idea of the theme which Anita Desai has developed in her novel *In Custody* later. One of the salient features of this short story is the use of first person narrative.

Another important short story by Anita Desai is *Surface Textures*, which is the study of a person who avoids responsibility, behaves non-seriously and is unable to carry on his duties. Harish is the chief character in this story. He is a clerk in a supply office, earning a meagre salary not perhaps sufficient for his wife and children. He neglects his work; even in his office, he tries to do as little as possible. He is derelict of his duties and his superiors have no confidence in his efficiency and calibre. He deliberately invites action against him so that he may be sacked from his job. He finds himself incapable of enduring the burden of his family any longer. He wants to relinquish this world to become a *sadhu.* He considers the life of a *sanyasi* far better than that of a clerk in an office, earning a meagre salary and surrounded by a number of worries and anxieties. He also thinks that once he becomes a *sadhu,* probably he will be profoundly respected by the people. He is an escapist and hence even his becoming a saint does not bring happiness to him. Being lazy and idiotic by temperament, he brings discredit to the life of a saint and puts a blot on sainthood by his various acts of omission and commission. His *surface texture* of incompetence and indolence, of indifference and antipathy, once boredom and tedium to him in office, are now equally impeding his new life of a *sadhu.*

In fact, this short story is an attack on evasiveness and pusillanimity, cowardice and irresponsibility of a person. The satiric vein runs throughout the story. Its tone is slightly bitter and more biting that of other short stories.

Private Tuition is a psychological short story, which deals with the psychology of a school teacher while engaged in private tuitions. Mr Bose undertakes tuitions to free his family from pecuniary strains. Students usually behave in a strange manner when their teacher teaches them. But with Mr Bose there are many other problems. The place where he imparts instruction is open to the view of all. Pupils know it well as to what Mrs Bose is doing at present in the kitchen. Radio is also on, which distracts the attention of his students. Moreover, Mr Bose's children are very naughty. They do all sorts of activities to divert concentration of other students. There is a lot of clatter of utensils, rolling of other domestic items and the students laugh in their sleeves. Mr Bose is upset; his pupils enjoy the situation. Added to all these, is the problem of certain students who need special care. Mr Bose feels that teaching a Brahmin priest's son is easier, but to teach a Bengali is difficult to upset (the girl in flamboyant garments, always giggling with irresponsible laughter) makes Mr Bose very much self-conscious.

Sale is a study of an artist whose paintings never sell. He is a painter gifted with unusual talents and calibre, but his misfortune is that nobody has the capacity to appreciate his creation in an unbiased manner. He complains of the degenerating aesthetic taste of the people. Once it so happens that three visitors come and make a long pursual of his paintings. They ask a number of questions from the artist ranging from professional to private affairs. However, the painter answers them well and he is quite hopeful that the visitors may purchase his paintings. Being encouraged a little by the interest shown by the visitors in his paintings, he tells them various specifications of his paintings in detail: "one cannot pinpoint any school, any style—one can only admit oneself in the presence of a continuous and inspired act of creation." But despite all his pleadings and persuasions, the painter fails to prevail upon the visitors: for, they do not find anything substantial in his paintings. As a matter of fact, Anita Desai has projected an idea of neglect of artists in the society through this short story. She considers the declining aesthetic taste of the people wholly responsible for the plight of the artists. Vulgar tastes demand vulgar arts and Anita Desai does not support the idea that an artist should ever make any compromise with the standard of his art just for the sake of money.

Studies in the Park deals with the genuine problems of a student named Suno who is preparing for his I.A. examinations. He does not find a conducive atmosphere for studies at his home: for, there are disturbances of all sorts. When he concentrates on his studies, his father listens to the news in six languages. His mother clutters in the kitchen, constantly pressing her glass of sugared milk on Suno. Not only this, other children make an intolerable noise rendering the whole atmosphere rent up with chattering and loud talking. He is completely enervated, but there is none to commiserate with him. To add to his plight, the water tap remains constantly splashing. His concentration on his studies is certainly impossible in such a disturbed atmosphere. He prefers a corner of a restaurant to his home, where too, the proprietor and the waiter, are both garrulous, talkative and glib liars. He then selects a park for his studies, but there too he finds a number of students already positioned with grimaced faces—some mentally dying, some physically constipated, some demented whereas some with wide lines of worries and anxieties writ large on their pale faces.

Suno feels disappointed, but his disappointment is transformed into hope and optimism, when he sees a pale, white, suffering Muslim lady in the lap of an elderly gentleman, who is looking like a benevolent scholar with a long beard and affectionate face. The lady is being tenderly caressed by the gentleman and there is an aura of immortal solace and succour around them. Suno feels that the burden of studies is decidedly useless in the face of love and kindness. Suno treats himself as a completely liberated soul at this juncture at the sight of the lady and the old man.

Almost a similar scene is there in *Where Shall We Go This Summer*?, where Sita feels liberated at the sight of a pale, weak Muslim lady being loved intensely by her anxious husband. The lady is about to collapse, but the husband embraces his hands around her in order to provide her strong protection. Sita regards these moments of love and sympathy as truly divine attributes and life spent during these fractions of time as an immortal bliss. For some time, she forgets all her anxieties and cares about Menaka and Karan: for, she treats life as not a lengthy span of right and wrong actions, but as small but beautiful, resplendent but satisfying experience. Raman, her husband, appears to her not as something to be hated and despised, but as a life-partner of very low and dull sensibilities. Her father, Deedar, appears to her truly an incarnate of virtue and her overall view of life is that of one who wants to fight the challenges with high spirits.

On Raman's insistence to reveal that event when Sita felt extremely happy in her life. Sita utters: "It was in the Hanging Gardens," she recalled, slowly pacing beside him. "One evening I book the children there. We were walking about. Near a tall hedge, on a bench, I saw a woman stretched out. A Muslim woman—She was wrapped up in her black *burqa*. Then she raised her veil and I saw her face. I saw her face lying in those black folds like a flower—a dead-white flower. Like a Persian lily, or a tobacco flower at night [...] fatally anemic—or fatally tubercular. Her head [...] lay in the lap of an old man [...]. He had spectacles and a long grey beard. He looked down at her and caressed her face—so tenderly, so tenderly [...]. But the man and the woman never looked at anyone else, they looked at each other with such, such a strange, strange expression—I can't forget it. I can't explain it. Tender, loving eyes [...] quite divine [...]" (105-06).

Sita is the protagonist in *Where Shall We Go This Summer*? Suno is the main character in *Studies in the Park*. The former is Anita Desai's novel, whereas the latter is her short story. Suno is just a micro, a short sketch of Sita: for, Anita Desai postulates her vision or outlook of life through Suno on a micro plane, whereas through Sita's on a macro level. However, Suno is the prototype of Sita in espousing a particular view for which Anita Desai is generally known. This view resembles Weltschmerz's, which means that notwithstanding a gloomy position of man in the scheme of things in this world, it is always worthwhile to struggle. This view is often mistaken as a pessimistic view, but Anita Desai's overall vision of life is not merely to feel helpless in the face of realities of life, but to face them boldly. Harish in *Surface Textures* is an escapist and his entire being just a psychograph of evasive personality—a personality of pusillanimity. He invites disciplinary action so that he can get rid of his family burdens and also to become a *sadhu* in order to lead a life where he had to do nothing but to prosper on other's earnings. This is a negative side or life, which Anita decidedly hates.

So far as the characterization of Desai's stories is concerned, it has both plus and minus points of its own. But it has the dominant impact of the CCV. For example, the character-sketches of Dr Rakesh in *A Devoted Son*; of Mr Misra in *The Accompanist*; of David in *Scholar and Gipsy*; of Ravi in *Games at Twilight*; of Suno in *Studies in The Park*; and of Mr Raman in *The Farewell Party*—have many traits in common. More or less, these human sketches weigh more towards good than bad. They are often obsessed with very probing questions of how to exist; how to survive in a society inhabited by frauds and mountebanks. David is a good tempered scholar of sociology but he is constantly tormented by Pat. Dr Rakesh wishes his father well, but his aged, diabetic father has a very peevish temperament and does not want to remain physically fit despite Rakesh's best prescriptions. Mr Misra wants to adore his mentor, it costs him his lifelong devotion and commitment. Ravi wants to see deeper meaning in life: for he looks upon his childish play just a very trite source of happiness. In his philosophical introspection, the child broods over the big problems of life and finds happiness, in a true Hardyian vein, just an occasional episode in the general drama of pain. Mr Raman has an altruistic motto: for, he finds great pleasure in feeling and entertaining others. In his altruistic pursuit, his wife Mrs Raman fully cooperates and on their promotion during the course of a party, everybody present feels unhappy to be separated from a couple really loveable and sociable.

Raghu, Ravi, Victor, and Suno are all children depicted as heroes in *Games at Twilight, Pineapple Cake* and *Studies in the Park* respectively. Their character-portrayal constitutes a very convincing child psychology. Ravi, Victor and Suno—all have many common personality traits: for, all of them have an introvert type of personality: all possess a pessimistic view of life: all want to live by idealism; and, moreover, all of them doggedly want to know the real meaning of life. Suno finds complete happiness not in studies of dry subjects of science and dead details of history, but insights full of commiseration and love. Tired of his home atmosphere which is full of din and clatter; getting bored of talkative restaurant proprietor and greedy waiter, he goes to the park fully crammed with all sorts of people, where the sight of a Muslim lady suffering from a terminal disease resting in the lap of an old, Commiserate scholar gentleman is highly soothing to Suno. In portraying child psychology, Anita Desai seeks to have closer affinity with Charles Dickens whose child heroes such as David and Pip are immortal creations from the points of view of child psychology.

Anita Desai's female characters have their own specific identity in her short stories. They fully exhibit their female sensibilities. Mrs Fernandez in *Pineapple Cake* is less educated but more wordily wise. She is used to the realities of life. At the time of wedding of Carmen Maria and de Millo, she eats a lot of pineapple cake, though a gentleman has just died and the cake appears as if it were a corpse to her son Victor. But she satisfies her lust for eating and does not philosophise like her son. She is, therefore, practical and has nothing to do with the contemplative side of life. Mrs Bose in *Private Tuition* is ill-cultured and does not possess sophisticated manners. Mr Bose is scared of her ill-manners as much as he is bored of his students. She makes a lot of noise in the kitchen when her husband is busy teaching his pupils. She is also incapable of controlling her children who start fighting the moment Mr Bose undertakes private tuitions. She brings disgrace to her husband in the presence of his students and makes his situation very precarious. Mrs Raman in *The Farewell Party* is a lady of good taste and good manners. She is always ready to help others. She considers helping others as more significant than glorification of the self. That is why others feel unhappy when the Ramans go elsewhere on their promotion. Everyone in the neighbourhood appreciates her for her good deeds and cooperative nature. Pat in *Scholar and Gypsy* is a lady of very independent nature. She does not like Bombay and Delhi. She goes to Manali, where she prefers the hippie cult to the accompaniment of her husband to America. She believes in the seamy side of life more than its realities. But Otima Bose in *Pigeons at Daybreak* is a very devoted lady.

Rakesh in *A Devoted Son*, Mr Misra in *The Accompanist*, and David in *Scholar and Gypsy* are fully-grown characters and they are, in a word, embodiments of virtue and good; for, Rakesh does everything possible to keep his father happy: David, likewise proves to be a devoted husband: and Mr Misra regards his master Ustad Rahim Khan as his God. Each one of them tries to search a meaning—a gainful meaning, indeed, in life. Amul Bose in *Pigeons at Daybreak* is a valetudinarian and he constitutes a class apart of his own.

Thus Anita has drawn the character-sketches of children, men, women, valetudinarians, mothers and wives in her short stories under the impact of CCV. Her child characters are very much convincing particularly from the point of view of psychosomatic delineations. Her sketches of full grown men and women too are quite convincing: but her treatment of good through these characters is more appealing than that of vice. The sketches of wives are certainly her forte: for, they are paragons of virtue not because that they have been made so intentionally but because their quest for higher values is extraordinarily convincing and of a universal appeal.

Her stories may have a thin substance, but even the thin substance that is there is certainly the substance, the elixir of life (CCV) that sustains us. In fact, her characters have unique capacity to move upward towards the higher side of life, notwithstanding the fact that they miserably fail many times while doing so. This tendency towards the good, the virtuous is an underlying strain even in her novels. For example, Gautama in *Cry, the Peacock* constantly endeavours to follow the path of detached actions, as his wife Maya truly explains: "He is fit to attain immortality who is serene and not affected by these sensations, but is the same in pleasure and pain [...] when he completely withdraws his senses from sense objects as the tortoise withdraws its limbs, then wisdom becomes well established" (108-09: Notes, 20).

In *Bye-Bye, Blackbird*, Adit and Dev, Sarah and Christine Langford—all struggle to seek a meaning in life in their own ways. There are moments of transformation and transmogrification in their life: there are moments of moral bliss which they find more valuable than anything else. On his departure to India, having a changed outlook, Adit tells, "as though he saw the Union Jack being lowered in sadness at his departure and saw the Indian tricolour rising upon the opposite horizon" (257). In *Where Shall We Go This Summer*? Sita and Deedar ruminate over the intricate issues of life rather doggedly and try to find a moral answer to them. Sita like Otima Bose feels cast down very frequently because she fails to find an appropriate answer to serious puzzles of life. Sita's postulate about life is worth consideration: "Life is a challenge to one's instinct for self-improvement. As soon as you have grasped one rung, reach for the next [...] followed, often, by a murmur of approval if not a roar of assent" (65: Notes, 21).

The same questioning strain to find a real meaning in life is copiously traceable in *Fire On The Mountain, Clear Light of*

Day, In Custody and in *The Village By The Sea.* Had Nanda Kaul had the gift of religious grace, spiritual faith, and had the rains come in time, there would have been no fire on the mountains. Raja, Bim and Tara see clear light of the day because they feel themselves spiritually and morally more evolved than other characters. *The Village By The Sea* is concerned with the problem of survival and change keeping moral proclivity alive and untainted. Despite the fact that Hari and Lila lead a life of want, their spirits have not been drooped from the point of morality: "their belongings, in tin and cardboard boxes, were perched on top bricks and stones along the edge. Some bundles hung from the bamboo poles that acted as rafters" (116). Yet they remain undaunted by their life of want and misery and try hard to exist, to survive. *In Custody* deals with Devan's higher aspirations to become a great creative artist and poet. His adoration of Nur is exactly the same as that of Mr Misra for his master Ustad Rahim Khan in *The Accompanist.*

The above appraisal of Anita Desai's short stories reveals the fact that she is a very conscious craftsman and assiduously works to produce the desired effect grounding her plots on the CCV. One very significant point about her excellence as a short story writer is that her art is certainly a process of growth. Only time will tell as to what will be the final stock of variety and diversity. As in her novels, one encounters a variety of themes changing from one novel to another, likewise in her short stories (only eleven studies in the only volume of her short stories named *Games at Twilight and Other Stories* hitherto extant) form a good variety. If *Games at Twilight, Pineapple Cake,* and *Studies in the Park* form one group dealing with child psychology, then *A Devoted Son, The Accompanist, Sale,* and *Scholar and Gypsy* form another category which deals with the problem of finding a meaningful existence in life. *Surface Textures* stands apart from other short stories forming an independent group: for, it deals with the problem of wilful negligence of duty and of escapism. *Private Tuition* deals with the child psychology *vis-a-vis* a teacher and this story may also be listed as forming its own separate category. Likewise, *The Farewell Party* cannot be bracketed with any other short story on the basis of its theme. *Pigeons at Daybreak* deals with the psychology of a valetudinarian, and hence this story, too, forms its own separate category on the basis of its plot and the foregoing thematic treatment is based more on the similarity of underlying idea than on anything else.

The people inhabiting the world of her short stories are children, fully experienced men and worldly-wise women, old fathers and mothers, artists, devoted sons and daughters, foreign ladies proselytizing into hippies etc. But the children such as Raghu, Victor and Suno appear to be more convincing than Harish, Pat, and David. Rakesh is a devoted doctor and an obedient son, but his father is an old man of very peevish temperament. Mrs Fernandez and Pat have not convincingly been drawn: for, they certainly lack an organic quality that might have enabled them to grow in accordance with the development in the story.

Desai has a marvelous mastery over language and style, fit to delineate a feminine sensibility. Her diction is highly sensitive, responsive, sensuous, but also nervous. Her style is fit for all modes of thought and tension. Whether she describes the morose Raghu or pessimistic Victor, or the derelict Harish, her language always catches the right words. As in her novels, the subtle nuances and shades have nicely been presented, so in her short stories, the thoughts, the modes and the tensions have excellently been narrated with the force and deftness of a big creative writer.

Her range of vision is certainly limited: for, most of her plots are sleek and airy dealing with the life of cities. The Hardyian touch of external details, the Meredithian effect of psychological growth, the Dickensian force of external specifications are commonly and often even conspicuously absent in her short stories and novels.

Despite all these limitations, Anita Desai has immense potential as a short story writer. As in her novels the Weltschmerz outlook characterises the whole treatment, likewise, in her short stories, her outlook on life is one that resembles *in toto* the Greek view of life, which clearly means that she has an unflinching faith in the inherent goodness of man and has nothing to do with the bestiality hidden in him. She is an incorrigible optimist: for, she is used to see life "steady and as a whole" which the Greeks were usually wont to. Her final vision of life seems to dictate: "*Live Naturally,*" which means that we should try to develop our adaptability as much as possible so that in the struggle for existence, we may survive for long. Sita's character precisely synthesises what Anita wants to convey by natural living. Sita compromises between *what is* and *what ought to be*: the struggle before us and the efforts which we should harness to surmount the struggle: "Life had no periods, no stretches. It simply swirled around, muddling and confusing, leading nowhere" (112). This is, in fact, the sum total of the semiotic circle of CCV. And, indeed, this approach to her novels and shorter fiction may truly point out Anita Desai's place as a forerunner to fight for the cause of Women's Liberation Movement (WLM) in India and abroad.

NOTES AND REFERENCES

1. Ram, Atma, Interviews with *Indian English Writers* (Calcutta: Writers Workshop, 1983).
2. Desai, Anita, *Voices in the City* (Delhi: Orient Paperback, 1965).
3. "The Ideology of Romanticism," in R.F. Gleckner and G.E. Enscoe, eds., *Romanticism: Points of View* (New Jersey: Prentice-Hall, 1970), 170.
4. Desai, Anita, *Cry the Peacock*. London, Peter Owen, 1963.
5. Sharma, S.D. *Thomas Love Peacock As A Novelist*. SPH, Delhi, Vol. I, Edn. I, 1986, 73.
6. Sharma, S.D., *Thematic Dichotomy of Writings in Indian English, Indology & Culture*. PBD Publication, Delhi, Vol. I, 1985.
7. Desai, Anita, *Where Shall We Go This Summer*? Vikas Publishing House Pvt. Ltd., Delhi, 1975 (hereinafter referred to as VPH). The protagonist (Sita) echoes the same views elsewhere too. "Sita felt a spasm of fear at her bravado, her wild words, her impulsive actions that had flung them all along onto this island surrounded by wild seas. It was no place in which to give birth [...]. The more physical details of the matter crowded her mind. Usually she repressed them with an agonized determination but the rain drumming. Thrumming, pouring all about her locked her in, locked her up, forced her to turn on herself."
8. Sharma, S.D., *Perspectives on Creativity* (ed.), Proceedings of the National Symposium, Faculty of New Education, G.B. Pant University, Pantnagar—263145, Vol. I, Edn. I, 1989, 152.
9. Sharma, S.D., *Longinus on the Sublime*. PBP Publication, Delhi, Vol. I, Edn. III, 1990, 190.

10. Sita makes similar socking cries seeing big buildings inhabited by murderers and frauds: "Crow formed the shadow civilization in that city of flats and alleys. She watched them from the balcony, hopping clannishly about the rocks on which the sea broke, scrambling to catch a rotten fish or scraps of edible flotsam left by the waves to stink in the sun. They even East on the edges and balcony rails of the flats, waiting for lazy cooks to throw out a bucketful of kitchen garbage into the alley—scraps were caught by them in mid-air, expert for all their clownishness, tattered wings holding them aloft as they twisted and flapped to get the largest bigs," 25.
11. Sharma, S.D. *Semantics and Syntax*. PBD Publication, Delhi, Vol. I, Edn. I, 1990.
12. Sita elsewhere feels: "She felt the long, straight monotonous track of her life whip itself round her in swift circles, perhaps a spiral, whirling around and around till its very lines dissolved and turned to a blur of silver, the blurred silver of mirror—like windowpanes. All was bright, all was blurred, all was in a whirl. Life has no periods, no stretches. It simply swirled around mudding and confusion, leading nowhere," 112.
13. Sita's faith in the supernatural powers of Manjori may appear to be most unscientific, but it often works wonders. Note her faith in the magical world of the island: "If reality were to be borne, then illusion was the only alternative. She saw that island illusion as a refuge, a protection. It would hold her baby safely unborn, by magic. Then there would be see—it would wash the frenzy out of her, drown it. Perhaps the tides would lull the children, too, into smoother, softer beings. The grooves of the trees would shade them and protect them," 72.
14. Desai, Anita, *Bye-Bye, Blackbird*. Delhi: Hind, 1971.
15. Desai, Anita, *Fire On The Mountain*. London: Heinemann, 77.
16. Desai, Anita, *Clear Light of Day*. Delh: Penguin Books, 1980.
17. Desai, Anita, *The Village By The Sea*. London: William Heinemann, 1982).
18. Desai, Anita, *In Custody*. London: Heinemann, 1984.
19. Sharma, S.D., *Dr Johnson's Preface to the Plays of Shakespeare*. PBD Publication, Delhi, Vol. I, Edn. III, 1986.
20. Sharma, S.D., *Makers of Criticism*. PBD Publication, Delhi, Vol. I, Edn. I, 1985.
21. Sharma, S.D., *Aristotle's Poetics*. S.S. Publication, Delhi, Vol. I, Edn. II, 1984, 170.
22. *Games at Twilight and Other Stories*, first published by W. Heinemann, London, 1978, Penguin Books, 1982.
23. Palgrave, F.T., *The Golden Treasury*. Macmillan, 1969, 275.
24. *Cry, the Peacock*. Maya also struggles to find a meaning in life. Her dialogue with Gautama is worth quoting: "I live my life for you [...] you

are untouched [...]. You shall never help me. It is all true one of us will win, the other must lose," 114.

In *Voices In The City*, Nirode and Dharma struggle for higher values of life. Nirode finds life in city boring with "muddy river air" superseded by "exhilaration, determination and pride," 11.

25. *Where Shall We Go This Summer*? 65 (Elsewhere, too, Sita utters similar words which reflect upon his delving deep into a quest for higher issues: "Everyone around her winced—she saw them wincing at her harshness, her wildness that they so dreaded. But she could not stop herself now, not even Karan's sake. Their betrayal had torn her open with such violence, now violence poured from her like blood. In it was also the shame, the disappointment: he had not come to see her, to fetch her, as she had supposed: he had come because Menaka had called him. He had betrayed her too. They had all betrayed her. Why?").

6

Marital Disharmony in Anita Desai's Novels

BASAVARAJ NAIKAR

Of all the contemporary Indian English novelists Anita Desai is, perhaps, the most perceptive and consistent explorer of the inner life, especially that of Indian women, convulsed by an acute sense of helplessness in the face of the onslaughts of an unfeeling world and the resultant mental agony. Even in her very first novel, *Cry, the Peacock,* she attempts to portray the turbulent inner world of its protagonist, Maya, whose neurotic condition is brought about by a variety of factors including marital discord and barrenness and psychic disorder. Using a tripartite structure and third person narration, which affords opportunities for authorial comment, Anita Desai traces Maya's gradual descent into a state of madness, impelled by her responses to the developments in her outer life, as it were.

Married at an early age to Gautama, a friend of her father and leading lawyer, who is of twice her age Maya seems destined to suffer from emotional starvation especially since she is childless. The first emotional crisis she faces arises at the death of her pet dog, Toto, on whom she has been lavishing all her affection. The opening chapter detailing it reports how Maya first could not stand the sight of her beloved dead dog and that she rushes to "the garden tap to wash the vision from her eyes" (5). Maya thinks that "she saw the evil glint of a blue bottle" (5) and grows hysterical and finds the setting sun "swelling visibly like [...] a purulent boil" (6). Her condition is aggravated by Gautama's causal and unfeeling remarks: "It is all over, come and drink your tea and stop crying. You mustn't cry" (7). Further, instead of consoling her in her grief at the loss of her Toto, he leaves her to meet a visitor who has come to see him and forgets all about the dead dog. This incident brings out the contrast between Maya, who is highly sensitive and imaginative and of a neurotic sensibility, and Gautama, who is unimaginative and pragmatic and unsentimental—a contrast accentuated by communication gap on account of his being wrapped up in his professional preoccupations. It is, therefore, not surprising that they have been constantly quarreling with each other even over trifles. Maya, reflecting on her unhappy marriage, observes:

> It was discouraging to reflect on how much in her marriage was based upon a nobility forced upon us from outside, and therefore neither true nor lasting. It was broken repeatedly, and repeatedly the pieces were picked up and put together again, as of a sacred icon with which out of the pettiest superstition, we could not bear to part (45).

Although, they continue to live together, they find their temperaments irreconcilable and their sensibilities marked by divergence. Surprised by Gautama's inability to differentiate between the smell of lemons and petunias Maya muses:

> The blossoms of the lemon tree were different, quite different; of much stronger, crisper character, they seemed cut out of hard moon shells, by a sharp knife of mother of pearl, into curving, scimitar petals that guarded the heart of fragrance. Their scent, too, was more vivid—a sour, astringent scent, refreshing as that of ground lemon peel, a crushed lemon leaf. I tried to explain this to Gautama, stammering with anxiety, for now, when his companionship was a necessity, I required his closest understanding (21).

It is not merely Gautama's insensitivity as is implied in his inability to distinguish between the two smells but his being inured to the beauty of the natural world and unresponsive to her feelings traceable in part to his philosophical detachment that makes for their estrangement. Maya feels sorry for her husband:

> [...] Poor Gautama. Not to be able to notice the odour of limes, not to hear the melancholy voice singing

> somewhere behind the plantains, not to have time to count the stars as they came out one by one—poor Gautama, my poor, poor husband [...] (237).

Indeed, she feels that Gautama "had never lived, and never would" (240). The temperamental incompatibility that characterises their relationship brings about an unbridgeable gulf between them causing acute mental agony to the highly strung Maya whose condition is aggravated by her father-fixation, as observed by the perceptive though unresponsive Gautama, when she harks back to her childhood memories to avoid the present:

> If you know your Freud, it would be very straightforward [...] you have a very obvious father-obsession which is also the reason why you married me, a man so much older than yourself. It is a complex that, unless you mature rapidly, you will not be able to deal with, to destroy. But then, it will probably destroy itself in the end, since passion of this sort is almost always self-consuming, having no object within its range that it can safely consume. Any little setback destroys it [...] (168-69).

Indeed, it is her 'father-obsession' which has made her marry Gautama, so much older than herself and a friend of her father and which accounts for her turning to childhood memories and lapsing into childhood behaviour as evidenced by her crying and bursting out into a fit of furious pillow-beating to seek release from the oppressive present. Maya even remarks: "The world is like a toy specially made for me, painted in my favourite colours, set moving to my favourite tunes" (41).

Further, her neurotic condition has worsened by her recollection of a prediction by an albino astrologer in her childhood:

> My child, I would not speak of it if I saw it on your face alone. But look, look at the horoscope. Stars do not lie. And it is best to warn you, prepare you [...]. Death to one of you. When you are married—and you shall be married young [...]. Death—an early one—by unnatural causes (33).

Obsessed with the albino astrologer's ominous prediction, Maya muses:

> It must be a mark on my forehead, which had been so clear to the opaque eye of the albino who had detected it, upon which the stars now hurled themselves vengefully, and which prophesied a relentless and fatal competition between myself and Gautama. I tried to define the mark, give it a name, a locality. Was it an arrow? A coffin? A star? Was it between the eyes? At the temple? Was it dark? Was it pale? And what made the gods reach out and touch it with their cold fingers, as they considered the prospect of a murder? (122)

Further, she is aware of her being confined to her private hell: "Torture, guilt, dread, imprisonment—these were the four walls of my private hell, one that no one could survive in long. Death was certain" (117). Her obsession with death reinforced by the death of her pet dog plunges her into a state of insanity of which she is uncannily conscious as she herself observes:

> Yes, I am going insane. I am moving further and further from all wisdom, all calm, and I shall soon be mad, if I am not that already. Perhaps it is my madness that leads me to imagine that horoscope, that encounter with the albino, his prediction, my fate? Perhaps it is only a phenomenon of insanity? (124)

Maya is convinced that she is becoming insane as she herself remarks:

> This is not natural, I told myself, this cannot be natural. There is something weird about me now, wherever I go, whatever I see, whatever I listen to has this unnaturalness to it. This is insanity. But who, what is insane? I myself? Or the world around me? (167)

In her insane condition she becomes all the more obsessed with death, which makes her think that "it was now to be either Gautama, or I." Faced with such a terrible choice she decides that Gautama has to die as he is detached from and indifferent to what makes life livable.

It is significant that even before becoming insane she contemplates murder as is brought out by her remark that murders are committed "only for the sake of money, or property—or anything solid, and dirty. Not for love, or life or basic things" (23). That she should think of it at all suggests her longing for a life of freedom possible only through the death of Gautama, which later becomes accentuated when she receives a letter from her brother, Arjun, informing her of his having 'rebelled' against their father and the socio-cultural tradition that have inhibited the development of his individuality. Ironically enough, her yearning for freedom seems fulfilled by her insanity which drives her to murder her husband. What is 'heard' at the end of the novel is not the shriek which a gruesome murder would cause but "the patter of a child's laughter cascading up and down the scales of some new delight—a brilliant peacock feather perhaps?" (251) followed by silence as she commits suicide which represents her release from the grasping world. The novel traces the disintegration of Maya as her overwrought mind plunges her into darkness of death.

Anita Desai's fourth novel, *Where Shall We Go This Summer* (1975) like her first novel, *Cry, the Peacock,* focuses on marital disharmony which accentuated the emotionally highly strong nature of their protagonists, Sita and Maya, respectively. In some respects, *Where Shall We Go This Summer*? is reminiscent of D.H. Lawrence's story, "The Woman Who Rode Away," although the comparison between the two cannot be sustained as they sharply differ in their essential thematic concerns. However, like the heroine of Lawrence's tale, Sita, the protagonist of Desai's novel, faced with an unwanted fifth pregnancy goes away from Bombay along with her two children, Menaka and Karan, leaving behind her husband, Raman, in despair. Sita after her marriage finds living in her husband's parents' house, "their age-rotted flat," unbearable in that it is marked by "sub-human placidity, calmness and sluggishness" and feels that "their subhumanity might swamp her." To preserve her individuality, she behaves in a way, which appears to be outrageous to the other members of the family by smoking openly and talking "in sudden rushes of emotion, as though flinging darts at their smooth, unscared faces." Indeed, she regards most of the people as animals: "They are nothing—nothing but appetite and sex. Only food, sex and money matter—Animals" (31-32). She compares them to pariahs:

> My pet animals—or wild animals in the forest, yes. But these are neither—They are like pariahs you see in the street, hanging about the drains and dustbins, waiting to pounce and kill and eat (32).

Later, she shifts to a small flat with her husband and children but does not find life any better as she has to endure visits by people whose "insularity and complacence" (33) "as well as the aggression and violence of others" (33) act as "affronts upon her tiring nerves" (33). Further, Sita becomes increasingly alienated from the world as she is paid little attention to by her husband because of his being absorbed in the management of his business and her children because of their growing independent with the result that she is faced with intolerable boredom that can prove destructive:

> She herself looking in it saw it, stretched out so vast, so flat, so deep, that in fright she scrambled about it, searching for a few of those moments that proclaimed her still alive, not quite drowned and dead (33-34).

Indeed, Sita has had to suffer boredom and loneliness to which modern man seems sentenced and her plight is reminiscent of that of Antoine Roquentin's in Jean Paul Sartre's *Nausea,* who is tormented by his traceable to ennui and alienation. Though bearing the legendary names, Sita and her husband Rama, they spell a relationship, which is a travesty of that immortalised by the characters concerned in *Ramayana.* Sita being highly imaginative and emotional and Raman being 'a middling kind of man,' prosaic and phlegmatic, they are temperamentally poles apart which accounts for their being unable to forge a harmonious marital relationship. For instance, recalling a month later, their encounter with a stranger on their way back home from their visit to Ajanta and Ellora:

> "He seemed so brave," she blurted when Raman asked her why she had once more brought up the subject of hitch-hiking foreigner, months later. "Brave? Him?" Raman was honestly amused, "he was a fool—he didn't even know which side of the road to wait on."

> "Perhaps that was only innocence," Sita faltered, "and it made him seem more brave not knowing anything but going on nevertheless" (34).

Sita's comment which must have seemed absurd or irrational to her husband highlights the psychological distance separating them as also their sharply differing perceptions traceable to her yearning for a life of freedom and his matter-of-fact attitude to life respectively. Her anguish has become unbearable when she finds herself pregnant once again—for the fifth time and deciding to have 'a bewitched life' for herself and her unborn child, she leaves for Manori, a small island off the Marve island, where her father has built a house, hoping to "achieve the miracle of not giving birth," taking her two children, Menaka and Karan, with her. Moses, the caretaker of the house, escorts them across the sea to her father's island house which being unoccupied for twenty years is in a sorry state:

> [...] then she went in at last and saw what had become of the house in twenty years of absence—a waste of ashes she saw, the cold remains of the bonfire her father had lit to a blaze [...] the odour was of bate and mildew; and silence boomed like the silence of undersea caves. It had no air of providing shelter from the sea or beach—it was much a natural part of them as an abandoned shell or lump of twisted drift-wood (18).

After unpacking her things and lying down with her children, Sita ruminates recalling her unhappy married life and her childhood spent on the island with her father who had become a legend in his lifetime having brought water from the well to the inhabitants of the island and taught them more profitable ways of farming, although she was sceptical about his being a messiah as she found his relationship with her own elder sister, Rekha, who later on became a national celebrity, rather incestuous. Indeed, recollecting her father, she wonders whether her father was really a true saint and patriot and what had made his second wife desert him and her children and live a life of seclusion secretly in Varanasi and significantly, she is not able to find answers to those questions which remain unanswered in the novel. Interestingly, while her father plays a Prospero-like role in Manori as in Shakespeare's *Temptest,* Sita does not behave like Miranda although she views "the island as a piece of magic, a magic mirror."

Her reverie-like reminiscing, presented as a stream of consciousness, is reminiscent of Mrs Ramsay's in Virginia Woolf's *To the Lighthouse* in that it underlines the tension between the materialist male world and the female world marked by sensitivity, although the comparison between the two novels cannot be pressed far beyond the fact that both exemplify in different ways "fiction of intensified sensitivity." Significantly, Sita's daughter, Menaka, does not share her mother's poetic or artistic temperament or perception as is evidenced by an argument she has with her. Sita discussing the poverty of science and the opulence of art observes: "Science don't be as satisfactory. It is all—all figures, statistics, logic. Science is believing that two and two make four—pooh" (85) and adds "It leads you to a dead-end. There are no dead-ends, now, in art. That is something spontaneous, Menaka, and alive and creative" (85). Menaka brushes aside her argument terming it "all nonsense."

Sita's attempt to overcome her existential despair stemming from her alienation from her husband and her children, who long for the comforts and excitement of city life, proves abortive. Menaka writes to her father asking him to take them back as she has to apply for admission to the Medical College. Seeing how excited her children are at the time of her husband's arrival, Sita feels "that they were being disloyal to her, disloyal to the island and its wild nature" (94). Raman's arrival and the conversation that she has with him have the effect of confronting her with the stark actualities of life, which cannot be wished away. She realises, though painfully, like the heroine of R.K. Narayan's *The Dark Room,* that there is no escape from one's responsibilities and that life must be continued:

> [...] Life must be continued, and all its business—Menaka's admission to medical college gained, wife led to hospital, now child safely brought forth, the children reared, the factory seen to, a salary earned, a salary spent [...] (101).

She even felt herself to be an escapist and coward:

> She had escaped from duties and responsibilities, from order and routine, from life and the city, to unlivable island. She had refused to give birth to a child in a world not fit to receive the child. She had the imagination to offer it an alternative—a life unlived, a life bewitched. She had cried out her grand "No" but now the time had come for her epitaph to be written—*che fece per viltate il gron refiute.* Very soon now that epitaph would have to be written (102).

Just as R.K. Narayan's heroine returns home after quitting it like Nora of Ibsen's *The Doll's House,* Sita picks up her belongings and prepares to leave the island with her husband and children, feeling "like a player at the end of the performance, clearing the stage, packing the costumes, in equal parts saddened and relieved." She regards her sojourn on the island as an episode in a drama—the drama of existence, in her case:

> [...] Her time on the island had been very much of an episode on a stage, illuminated by gaudy sunset effects and played to thunderous storm's music, the storm ended, the play over, the stage had now to be cleared—then the player could go home. Instead of being a person who for many years had had to perform on a false stage and had only her, on the island, begun to live a life of primitive reality, she had actually been playing the part here of an actress in a theatrical performance and was now to return to a life of retirement, off stage (110-11).

Sita's frustration is traceable to her futile attempt to relive her past as she did in her childhood forgetting that the passage of time inexorably alters everything including herself, which explains why she finds the islanders unresponsive and critical of her, comparing her with her father. Further, she is made to admit to herself "that destruction may be the true element in which life survives and creation merely a freak, temporary, and doomed event" (37-38) as she battles to save her unborn child from the violence-ridden world. Significantly, she becomes aware of it when she helplessly watches her children acting violently:

> Karan kicked over a tower of blocks and howled with

> maniac glee to see them tumble; Menaka sat calmly tearing her Sunday water colours into long strips of meaningless colour, her husband casually handed her the newspaper on his way out to the office. They all hammered at her with cruel fists [...]. They were hand-grenades all hurled at her frail gold fish-bowl belly and instinctively she laid her hands over it, feeling the child there play like some soft fleshed fish in a bowl of warm sea-water. She folded her hands over it, frightened, certain now that civilization had been created by the god-like efforts of the few, in the face of timeless war of destruction that had begun with time and was now roaring around her, battering her and her fish-foetus so that survival seemed hopeless. How could civilization survive, how could the child? How could she hold them whole and pure and unimpeached in the midst of this bloodshed? They would surely be wounded, fall and die (37).

The island to which she goes in the hope that it will provide a sanctuary for her tortured self seems as suffocating as the city, confronting her with a kind of primitive reality that proves as unbearable as the dreary reality that her home in the city spells to which she has to be reconciled if she is to commit herself in life and motherhood.

Where Shall We Go This Summer may thus be seen as a parable on the inability of human beings to relate the inner with the outer, the individual with society. It is a story of illusions melting away in the cold light of the everyday and the commonplace. It does suggest that a life of complete inwardness is not the solution to the problems of life. Nor is the other extreme of complete conformity and total draining out of the individuality and of the imagination of the human being the proper way out of the dilemma. It shows that human happiness consists in harmonising the opposites of life.

REFERENCES

Anita Desai, *Cry, the Peacock.* Calcutta: Rupa and Co., 1980.

Anita Desai, *Where Shall We Go This Summer.* Delhi: Vikas Publishing House, 1975.

7

Discovery of the Self: An Interior Journey in Margaret Atwood's *Surfacing* and Anita Desai's *Where Shall We Go This Summer?*

S.N. VIKRAM RAJ URS

In this paper an attempt is made to focus on the basic quest of a solitary individual as dramatized in Margaret Atwood's *Surfacing* and Anita Desai's *Where Shall We Go This Summer*? These novelists hailing from totally different cultural contexts take up the interior journey of a human being, an archetypal figure who struggles for a new pattern of order. Their protagonists try to rediscover a creative possibility within the invisible layers of their self. The woman, in these two novels, is the archetypal figure who tries to find her moorings to extricate herself from her anguished state. There are striking similarities in the respective approaches of Anita Desai and Margaret Atwood. They share a similar belief in concentrating on the submerged inner world of an individual.

Anita Desai explains in a key passage that, 'writing is to me a process of discovering truth—the truth that is nine-tenth's of the iceberg that is submerged beneath the one-tenth visible portion we call Reality. Writing is my way of plunging to the depths and exploring the underlying truth.'

A study of the fiction of Anita Desai reveals the creative potentialities of a human being who is cramped in by her associations with social mores and conventions which reflect her connections with the objective world. Maya (*Cry, the Peacock*), Sita (*Where Shall We Go This Summer*?), and Bim (*Clear Light of Day*) explore a definite meaning for their existence. Maya searches 'for an order of lines and designs, a symmetry' in order to discover solace for her inner rage. Sita travels back to her past to find out a meaning to her present life. Similarly, Margaret Atwood's *Edible Woman* and *Surfacing* in particular deal with the theme of confronting the submerged layers of the self. The outer skin of an individual is peeled off and the essential core is in perfect union with the cosmos. *Surfacing* is an archetypal search of a nameless narrator to find out the creative sources of life. This search for a new being is fully probed in *Surfacing* and *Where Shall We Go This Summer?*

Where Shall We Go This Summer? deals with the story of a young disillusioned woman, Sita. She wishes to go back to her childhood past, her parental house, Manori. The island of Manori is cut off from the mainland. She also wishes to cut herself off from the mainland, Bombay. It is her desire to go to the island and live where her father was a respected figure. He was a Gandhian who has left his unmistakable stamp on the island. She desperately tries to recapture her childhood days when she was happy and secure in the company of her father.

The starting point of plunging into the invisible mysterious past is that she decides to go back to the island. The island is a romantic metaphor for Sita who values the heroic and redeeming qualities of her father. But when she travels back to the island which is almost deserted, she painfully reconstructs her submerged past. She discovers that her father was not a true Gandhian at heart. She also realizes that the sea is dangerous and evil. It is not the sea which once represented her childhood memories. The very name Sita reminds us of the suffering qualities of the exiled Sita in *The Ramayana*. This Sita is an extension of the archetypal figure of Sita. She makes a deliberate choice and she is exiled from her disillusionment with her husband and from false social values.

There is an attempt to understand personal relationships through the character of Sita. An intimate rapport with Raman her husband is possible only if Sita tries to re-adjust her inner realities to the outside 'meaningless' world. The novel develops from the germinating idea that it would be impossible to go on living in a state of inner contradictions. A sensitive individual will have to make a sacrifice of giving a part of oneself to make way for a meaningful personal relationship.

Sita has an answer to her dilemma in Cavafy's poem. She quotes from the poem and it consoles her to a great extent. The poem reappears in the final section of the novel. She is not sure whether to say the 'great Yes' or the 'great No.' The essence of the poem is that an individual who has the courage to say 'the right No' is absolutely 'free' from life's 'dull-lit empty shell.'

The innermost urge of Sita is to identify herself with 'the right No.' She almost says 'the right No' to the 'order and routine' life with Raman. But she is not fully prepared to go to that extent of defying the ordinariness of her existence. She meekly submits to Raman's wish to take her back to the mainland. But she is determined to wage a ceaseless 'battle between his brand of courage and hers.'

On the surface, Margaret Atwood's *Surfacing,* recounts the experiences of a young Canadian divorcee who returns to her home of the childhood with three friends. She fails as a painter and her name is not mentioned. Her lover Joe accompanies her. He is a potter who does not make the grade. Her other two friends, David, a failed rebel and Anna, a failed wife also go with her in search of her 'lost' father. The nameless narrator wants to investigate the sudden disappearance of her father from an isolated island in one of the large lakes of Northern Quebec.

When she returns to the island she is exposed to memories of her childhood. The wild island exerts its elemental hold on the consciousness of the nameless narrator. The search for her father leads onto something else—an exploration of her inner self, her nature as a woman and her place in Nature. She is submerged into a mystical vision when she dives into the lake from which she surfaces to re-discover her lost innocence, with a new acceptance of herself and her spiritual powers in the natural world.

Like Sita, the nameless narrator rejects her oppressive environment. She rebels against the false materialism and vulgarity of the American society. She rejects her marriage. She distrusts love as a form of male possessiveness. Sita too does not want love to be an aspect of male domination. The nameless narrator is a divorcee with a sense of guilt. The dead body of the child under water brings a sudden memory that she had had an abortion. She travels back to the lonely island disgusted with the false notions of floating on the surface life. Similar to the agitated self of Sita who is fed up with the ugly life of Bombay, the nameless narrator has a strong desire to find out an order, a balance to her inner fury on the island. She tries to explore the rock paintings beneath the lake. She wants to understand the secret language. She plunges into the lake and many realizations occur to her. In the process of knowing her past, she is transformed into a new being.

The novel is a continuation, a renewal of life in the self of the nameless narrator. Her dive into the lake below the surface is a crucial event: she is descending into her subconscious. She has recognized her dead father. It is also a nightmare of her lost child. She dies a symbolic death beneath the surface:

> I couldn't accept it, that mutilation, ruin I'd made, I needed a different version.

She is separated into two parts, owing to the raging conflict within. One part exists on the visible world. Another part is buried under the surface. Her relationships with her ex-husband, her present lover Joe and David and Anna, her friends who are known to her very recently consist of one separate self. The direct encounter of her father's corpse leads onto the surfacing from death into renewal of life. She identifies through the dive into her invisible part, her 'free-floating' new born self. She realizes her twin-double:

> My other shape was in the water,
> not my reflection but my shadow,
> foreshortened, outline blurred,
> rays streaming out from around the head (141).

The re-living of the memories of her past is a process in her psychic quest.

She is able to capture lucid moments of pristine spiritual harmony with Nature through the re-enactment of her memory and by observing her relationship with her friends David and

Ann and her lover Joe, she emerges as a 'whole' woman cured of her sick disease of the mind:

> When I am clean I come up out of the lake,
> leaving my false body floated on the surface,
> a cloth decoy; it jiggles in the waves I make,
> nudges, gently against the dock.
> They offered clothing as a token, formerly;
> that was partial but the gods are demanding,
> absolute, they want all (178).

She joins herself into the mysterious, elemental forces of Nature. She is in a mystical travel. '[...] accepts me as part of the land' and 'Around me the space rustles; owl sound, across the lake or inside me, distance contracts. A light wind, the small waves talking against the shore, multilingual water are indications of the change that has happened.'

She sheds all she has acquired from society and lives alone. She lives like a wild beast on roots. She returns to a consciousness beyond her rational self. She hopes that her unborn child will be 'the first true human.' She has a vision of her father in which he realizes that he is an intruder upon Nature. The father makes a determined effort to destroy his cabin. The rational mind gives way to a heightened state. It is possible for a secret communion with the dark powers of Nature. Her return to 'my own time' will be based on new energies which are released from a life-enhancing 'power.'

The important difference lies in the fact that in *Where Shall We Go This Summer?* Sita goes to the mainland still clinging to keep her individual freedom secretly. But in *Surfacing,* the nameless narrator fully evolves into a new being who is free of guilt and shame. She merges with the living preserves of Nature. The dive into the lake and the surfacing point to a state of 'To Trust is to let go.'

REFERENCES

Anita Desai, *Where Shall We Go This Summer?* Vikas Publishing House, Delhi, 1975; Orient Paperbacks, Delhi, 1982.

Margaret Atwood, *Surfacing,* Virago, London, 1972. Rpt. 1983.

8

A Feminist Perspective on Anita Desai's *Fasting, Feasting*

ASHA CHOUBEY

In the days of Adam and Eve, inequality of sexes was not known but down the ages women have been relegated to an inferior position in the social set-up. From being the very incarnation of Power (Shakti) and Knowledge (Gnyan), women came to be held only as a child-bearing machine and their horizons have been supposed to be confined only to their familial role. Chiefly the blame was put on men and it was believed that male-domination does not allow women to flourish freely. But in recent times there have also been sensitive writers who have taken a humanist approach to the situation. They have taken a holistic view of the issue and have discovered that it is not only male-chauvinism that has caused havoc but also female-reluctance to face the challenges and even female-apathy that is responsible for this disparity. In the last couple of years *Difficult Daughters* by Manju Kapoor and *Fasting, Feasting* by Anita Desai are two attempts to take stock of the situation from this viewpoint. Primarily the story of human hungers, *Fasting, Feasting* merits appreciation from a feminist point of view. Like all women writers, Desai is not only sensitive to the woman-question but also all 'criticism of life' from her pen can be finally seen as gynocriticism (Showalter 1989: 4). This paper is an attempt to present a feminist approach to *Fasting, Feasting.* The novel, divided neatly into two parts, takes us to the centre of an extremely orthodox Indian family on one hand, and an unusually whimsical family in Massachusetts on the other. Apart from the head MamaPapa, Uma, Aruna and Arun form the Indian family whereas the family in Massachusetts consists of Mr and Mrs Patton, Rod and Melanie. Arun forms the link between these two families, which are socially, nationally and culturally different. Desai simply points out the emotional and human affinity that makes the two families one.

I

Primarily *Fasting, Feasting* is the story of Uma, who happens to be the most subdued—rather crushed member of the Indian family. Uma is like a catalyst whose presence is never noticed, never appreciated and yet whose absence may make all the difference. Uma is a woman lost in the jungle of duties—sometimes to her MamaPapa, at other times to her brother Arun and at still other times to her sister Aruna. She is expected to be an obedient daughter, an affectionate and motherly sister and everything but an individual. As a young girl, Uma has her dreams, her desires, but when her dreams come in conflict with the comforts of her parents it is she who has to sacrifice and she does. At the outset itself the novelist presents the contrast that exists between the colourful, happy life of her parents and her own dull and deary existence:

> Uma flounces off, her grey hair frazzled, her myopic eyes glaring behind her spectacles, muttering under her breath. The parents, momentarily agitated upon their swing by the sudden invasion of ideas—sweets, parcel, letter, sweets—settle back to their slow, rhythmic swinging (Desai 1999: 5).

The Atharva Veda says: The birth of a girl, grant it elsewhere, here grant a boy (vi, 23).

If this could be the prayer of an age when the condition of women was relatively better and they were granted an almost equal status in the society, we may very well imagine the poor lot of women in other ages. Even educated parents show their primitive, rustic face today when it comes to choosing between daughter and son. Girls are not only less preferred but also they are more burdened with responsibilities. Women are expected to take care of their siblings. A woman is never allowed to be a child, right from her childhood she is supposed to act as a mother to her younger brothers and sisters. Since the birth of her baby brother Arun, Uma has been trained to sacrifice her private pleasures at the altar of familial responsibilities. Much like Virmati of *Difficult Daughters,*

Uma is forced to nurse her kid brother, even when she is herself a child:

> When Mama came home, weak, exhausted and short-tempered, she tried to teach Uma the correct way of folding nappies, of preparing watered milk, of rocking the screaming infant to sleep when he was covered with prickly heat as with a burn. Uma, unfortunately, was her clumsy, undependable self, dropping and breaking things, frightenedly pulling away from her much too small, too precious and too fragile brother (17-18).

Desai brings into focus parental apathy which scars the daughters permanently. First it is parents craving for a boy that hurts the daughters because it makes obvious the truth of their accidental birth. Had the parents been given a choice they would never have liked to face the ignominy of giving birth to a female child. Then it is their ecstasy at the birth of a son that makes the wounds even deeper, beyond cure. Papa celebrates the birth of Arun as he had never done the birth of Uma and Aruna.

> Papa, in his elation leaping over three chairs in the hall, one after the other, like a boy playing leap-frog, his arms flung up in the air and his hair flying. 'A boy!' he screamed a bo-oy! Arun, Arun at last!' (17)

Feminists maintain that women are not mentally different since birth. The female-child is only biologically different but the parochial society conditions it into being a woman:

> One is not born but rather becomes a woman, says Simone de Beauvoir. She continues, "No biological, psychological, economic fate determines the figure that the human female presents in the society, it is civilisation as a whole that produces this creature, intermediate between male and eunuch, which is described as feminine" (Beauvoir 1957: 445).

Uma becomes a victim to the tendency of society to condition a girl-child to submit to the norms of the patriarchal set-up. Desai as a true humanist puts the blame not only on men who are suffering with the complex of male-superiority but also on women who oppress their own kind. It is not only the male-chauvinist that acts as the antagonist force but also apathetic female does more harm in terms of the loss of woman-soul. Uma is reduced to the status of a domestic help. All this because her mother has to fulfil her role of, 'Papa's helpmate, his consort' as 'After all Uma and Aruna and the ayah were there to stand in for her at Arun's cot' (31). No efforts to cow down the already docile spirit of Uma are spared. She is denied the pleasure of ordinary living. If she once enjoys a cheerful evening out with Ramu Bhai, she has to bear her mother's curse: 'Quiet, you hussy! Not another word from you, you idiot child!' [...]. 'You, you disgrace to the family—nothing but disgrace, ever!' (53)

'Marriage is the destiny traditionally offered to women by society,' say the feminists (De Beauvoir: 445). Twice MamaPapa try to get Uma married, and twice it is that she is put to much humiliation and disgrace. When both the attempts end in fiasco, it is accepted that Uma has to remain unwed all her life and with a heavy heart her parents accept this burden. Though she never rebels, never utters a word of complaint, she is certainly not an unfeeling brute. She suffers silently, and solace does not come even from the most expected quarters—her mother. To make the matters worse Mama also looks upon her as an object of laughter.

Uma's sister Aruna is married off into a respectable family and moves to Bombay. Her brother Arun goes to Massachusetts to pursue higher education but Uma is left behind to serve her parents untiringly, to become the object of their barbs and to live a life of desolation. In this apathetic, friendless world Uma finds refuge in her childhood memories when she was still studying in school. Those were the golden days of her life, never again in her life she gets to taste such bliss as she had experienced then. Whenever she finds her present aimless existence too dreary to tolerate, she escapes into that world again. She has carefully preserved the Christmas cards and snapshots belonging to that period and the very sight and touch of these thrill her with ecstasy:

> She runs her finger along the gilt crosses and embossed poinsettias, she plays with fragments of ribbon and lace, and reads through the merry little jingles that make her smile: they are so loving and bright with goodwill and friendship, she binds them all up again with string and stows them away like treasure—to her they are treasure.

> If anyone were to touch, their magic would be somehow defaced: that is how she feels about them (98-99).

Mama herself has no time for her family and home because she is always busy attending kitty parties and club meetings but when Mrs O'Henry invites Uma to a coffee party, much hue and cry is raised. Even a single phone call invites the wrath of Papa:

> 'Costs money! Costs money!' he kept shouting long after. 'Never earned anything in her life, made me spend and spend, on her dowry and her wedding. Oh, yes, spend till I'm ruined, till I am a pauper' (146).

In India, a woman is considered to be an: 'embodiment of sacrifice, silent suffering, humility, faith and knowledge' (Everett 1981: 76). MamaPapa are deaf and blind to the needs of their daughter. They forget that Uma is not a body but a soul as well. They, however, feel that if she is kept occupied with one or the other work, she shall not get time to think about her personal dreams, she shall not cherish dreams at all:

> All morning MamaPapa have found things for Uma to do. It is as if Papa's retirement is to be spent in this manner—sitting on the red swing in the veranda with Mama, rocking, and finding ways to keep Uma occupied (133).

The dreams of a free existence are not unknown or unimagined for Uma. The fact that Moyna Joshi is pursuing a career in Delhi, incites in her an aspiration to make a career, to leave home and to soar high. But her wings have been so badly and pre-maturely clipped, that she can simply flutter her wings, but cannot fly. Aeons of dumb, docile existence renders women incapable to act. They are trained simply to show obeisance to the orders of their rulers. They sulk, they struggle but they are never freed of their meaningless existence as secondary to their masters.

> These troubling, secret possibilities now entered Uma's mind—as Mama would have pointed out had she known—whenever Uma was idle. They were like seeds dropped on the stony, arid land that Uma inhabited. Sometimes, miraculously, they sprouted forth the idea: run away,

> escape. But Uma could not visualise escape in the form of a career. What was a career? She had no idea (131).

The romantic poetry of Ella Wheeler Wilcox opens up 'magic casements' before Uma. She is filled with the courage to rebel. But her timid ever-servile soul does not support her rebellion and at the most she registers her anger through an 'angry look at the door' when Mama knocks: 'She hears the door splintering, waits for it to give way, till it does, she will not move. She tightens her hold on the book' (136). Uma's existence has been reduced into an unfed servant who has so many duties but no rights.

II

The novel is certainly Uma's story, but Uma is a helpless member of an orthodox family that is again set in the parochial society. The patriarch happens to be the unchallenged ruler here. He holds the rein and commands all members and all activities inside the family. He has to cater only to the physical needs of the members, emotionally they are not expected to be alive. It is supposed that all members must ally their joys with the happiness of the patriarch. Like a truly devoted servant they are expected to work for his comforts and instead of expecting gratefulness from his side, they should rather feel privileged to serve him. Engels in his *Origin of Species* points out that the very concept of family is based on the presumption that wife belongs to husband. He says that the Latin word 'family' means the total number of slaves belonging to one man. The woman is 'given' in marriage and then she becomes 'his' to command. This sense of belonging is not mutual—husbands do not belong to their wives. Papa believes in the concept of male-superiority and is immodest enough to flaunt it at every opportunity. He is the very epitome of male-chauvinism. Feminists all over condemn this attitude which holds men as 'absolute' and women as 'subjects.' This is precisely what we see in MamaPapa's family. Papa exercises his authority at every little opportunity. Every activity, every moment of life is well within the grip of Papa. A family outing on Sunday evening turns out to be more of an exercise under the strict control of Papa and less of a pleasure trip.

Papa has two daughters but the desire for a son keeps troubling the patriarch. When Mama becomes pregnant for the third time, she has two grown up daughters and out of shame she wants to abort it. But the very thought that women have a right over their bodies is considered preposterous in a patriarchal society. This is what Kate Millett calls *Sexual Politics* 'whereby one group of persons is controlled by another' (Millett 1969: 23). In a male-dominated society women must always be prepared to allow their husbands to use their bodies for whatever purpose they desire. The perfect oneness of MamaPapa is disturbed when Mama refuses to oblige. But the tyrant wins again:

> Mama was frantic to have it terminated. She had never been more ill, and would go through hellfire, she wept, just to stop the nausea that tormented her. But Papa set his jaws. They had two daughters, yes, quite grown-up as anyone could see, but there was no son. Would any man give up the chance of a son? (16)

The irony of all this lies in the fact that the woman forgets all humiliation that she was subjected to. After the birth of the son, Mama again becomes one with Papa. Not only does she forgive the patriarch but also she joins him in his elation at the birth of a son. Mama takes pride in the fact that she has bred a son and for this heroic exploit she is ever grateful to the husband:

> He had not only made her his wife, he had made her the mother of his son. What honour, what status. Mama's chin lifted a little into the air, she looked around her to make sure everyone saw and noticed. She might have been wearing a medal (31).

III

Feminists all over blame not only male-possessiveness and chauvinism but also female reluctance, easy acquiescence and lethargy for the bad shape that women-existence is in. Male-gods are the unchallengeable legislators of a patriarchal society and women join them in their pride which makes the matters worse. Mama leaves all thinking and decision-making part for Papa. She simply obeys him and takes pride in her servility. This is quite common on the Indian scene but Desai explores the essential oneness of two apparently different cultures. In India Mama shows mute obedience to Papa and follows all his whims and caprices meekly and in

Massachusetts, Mrs Patton shows similar servile attitude. In a country of supposedly strong and independent women Mrs Patton has made compromises over every small matter. She is not free even in her choice of food. An ardent vegetarian, she has meekly taken to non-vegetarian food because Mr Patton feels that that is the only kind of food. All her life Mrs Patton yearned for vegetarian food but out of fear of disturbing the peace of her home, she did not do anything about it. Though she actually despises meat, in her effort to maintain equilibrium in this strained atmosphere, Mrs Patton pretends as if she enjoys eating meat prepared by her husband. She confides in Arun:

> I've always hated eating meat—oh, that red, raw stuff, the smell of it! I've always, always disliked it—but never could—never knew how—you know, my family wouldn't have liked it (179).

She loves vegetables and fruits and finally when she discovers a food-companion in Arun, she is rejoiced to no end. This leads to another imbalance in her life. She starts enjoying shopping at the food mart and develops an abnormal flare for it. The lady seems to be craving for an opportunity to shop for food, as Mr Patton and Rod eat meat only and Melanie has taken to nuts and candies as fish takes to water. When she reminisces about the good old days when she had to buy a lot of food for her family, she seems like a little girl talking about her most cherished dream:

> You should have seen the way I'd load a shopping cart when the children were small. I'd have Melanie sitting up here on the shelf, and there'd be such a heap of groceries under her, she'd have to stick her feet right up on top (196).

It seems that the lady has been starving for real food, and when she gets someone to shop for she makes the most of it. She wears T-shirts with the legend 'Born to Shop' and seems in full control of the situation while in the market. It is hard to believe that at home she is the same, lady with her 'tentativeness and timidity' (183). The seemingly independent woman was so much in awe of her husband that she is 'apologetic and deceitful' when gingerly she announces her decision to 'give vegetarian food a try' (185). Though the cultures, the setting, the socio-familial values are different, the reaction of the patriarch is everywhere the same. Mr Patton's reaction to his wife's vegetarianism is one of indifference, 'as if he had simply not heard, or understood' (185). Arun notices this oneness: 'his father's expression, denying any opposition, despair, all seem to him a mirror reflection of it' (185). In contrasted affinity we find the subversive forces working against women both in the parochial Indian society as well as the comparatively free Western society.

IV

Melanie Patton is again a study in psychology. Like Uma this girl also becomes the victim of parental indifference. Her need and thirst for a little love and affection is as intense as that of Uma but unfortunately it is as much in vain as that of her Indian counterpart. On the Indian scene a normal, healthy Uma becomes a patient of Globus hystericus (Hysteria) and on the Western side the insatiated desire for parental affection and attention, makes Melanie a victim of anorexia and bulimia. The novelist writes:

> Then Arun does see a resemblance to something he knows: a resemblance to the contorted face of an enraged sister who, failing to express her outrage against neglect, against misunderstanding, against inattention to her unique and singular being and its hungers, merely spits and froths in effectual protest. How strange to encounter it here, Arun thinks, where so much is given, where there is both licence and plenty (214).

Melanie's alienation from her family points out the essential hollowness of the so-called developed world. Despite all efforts on the part of Mrs Patton, Melanie remains hungry biologically as well as emotionally. She herself does not know what she wants and keeps venting her anger on her poor mother.

V

Apart from Uma and Melanie, Mira Masi, Mama, Aruna and Anamika make the feminist study complete by presenting various aspects of feminism. Mira Masi is the prototype of an Indian widow: '[...] quite alone, safe in her widow's white garments, visiting one place of pilgrimage after another like an obsessed tourist of the spirit' (38). All these women have their own hungers (fasting) and all of them crave for a little satiation (feasting). Aruna is what feminists label a truly 'feminine' woman (Shiela Rowbotham). She has no ambition apart from winning a suitable coveted groom for herself by dint of her beauty and coquetry. Since Anita Desai is concerned more with the "exploration of the inner sensibility rather than the outer world of action," (Iyengar 1973: 392) all her characters merit interpretation from the psychosomatic perspective. As a child Aruna has been a mute witness to her father's hilarity at the birth of a male child. His shameless display of ecstasy had one effect on Uma and altogether different effect on Aruna. Her show of beauty and her coquetry are simply a result of that impact. It is her unique way to show her superiority, it is what may safely be called her self-assertion. This superiority complex becomes strong and takes root as she enters into marriage with Arvind and moves on to a better, richer and more fashionable world of Bombay. The hurt left on her heart since childhood, pushes her towards the quest for a flawless world. The novelist herself writes:

> Clearly Aruna had a vision of a perfect world in which all of them—her own family as well as Arvind's—were flaws she was constantly uncovering and correcting in her quest for perfection (109).

Not all women are Aruna, most of them are born with a stamp of ill-luck on their foreheads. The tragedy of such women is caused by the fact of their birth in a patriarchal society which fails to respect women as individuals. The lot of women is no way better than that of tragic hero—even the most perfect of them is crushed and doomed. However, there is one clear difference—in women's case 'Hamertia' happens to be no fatal flaw of their own but the bare fact that they belong to the female sex. Anamika—the lovely, intelligent and modest cousin of Uma—presents an example of sheer sacrifice of young, talented lives at the altar of the norms of a male-dominated society. Anamika has all that it takes to go places:

> She was simply lovely as a flower is lovely, soft, petal-skinned, bumblebee-eyed, pink-lipped, always on the verge of bubbling dove-like laughter, loving smiles, and with a good nature like a radiance about her. Wherever she was, there was peace, contentment, well being (67).

She is not only lovely but also good at studies. She wins a scholarship to Oxford but her parents look upon the letter of acceptance as a trump card which shall be useful in their search for a husband for her. It is this letter of acceptance only that brings about her nemesis. Her scholarship wins for her a husband, who is not only superb but he is also aware of his superbness. He does not care a straw for Anamika. He has a mother-fixation and has no time or attention to waste on his wife. Marriage according to Kate Millett is a game of 'power-politics.' Men marry, not because they need a companion or a soul-mate but because marriage gives them a licence to show power. Thus politics enters into marriages. Anamika is also an instrument for her husband 'to enhance his superiority to other men' (70). Though there is no love for her, he does not waste time before impregnating her as a means to crush her even more. But the pregnancy ends in abortion as she is beaten by the mother-in-law. The agony of a woman who is trapped in a wrong marriage is not realised by members of her own race. Though Anamika is experiencing hell, even her own parents do not interfere, neither do they want her back in their home. Anamika's sad saga is a strong statement against a cruel, apathetic society which does not care for lives, instead it gives more importance to its customs and rules. Uma, in her innocence, keeps hoping that Anamika shall be sent back to her mother and all will be well. But she is reproached by her mother with these words: 'You are so silly, Uma. How can she be happy if she is sent home? What will people say? What will they think?' (71). It is this fear of society that leads to the loss of many unfortunate lives. It is this unwillingness to act that results in Anamika's death—rather murder at the hands of her husband and mother-in-law. It is the irony of this unfeeling society that even her death fails to cause a stir or to shake the souls in slumber. They are resigned to their lot. Desai's tone becomes satirical here:

> What the husband said was that he had been away on a business trip and returned only that afternoon on hearing the news.
>
> What the mother-in-law said was that she always had Anamika sleep beside her, in her room, as if she were a daughter, her own child. Only that night Anamika had

insisted on sleeping in her own room. She must have planned it, plotted it all.

What Anamika's family said was that it was fate, God had willed it and it was Anamika's destiny.

What Uma said was nothing. (151)

A promising life is reduced to ashes and people who form society still talk instead of taking action. This lethargy and inertia on the part of women has contributed a lot towards the atrophy.

Fasting, Feasting is an indictment against men who believe in holding their women in their grip, it is a statement against women who take pride in their servility, it is again an indictment against men who trade in marriages as a means of increasing money and power, it is a strong criticism against women who, like fish, devour their own frail sisters, above all *Fasting, Feasting* is a plea from a woman in favour of her less fortunate counterparts. It is a strong statement against male-chauvinism, female apathy and reluctance and it is a woman's voice for freedom and emancipation.

REFERENCES

1. De Beauvoir, Simone, *The Second Sex.* 1953. Trans. and ed. H.M. Parshley. Harmondsworth: Penguin, 1983.
2. Desai, Anita, *Fasting, Feasting.* London: Chatto and Windus, 1999.
3. Engels, Frederic, *The Origin of the Family, Private Property and the State.* 1884; rpt. Moscow: Progress, 1972.
4. Everett, Jana Matson, *Women and Social Change in India.* New Delhi: Heritage, 1981.
5. Millett, Kate, *Sexual Politics.* 1969; rpt. London: Rupert Hart-Davis, 1971.
6. Srinivas Iyengar, K.R., *Indian Writing in English.* New Delhi: Heritage, 1973.
7. Showalter, Elaine, "Introduction: The Rise of Gender" in Showalter, Elaine, (ed.), *Speaking of Gender.* New York: Routledge, 1989.

9

Anita Desai's Short Stories: A Study of *Diamond Dust*

BASAVARAJ NAIKAR

Anita Desai, who is basically known as an Indian English woman-novelist, has now published her *Diamond Dust,* a collection of nine short stories. As in her novels, she has exhibited her creative talent in the short stories also. One of the striking features of her writing happens to be her typically feminine point of view, which is expressed through her microscopic observation of life in a very subtle and lyrical language. Whether the setting is Indian, Canadian or British, she has a remarkable power of evoking the atmosphere in a photographic but poetic way. Like a good story teller, she selects a single event or thematic unit and explores its intricacies and highlights its significance in a very subtle manner. Like a goldsmith or an embroiderer, she deals with superfine aspects of life with a microscopic vision. Her stories, therefore, add to the beauty and richness of the genre of Indian short story.

In the first story entitled, "Royalty," the authoress picturizes the contrast between east and west, poetic and prosaic life and nostalgic attachment to one's past. The protagonist of the story, Raja has returned to India from California where he teaches Sanskrit and composes poetry. Now, he is returning from South India to Delhi in a train. Though he is used to flying in America, he prefers to travel by train. His sister Sarla does not understand why he prefers the tedious train journey. Raja has a deep nostalgic attachment to Indian things. That is the reason why he dresses himself in a South Indian *dhoti* and shirt and travels in train to Delhi in order to relive his past and renew his relation with Indian reality and see some (subtle and higher) beauty even in drab and ugly things. Raja easily brings Raja Rao or Ramaswamy to our mind. Sarla who is a practical woman comparatively fails to understand Raja's poetic approach to life. Raja who believes in unity of being, laughs at the double standards of Ravi (Sarla's husband) who dresses himself in tweed suit and hats and pretends to be a patriot. Raja finds spiritual peace in his nostalgic engagement with India. He visits the tomb of Nizamuddin and seems to be deeply moved by it. Similarly he enjoys poetic trance in the observation of the beauty of the Himalayas. Endowed as he is with a poetic and philosophical sensibility, he cannot only see but also show to others extraordinary beauty in ordinary things. He enjoys the Indian music with real gusto. Thus, his visit to India enables him to have an intense poetic ecstasy and share it with others. Perhaps there is no greater royalty than the rich artistic experience one undergoes. Anita Desai, thus, explores the psyche of an artist by contrasting it with that of the ordinary ones.

"Winterscape" delineates the widening gap between people of different generations and cultures resulting in a sense of alienation and lack of communication. The story highlights the contrast between Hindu culture and Christian culture. Whereas in Hindu culture filial bonds transcend the barriers of technical relationships of kinship, in Christian (and Western) culture, they are restricted by technical bonds. Whereas Hindu culture believes in a collective happiness, Christian (Western) culture believes in the individual happiness. This contrast is brought out in a subtle fashion by the writer. In a Hindu family there are two sisters, Asha and Annapurna (or Anu). Asha, the elder sister gets married, but does not have any child. A little later Anu, the younger sister also gets married and has a child named Rakesh in course of time. The childless Asha nourishes Anu's child very affectionately and experiences the joy of surrogate motherhood. Anu gives her child to the care of Asha happily and willingly. Meanwhile, Asha's husband dies most unexpectedly in a gun-accident. This event brings the two sisters emotionally closer. As the child Rakesh grows into a youngman, he cannot differentiate between his mother and aunt on account of their equal affection for him. He, therefore, thinks that he has two mothers instead of one. As he wishes to go to Canada for further education, both the mothers sacrifice their individual pleasure and arrange for the financial support for his education by selling their lands. The Hindu collectivism is contrasted with the Western individualism and selfishness. After completing his education in Canada, Rakesh, like many ambitious Indian youngmen, refuses to return to India and settles down in Canada by marrying a Canadian girl called Berth. When Rakesh wants to invite his two mothers to Canada for a short trip, Berth, like a typical individualistic, Canadian and Western lady, cannot understand how Anu could give her baby to her sister. Berth's mother Doris wonders at Rakesh's having two mothers. That the West cannot understand the East is easily borne out by this situation. The theme of cultural contrast is intersected by that of generation gap and time-gap. When the two mothers go to Canada to stay for a few days with Rakesh and try to remind him of his childhood days, he finds that he has forgotten the past because of the long interval of time as well as his long stay in a foreign land and culture. His growth of personality also adds up to the lack of communication with his two mothers. He is no longer a boy, but a grown up and highly educated man who finds it difficult to communicate with his mothers who are illiterate. Likewise the mothers also feel a sense of alienation. Although Rakesh and Berth try their best to take care of them by buying new cloths for them and taking them out, the two mothers begin to feel bored with the Canadian life and watch the Canadian winter with curiosity. Their watching the winter from the window is captured by Rakesh in his snap of photo. They fall ill because of the cold weather. The winter is not only real but grows metaphorical for them. There is no real communication between the two mothers and their son. Rakesh, therefore, sends them back to India. His wife heaves a sigh of relief when the two mothers leave for India. In this story, Anita Desai has shown the contrast between an Indian mother and a Canadian mother in a very subtle fashion.

The title story, "Diamond Dust" depicts the theme of unusually intimate relationship between man and animal, between Mr Das, the protagonist and his pet dog called Diamond. The dog is a terror to the neighbours. People who are scared of it try to avoid going to Mr Das's compound. The postman tries to avoid it by throwing the mail into the hedge. The dog breaks its chain and goes out for mating bouts with stray bitches and comes back with bloodstains on its genitalia. Mr Das heaves a sigh of relief on its arrival after the first outing. When it goes out for the second time, it is caught by the police and taken away in the police van. Mr Das grows anxious about its absence from home and begins to search for it at every possible corner of the city. But when he finds it in the police van, he climbs the rear side of the van and dies when he is jerked back by the vehicle. His deep attachment for the pet dog makes him reckless and costs him his life. Anita Desai seems to teach the lesson that all over—whether of man, or woman, bird or beast—requires some kind of sacrifice.

In "Underground," Jack Higgins and his wife Meg go in a car in search of a hotel on a hot sandy beach. Meg has recently been treated in the hospital and needs rest now. Her husband has brought her in the car in the hot sun and searches for a hotel. But everywhere he gets a negative answer. Finally he has to be satisfied with an underground room. The story is episodic and the motif is not sufficiently clear, although it contains very fine description of the coastal atmosphere.

"The Man Who Saw Himself Drowned," is a psychological fantasy. It shows the death of the protagonist's double by drowning in the river. He attends his double's funeral. The protagonist is nameless. The story has the quality of a fable and is conspicuous for its psychological significance. It easily brings the novels of Kafka to our mind.

"The Artist's Life," presents a picture of the paradox of an artist's life. It shows how an artist has to create beauty in spite of being surrounded by physical and behavioural ugliness. Miss Polly attends a summer school where she is taught by Miss Abigail to paint according to her dreams. Tom is Miss Polly's brother. They have a tenant called Miss Mabel Dodd who is an artist teaching the delinquents in a school. But Miss Mabel, in spite of being an artist, has not cleaned the surroundings of her cabin. Miss Polly's mother is puzzled by Miss Mabel's negligence and wishes to remind her of the need for cleaning. She, therefore, leaves a few garbage cans outside her cabin. Miss Mabel perhaps takes a cue from this and brings a black youth and cleans the surroundings every Sunday. But one day, Miss Polly and her mother are surprised to see that somebody has written 'PIG' on her car with excrement. They cannot guess as to who must have done the filthy thing. The police are called to investigate the matter. It is suspected that one of Miss Mabel's delinquent students or the black youth must have done the heinous thing. This is the fate of an artist dealing with morally ugly people.

In "Tepoztlan Tomorrow," Anita Desai highlights the generation gap between the old and the young, one's nostalgic attachment to one's native city and the progressive deterioration of the city. Louis, son of Teresa, who is the protagonist of this story goes to Tepoztlan and meets Dona Celia. While having his dinner, he inadvertently refers to Pedro and spoils Dona Celia's mood. It is very unpleasant for Dona Celia to remember Pedro who was her suitor but whose family she had disliked. Next morning Dona Celia and her daughter Nadyn complain to Louis about a neighbour who is a professional garbage picker and who disturbs them with the stinking smell and the loud music of radio and TV and by her other dirty habits.

Louis meets his friend Arturo and talks about the past very nostalgically. Arturo invites him to the golf club for having some fun. Then he meets Don Beto who enquires about his thesis and study at the University of Houston and advises him to write polemical articles and to oppose the golf club. Later Louis goes to the golf club where he sees Alesandro playing guitar and Arturo. Then he sees some parts of the city, returns to Dona Celia's home and takes his leave with the pretext of continuing his research. The story, thus, shows a picture of decadence of the city in various ways, quite in line with Nirad Chaudhuri's picture of American decadence as part of global decadence.

"Five Hours to Simla or Faisla," is one of the successful stories in this collection because of the clarity of motif in it. It is a humorous story about the adamant attitude of a sardarji causing a good deal of tension to the travellers on the way to Simla. A family is going to Simla in a car. They have to travel another five hours to reach the place. But on the way, they are forced to stop the car as an unexpected difficulty crops up. When the sardarji is driving his truck along the road, some goatherd pelts a stone at his vehicle as a consequence of which the windscreen of his truck is broken. Now the sardarji gets angry, parks his truck across the road thereby blocking the traffic from both sides. He demands compensation for the breakage of his windscreen by the goatherd. There is a traffic jam for two miles. The sardarji sits leisurely on the bridge wall without heeding for the tension of other travellers. They do not know how to tackle him because of his irrational demand. Some people go in search of the goatherd. Some others go to the nearest city to find out a police station. Meanwhile a temporary market gathers there. The members of family feel restless and helpless in the car. Beggars, hawkers, tea-vendors and toy-vendors gather there to make the best of the situation. During the four or five hours of tension and waiting, the members in the car compromise with the situation gradually. Necessity impels them to neglect the ideal of hygiene. They are forced to eat and drink the cheap stuff that is available with the hawkers and vendors. After a long and tedious waiting, they are surprised to see a police van come from a nearby town. All the travellers are expecting an exchange of words between the sardarji and the police officers. But to their surprise, the sardarji, far from asking for any compensation, climbs into his truck, starts it and drives away from there without any demur. The family heave a sigh of relief after great tension. The sardarji's behaviour is, obviously, as adamant as irrational and humorous.

"The Rooftop Dwellers" deals with the problems of a working single woman in Delhi. Moyna is a young lady who has passed her M.A. in English and who wants to earn her livelihood in the metropolitan city of Delhi. She joins as a sub-editor of a literary magazine entitled *Books*. Tara happens to be her senior colleague whose husband Ritwik is a teacher in Jawaharlal Nehru University at Delhi. Moyna cannot afford to hire an expensive house or apartment. Besides, space is a big problem in the overcrowded capital city. Moyna, therefore, hires a rooftop *barsati* and suffers from minimalism, lack of social life and insecurity. She has to get up early in the morning to collect water from the tap as there is no facility for storing it. The owners of the house suspect her character when she brings male friends to her room. Once when she returns in the evening, she is surprised and shocked to learn that the things in her room are stolen by somebody. In course of time she realises the impracticability of running a literary magazine. The politician who is financing the magazine decides to wind it up. Finally Moyna is called by her mother to meet a bridegroom who has returned from America. Though simple, the story throws light upon the contemporary Indian society by highlighting the problems of an unmarried working woman like the financial, social and emotional ones. An educated woman in India has to face many odds in her adventure of achieving her identity. Anita Desai's depiction of women's problems has a ring of authenticity and sympathy.

On the whole, the stories in *Diamond Dust* are written from an omniscient point of view. Out of the nine stories, five are set in Canada and England and four in India. They are conspicuous for their remarkable and microscopic description, evocation of relevant mood and atmosphere and insight into the subtle working of the human mind. Sometimes her virtues become her vices in that the abundance of descriptive element tends to slacken the pace of the stories. As the blurb says, "In this brilliant new collection of funny, sad, compassionate and charming stories, Anita Desai shows us ordinary lives in a disconcerting world, where hopes and dreams clash with disappointment and the human spirit shines strongly from India to Canada and England." One cannot but agree with *The Times* which says, "These are stories whose beauty is in the detail, and their knowledge of the human psyche. They sparkle, not with the brash glitter of rhinestones, but with the intenser, more complex fire of real diamonds." Obviously, the stories of *Diamond Dust* add to the beauty and richness of the genre of Indian English short story.

REFERENCE

Anita Desai, *Diamond Dust*. London: Vintage, 2000.

10

Trauma of a Housewife: Anita Desai's *Fire on the Mountain*

RAMESH KUMAR GUPTA

Fire on the Mountain, published in 1977 in London, has placed Anita Desai's reputation as one of the best Indo-Anglian novelists. She has been awarded the Royal Society of Literature's Winifred Holtby Memorial Prize and the 1978 National Academy of Letters Award for this novel. The title of this novel is perhaps taken from William Golding's famous novel, *Lord of the Flies*, the second chapter of which is entitled 'Fire on the Mountain.' It symbolises fire which burns in the heart of an old lady, a great-granddaughter of Nanda Kaul, and her emotional world is the theme of the novel. In this novel the title refers to the words of Raka, the great-granddaughter of Nanda Kaul, who says at the end of the novel: "Look, Nani, I have set the forest on fire. Look, Nani-look-the forest is on fire" (*F.O.M.*, 145). For this purpose R.S. Sharma rightly states that, the words are expressive of Raka's resolve to destroy a world where a woman cannot hope to be happy without being unnatural.[1] Mrs Desai makes use of the flash-back-technique in describing the central theme of the trauma of a housewife in the novel and the novel centres round the character of Nanda Kaul.

Anita Desai's *Fire on the Mountain* presents a study of trauma of a housewife, the trauma that takes refuge in seclusion. The life-long faithlessness of Mr Kaul to Nanda Kaul and the hypocritical situation force her to avow this severance. Nanda Kaul has conceded this after passing through psychic suffering and bitter experiences of a marital life. This wedding is veritably based on physical lust and circumstantial convenience for Mr Kaul. Mr Kaul does not love her as a wife. She plays the gracious hostess all the time and enjoys the comforts and social status of the wife of a dignified person. Nanda Kaul becomes a mother, grandmother and great-grandmother of many unwanted and unloved children. Her life as the Vice-Chancellor's wife though crowded and full of social activity, was truly purportless and insatiating. There have been too many guests coming and going all the time, leaving little privacy for her. She ever passes her life to arrange the dinner table as a hard working hostess.

The novelist presents the trauma of a housewife through the following passages:

> The old house, the full house, of that period of her life when she was the Vice-Chancellor's wife and at the hub of a small but intense busy world, had not pleased her. Its crowding had stifled her [...]. There had been too many guests coming and going, tongas and rickshaws piled up under the eucalyptus trees and the bougainvilleas, their drivers asleep on the seats with their feet hanging over the bars. The many rooms of the house had always been full, extra beds would have had to be made up, often in not very private corners of the hall or veranda, so that there was a shortage of privacy that vexed her. Too many trays of tea would have to be made and carried to her husband's study, to her mother-in-law's bedroom, to the veranda that was the gathering-place for all, at all times of the day. Too many meals, too many dishes on the table, too much to wash up after.
>
> They had had so many children, they had gone to so many different schools and colleges at different times of the day, and had so many tutors—one for mathematics who was harsh and slapped the unruly boys, one for drawing who was lazy and smiled and did nothing, and others equally incompetent and irritating. Then there had been their friends, all of different ages and sizes and families (*F.O.M.*, 29-30).

The novel depicts Nanda Kaul's intense awareness of 'lost privacy and busy world.' The following lines explicate the point:

> She would go to the kitchen to see the milk taken out of the ice-box, the layer of cream drawn off, the row of mugs on a tray filled and carried out to the green table on the veranda around which the children already sat on their low cane stools—the little girls still having their long hair plaited and their fresh cotton dresses buttoned, and the boys throwing themselves backwards and kicking the table legs and clamouring with hunger. Then there was the bread to be spread with butter, jam jars opened and dug into, knives taken away from babies and boys, girls questioned about homework, servants summoned to mop up spilt milk and fetch tea, and life would swirl on again, in an eddy, a whirlpool of which she was the still, fixed eye in the centre (24).

The above quoted passage depicts the liabilities of a housewife but the word "eddy or whirlpool" indicates traumatic *et al.* of Nanda Kaul. Externally everything appears to be free from harshness but internally Mrs Kaul burns with a fire of frustration. She feels lonely and neglected. Above all Mr Kaul carried on a life-long illicit affair with Miss Davidson, a member of the teaching staff. He invites her for badminton parties, and compels her to stay at night and comes back secretly to his separate bedroom. Here it is to be worth noted that there is no Hindu wife who could endure such an illicit relationship between her husband and another lady. In spite of this she appears as smooth and free from heart-breaking agony. Mostly traditional women are seen as insane ones immolating their lives in such a critical and pitiable plight. Even the modern women cannot endure it. They can break the marital bond and live independently. But Nanda Kaul keeps the congealed smile on her face. She looks after the children, family, his house, servants, shutting the doors, cooking food, lunch, dinner and guiding supper table, keeping the visitors at ease and waiting, ever waiting with a singular, burning, soul-destroying enmity for her husband and to stop all these perpetually, she craves for a blessed widowhood, the complete separation sans man and children around. These are the situations which have forced her to get such a dreamed house at Kasauli *viz.*,

> Nor had her husband loved and cherished her and kept her like a queen—he had only done enough to keep her

> quiet while he carried on a life-long affair with Miss David, the mathematics mistress, whom he had not married because she was a Christian but whom he had loved, all his life loved. And her children—the children were all alien to her nature. She neither understood nor loved them. She did not live here alone by choice—she lived here alone because that was what she was forced to do, reduced to doing (145).

It produces in Nanda Kaul such a disease of spirit that she distrusts all attachments and affairs: "After the death of her husband she has been so glad when it was over. She had been glad to leave it all behind in the plains, like a great, heavy, difficult book that she had read through and was not required to read again [...] 'discharge me' she groaned, 'I have discharged all my duties. Discharge'" (30). The novel presents marital incongruity. Nanda Kaul attempts to conceal it, she has been violently injured and disappointed in her earlier life as a wife, mother and housewife. She prefers seclusion not because she favours it but to rest her pain-filled psyche, her stagnated pulses, bits and pieces of identity that she attempts to get in the shelter of Carignano doubtless need that rock-like exterior to give them a wholesome structure, a hopeful destination. She is gruesomely afraid to be injured again by the insensibility or harshness of the outside world and encourages no obstruction, no trespassing in her place of refuge. Mrs Kaul strives to concentrate on the soothing scene outside. But she feels upset and perturbed, puzzled and disgusted, she asks: "Have I not done enough and had enough? I want no more. I want nothing. Can I not be left with nothing? But there was no answer and of course she expected none" (17).

When the novel opens we find Nanda Kaul a solitary figure in the hills of Kasauli. Most of her experiences find no place within the span of the novel. We get to know her past through her reactions of withdrawal and fantasy. Her emotional coldness is a pose that she carefully cultivates to convince herself and the world that has rejected her, her self-reliance and her self-sufficiency. Her withdrawal from life and family is not the result of any existential realization of man's ultimate aloneness but she has just been 'reduced' to such a state.

She prefers her lonely isolated existence guarding her privacy fiercely and the news of her great-granddaughter Raka's arrival, conveyed to her through a letter, unsettles her. In the authorial description on Part I a comparison has been shown between her and a tree:

> She was grey, tall and thin and her silk saree made a sweeping, shivering sound and she fancied she could merge with the pine trees and be mistaken for one (1).

The novel presents the traumatic self of Nanda Kaul, an old woman, who has had too much of the world with her and so longs for a quiet, retired life. Her busy past now looks like "a box of sweets" (31) positively sickening.

Nanda Kaul performed the duties of her married life very well, but her husband and children never bothered about her inner psyche. This indifference of her husband and children made her pine for privacy which could be hers only. It is because of this very reason she pines for seclusion in Carignano, and does not like the idea of Raka's staying with her. Her interior feeling prevails her life as she desires and is suggestively painted through an eagle:

> An eagle swept over it, far below her, a thousand feet below, its wings outspread, gliding on currents of air without once moving its great muscular wings which remained in repose, in control (19).

The eagle is the emblem of total detachment here, a free soul that is not bound by any type of responsibilities or duties, and is not attached to any place or person. Though the use of a poem is not so significant in the novel yet it has some connection with the character of Nanda Kaul who quotes it and the poem depicts her desire to be away from the humdrum of life and far from the madding crowd. And the poem is:

> I have desired to go
> Where springs not fail,
> To fields where flies no sharp and sided hail
> And a few lilies blow,
> And I have asked to be
> Where no storms come
> Where the green swell is in the havens dumb
> And out of the swing of the sea (58).

Now it is clear that Carignano is presented in the novel as a contrast to the life of the city. Mrs Kaul's dislike for the city life results in her seclusion to Carignano. She has no interest in her family. Asha in her letter to Nanda mentions about the heat of Delhi and the dust, tempest in summer. Asha thinks it would be very fine for Raka to stay at Carignano for the rapid recovery of her health. Raka, the great-granddaughter of Nanda Kaul, is not a normal child by any standard: "Amongst them she appeared a freak, by virtue of never making a demand. She appeared to have no needs [...]. Raka wanted only one thing—to be left alone and pursue her own secret life among the rocks and pines of Kasauli" (47-48). Mrs Desai calls her a natural recluse and this way compares her with Nanda Kaul: "If Nanda Kaul was a recluse out of vengeance for a long life of duty and obligation, her great-granddaughter was a recluse by nature, by instinct. She had not arrived at this condition by a long route of rejection and sacrifice—she was born to it, simply" (48). It is however logical that Raka is not a born recluse. She becomes an introvert because of the abnormal circumstances around her. She is the prey of parental perturbations *viz.*,

> "Somewhere behind them, behind it all, was her father, home from a party, stumbling and crashing through the curtains of night, his mouth opening to let out a flood of rotten stench, beating at her mother with hammers and fists of abuse—harsh, filthy abuse that make Raka cover under her bedclothes and wet the mattress in fright, feeling the stream of urine warm and weakening between her legs like a stream of blood, and her mother lay down on the floor and shut her eyes and wept" (71).

Raka's psychic balance and deteriorating physical power render her miserable and helpless. Her father has no time to pass some pleasant period with her. So she is deprived of her father's love and care. William Walsh lays stress on the significance of love for the wholesome growth of a child in this way:

> The child's consciousness, which is partial and successive, does not include a sense of the past or the future. It has to be discovered, and the provocation to learn it, is

> love. Affection is the seed of time. It is love—intensifying the delight in the present and correspondingly bringing discomfort in absence—which introduces an element of permanence into the child's experience.[2]

We find that Raka is undoubtedly, a "freak" child but after all she is a human being and needs love, protection and attachment to grow into an individual. Her parents do not fulfil her basic demands. L.H. Scott rightly says that Raka is a victim of "emotional deprivation."[3] Horney, in this regards, also remarks a person's craving to "strengthen his inner position by being accepted, approved of, needed, wanted, liked, loved, appreciated."[4] Nanda Kaul is filled with tenderness for Raka. Mrs Kaul wants to help the child in going to bed: "Habit would rear its hand inside her, make her prepare to follow, tell her to tuck the child in, read her a story and lead her safely into sleep" (80).

Nanda Kaul's granddaughter, Tara too, suffers a gruesome fate of a chronic nervous breakdown as a result of her marital incongruity. Another dire and despised marriage is that of Ila Das. Nanda Kaul is, directly, related with their problems and these are the traumas of her life.

In the novel, we find that, there is another intruder at Carignano—Ila Das, who is a pathetic, slightly comical creature, nevertheless draws out our sympathy at the end of the novel. Her voice is such, "no human being ought to have had: it was anti-social to possess, to emit such sounds as poor Ila Das made by way of communication" (111). When Ila Das informs Nanda of her arrival at Carignano, Nanda becomes confused for some time. She murmurs on the telephone and Nanda turns her head the other way in an effort to run away but she finds a white hen dragging out a worm. Nanda compares herself to this worm. The boys of the locality tease Ila Das like langurs. Ila Das, a piano teacher, discharges her duties as a welfare officer in the area promptly and efficiently. She is brutally assaulted, raped and murdered by Preet Singh only because she has just tried to stop the disastrous child marriage of Preet Singh's daughter. "Crushed back, crushed down into the earth, she lay raped, broken, still and finished" (143). The news of the tragic death of Ila Das shatters Nanda Kaul's inner world. The fallacious world which she had constructed as an emotional refuge absolutely breaks down. Dropping the telephone she began to cry: "No" no it is all lie! No it cannot be. It was a lie! Ila Das was not trapped, not dead she had lied to Raka, lied about everything" (145). Ila Das's life indicates the tragic life of a woman in our society. Nanda Kaul was very much attached to her. They were friends. They were very close to each other. When a police officer gives the news of Ila Das's tragic death she is shocked and faints. When Raka returns home, setting fire to the forests, she finds her sitting. Nanda Kaul dies on the stool with her head hanging, the black telephone hanging the long wire dangling" (145).

This way, *Fire on the Mountain* unfolds the trauma of a housewife. It presents Desai's tragic view of life, in which innocent people are bound to suffer and pay a heavy price for their goodness. The fire on the mountain becomes the emblem of destruction and purgation, the destruction of an unkind world of many Nanda Kauls and Ila Dases, of an unequal situation in which women suffer from the slings of misfortune, social inequities and injustices committed on them by a savage society of men. The title of the novel is emblematic of the revolt of the new generation of women against the male chauvinistic society. That is why Anita Desai, commenting upon the importance of such feelings, remarks in an interview: "But I'm quite sure that even life contains many traumatic experiences."[5]

NOTES AND REFERENCES

1. R.S. Sharma, *Anita Desai,* Allied Publishers, New Delhi, 1979, 145.
2. William Walsh, *The Uses of Imagination,* Chatto and Windus, London, 1959, 166.
3. Leland H. Scott, *Child Development,* Rinehart and Winston: New York, 1967, 317.
4. Karen Horney, *Neurosis and Human Growth,* Routledge and Kegan Paul, London, 1965, 216.
5. Jasbir Jain, "Anita Desai: Interviewed," Rajasthan University Studies in English, 12, 1979, 60-61.

11

Fasting, Feasting: An Attempt at Fusion of Continuity and Experiment

J.P. TRIPATHI

Beginning from *Cry, the Peacock* when we survey the literary career of Anita Desai we note that she has at least some special areas of insight although her genius is a multisided one. Some of these areas are the painting of familiar domestic and familial scenes, deep penetration in the mental states of men and women, a philosophical and reflective penetration into life's realities, a sympathy for the suffering mankind and particularly the woman kind. In her newly published novel *Fasting, Feasting* there is a fusion of experiment and continuity. Usually Anita Desai, like Jane Austen, concentrates on domestic Indian scenes. Here for the first time a flight to the American scene is visible. British and European scenes were already touched upon in *Bye-Bye, Blackbird* and *Baumgartner's Bombay* but America somehow got left out, perhaps, because like Jane Austen, she concentrated on her "two inches" of ivory. However, she extends her range and touches new scenes in the American hemisphere in the present novel.

The reflective and philosophical note is an old strain in Anita Desai, the perfect expression of which was found in *Journey to Ithaca*. There are no spiritual flights in the present novel but the tone of detachment and serenity, a harmony of equanimity in the ups and downs of life is everywhere visible. In the earlier works Anita Desai seemed to be feverishly and hectically concerned with and involved in her material and characters. In the present work she takes a detached view of things and her material. This is the result of a long-time familiarity with the experiences of life and its involvements.

In this sense the present novel is different from other novels of hers.

The law of artistic growth of a writer is a mysterious phenomenon; the deciphering of the factors leading to it is rather difficult. Review of the literary careers of great writers reveals that there are many ups and downs in so far as positive development of the artist is concerned. The process of growth is thus more esoteric than mechanical. As a novel *Fasting, Feasting,* if a graph of growth is drawn, will show not an ascent but a rather flat ground, except in the lifeview. By way of philosophy, in addition to a sense of harmony and equanimity, the novel focuses on a sense of deep-seated paths over the plight of mankind and particularly women all over the globe. Another significant point that emerges is that most of life is unavailing, confirming the view that life is a vanity of vanities. Still, higher pursuits are to be undertaken such as that by Mrs Patton, and, people like Mr Patton and his son, and Arun will explore life through ceaseless adventure and struggle.

As a novel the book is commendable and covers a wide range of life spectacle and themes in two countries and continents. May be that the sharpness and brilliance which is attained by Anita Desai in the novels with a limited range is not attained here because pictures grow into silhouettes and landscapes into dim and hazy outlines on a large canvas and definitely the canvas in the novel is a very large one. However, the artistic wisdom and integrity of the novelist lies in the fact that she focuses only on two scenes, one native and the other American. And the character who binds the two threads of the plot is Arun.

For forming an idea of the novel and its impact on the readers we must first make a perusal of its themes. The novel opens with the parents dozing over a swing:

> The parents set, rhythmically swinging, back and forth (3).

The vital idea is that the identities of the parents have fused and blended and they have become one: "Mama and Papa. Mama Papa, Papa Mamma" (5). With great verisimilitude the novelist shows a very important aspect of the life of Indian couples when they become one:

> Having fused into one, they had gained so much in substance, in stature, in authority [...] they did not need separate histories and backgrounds [...] (6).

A lack of proper proportion and sense of responsibility among parents is an eternal theme in Anita Desai, like that in the novels of Jane Austen. The parents' indifference to the children and over self-indulgence in personal life leave a bad impact on children. Open night adventures of parents in the knowledge of children are a well-established fact in some Indian families and Anita Desai's keen eyes paint them vividly.

"Aruna's vision was more domestic-petticoats and saries lifted, legs thrashing, naked legs, in the night, under the mosquito net. They'd heard sounds, muffled, escaping involuntarily behind curtains. No doors were ever shut in that household: closed doors meant secrets, nasty secrets, impermissible" (15). Another psychological phenomenon of curiosity among children for the sexual sports of parents is also pointed out. "But when it came to parents, one did not look. One looked down at oneself, ashamed" (16). There is a subtle irony in the suggestion that even if the parents have no sense of shame, the children have.

In the novel Anita Desai brings out another important feature of Hindu families in India—the supremacy of the male child. The above mentioned adventures of the parents of Aruna and Uma lead to a delayed pregnancy and childbirth, and luckily the child born is a male one. The daughters of the family are expected to help in childcare and house keeping; mother talks about the marriage of Uma. "Till then, you can help me look after Arun. And learn to run the house" (22). This is the lot of Indian female child, though not very bleak.

Presenting the pathetic state of Indian women, particularly widows is an important theme in Anita Desai treated in many of her novels. First the novelist takes up the pathetic plight of Uma who fails to get through her examinations for a second time and the parents want her to discontinue her education, which she does not relish. In her depression and despair Uma becomes a patient of fits. After failure, Uma goes to Mother Agnes for promotion in the class, which, when refused makes her faint: "Uma suddenly went limp and crumpled and the next thing Mother Agnes knew was that Uma was lying stretched out on the cotton rug by her desk [...] she was writhing, frothing a little at the mouth and moaning, banging her head to one side, then the other" (29). Uma's fainting is the result of general depression. Uma's failure to get through for the second time is definitely due to her poor intellect. The birth of the male child further cements the bond of oneness between the parents of Uma.

The fasting-feasting contrast is demonstrated in the Indian scene by the contrast between the feasting parents—both sexually and in the matter of pleasures of life, and the fasting from all pleasures on the part of Uma. In the American scene the feasting theme is represented through Mrs Patton who delights in filling her freezer with all kinds of cooked material. But the self-indulgence element represented in the feasting theme of Uma's parents is totally lacking here. Melanie's feasting and over-eating results in vomitting and the feasting is as good as fasting or rather sickly and unbalanced. Melanie who lives in a world of opulence and prosperity and eats what she likes and has no commerce with poverty is no better than Uma. On the contrary, her feasting-indulgence into eating—is not only equal to fasting but worse than it—it is positively painful:

> She twitches and grunts [...] then rubs her face with her hands. It is smudged with dirt and soiled with vomit. Her eyes are tightly shut [...]. Then, with a groan, she lifts herself onto her knees, thrusts her finger down her throat and vomits again, copiously (223).

The pathetic condition of Indian women, arousing a feminist ire in the novelist, finds expression in the case of Uma in India and Melanie in America. But in fact in the case of Anita Desai this feminist consciousness is subordinate to higher considerations. Uma seems to be victimised more by her destiny than anyone else. She possesses an inferior and substandard brain which is incapable of making her get through examinations. Her facial and bodily features are also not attractive enough to please men so that marriage offers do not fructify. When the marriage arrangement does take place it proves to be a fraud and her parents are shorn of their major part of income. They always offer a fair dowry to the aspirants for Uma's hand in marriage but in vain. Melanie also does not lack money. Opulence leads to her over self-indulgence and that to neurosis.

As mentioned earlier the thematic range of the novel is broad and almost cosmopolitan. The Indian and the American ways of life are represented without any bias. Vegetarian-non-vegetarian dietary habits are also mentioned. Arun is by nature a vegetarian against the wishes of his father who thinks that meat-eating is a mark of advancement. He faces difficulties due to his vegetarianism in America also. His vegetarianism speaks of his character and also is a model for Mrs Patton who takes to vegetarianism and later to yogic practices. In other words he inspires higher value in others.

Another important theme in the novel is the widowhood of Mira-masi, it is the typical widowhood theme in Hindu society, particularly described in Bengali fiction, Mira-masi, the widow constantly describes and spreads news of "births, marriages, deaths, illnesses, scandals, litigation, gossip, rumours, prattle, tittle-tattle" (39) about relatives. This is her social role. Besides, she has another role also—"Ever since her widowhood, she had taken up religion as her vocation" (39). She makes Uma also share some of her sentiments and enjoys tales of Hindu myths. Mira-masi's participation in religion along with Uma's is considered as a 'mischief' by Uma's parents. Uma's visit to the Ashrama, her being possessed, Mira-masi's sickness in the Ashrama show the mixed form of religion. In the Ashrama Uma feels some tranquillity—"That was what Uma felt her own life to have been—full of barks, bowls, messages, and now silence" (61).

Another significant theme in the novel is that of Anamika's marriage to one who is impervious to her beauty and graces. Although from every point of view Anamika is a perfect girl, she is beaten by her mother-in-law and has miscarriage and is permanently damaged as a woman (71). The tragedy of arranged marriages is thus exposed by the untimely death of Anamika. There are many such Anamikas in India and deaths of this type are caused by the Indian marriage system, or perhaps social disease of dowry or destiny. Another important idea also hinges around the theme of women or girls—whether to give them convent education or to marry them off. The tragedy of a girl rejected by many parties in marriage is pathetically drawn in the case of Uma. She is drawn into another deceitful marriage with Harish, an already married man with children, only for the sake of a dowry, after this marriage she is considered a blighted 'ill-fated" (16) girl. The pathos of situation in such cases lies in the fact that such unlucky girls are not allowed even genuine remedies and cures—Uma is prevented by her parents from going to Bombay to her own sister Aruna for an eye-test (108).

The theme of equality of fasting-feasting, equanimity between pleasure, pain, happiness and unhappiness, as indicated by the title, pervades the whole novel. The idiotic, hysteric Uma is quite discontented. And similarly, the seemingly prosperous and happily-married Aruna, who is beautiful and mentally sharp, and enjoys dazzling pleasures of life is discontented. She is irritated by her husband's shirt not matching with his trousers and such petty things and not only once but almost all through the day. Aruna's "vision of a perfect world" (109) is always disturbed by petty things such as the sinking of pudding, Arvind's coming to dinner in bedroom slippers, Papa's wearing a shirt with a hole; this inspires pity in Uma for Aruna and a doubt regarding "the realm of ease and comfort" for which Aruna pined all life. "Certainly it brought her no pleasure: there was always a crease of discontent between her eyebrows and an agitation that made her eyelids flutter, disturbing Uma who noticed it" (109). Thus from contentment point of view Aruna's and Uma's cases are at par confirming thematic implication of the title.

The typical discrimination against a female child is another part of the theme: parents aim at promoting "education" of Arun, a male child whereas the girls are [...] "being raised for marriage." Arun is allowed to go to U.S.A. for best education whereas Uma's going to the convent close to home is not permitted.

The underworld theme of Uma's nihilistic feelings at moments is described. Mira-masi tells Uma that she has been picked up by God for Himself at which Uma begins to thrash her arms around but at Mama's scolding she would subside, and "as she subsided, feel herself drawn by an undercurrent into a secret depth, so dark that she could see nothing at all—just the darkness" (132).

We have already noted that Mira-masi's religious faith is presented in a way so that it might appear very sincere to some and very flippant to others. The case in point is her finding the stolen image of her Lord in a shop at Benaras (139). Some regard it as a consummation of her devotion and others as a matter of chance.

Anamika's suicide is another representative theme in modern Indian life. "She filled a can with kerosene oil. She unlocked the kitchen door and went out on the veranda. Then she removed her cotton clothing. She wrapped a nylon sari about her. She knotted it at the neck and knees. Then she poured the kerosene over herself. Then she struck a match. She set herself alight" (150-51). The incident inspires not only pathos but a sense of horror.

The East-West encounter theme is particularly represented by Arun's visit to U.S.A. and his experiences there. The liberal and accommodating nature of Mrs Patton, cooking vegetarian diets for Arun and becoming a vegetarian, is also an important part of this theme. East-West encounter theme is characterised by mutual attraction and also disenchantment. The enchantment theme is represented by Mrs Patton's attraction for India. And the disenchantment theme is represented by Melanie's disgust with Arun and his ways, and Arun's dislike for habits of Rod and Melanie, Mrs Patton's children. Arun's attraction for American male life of the Pattons seeing baseball on the screen with legs outstretched and beercans on the floor beside them is great—"the scene is so convivial, so inviting" (191).

Another vital theme is Arun's desire to discover the American spirit, the American life, the mystery of the American will to struggle and go ahead: and this he thinks he can partly touch and taste by jogging like Americans in its vast terrains:

> "But he will jog and jog—like Rod, like all those others, he has seen their contorted faces, their closed eyes, their shut expressions as they struggle to leave behind the town, the suburbs, the shopping malls, the parking

> lots, struggle to free themselves and find through endeavour most primitive, through strain and suffering, that open space, that unfettered vacuum where the undiscovered America still lies" (200) such journeys of quest are ceaseless, therefore, he "must go further, further [...]" (200). Then follows a discussion as to who are the inheritors of the pioneers of the dream of the golden New World—the joggers or the men with the cars? The answer is the men with the cars, that is, science and technology together will help man in the fulfilment of the dream: "It is they, not the earth-bound joggers, who are descended directly from the covered waggons and the trusty horses, who are the inheritors of the pioneer's dream of the endlessly postponed and endlessly golden west. They alone can challenge the space and the desolation, pit their steel against the wilderness and the vacuum [...]" (201).

Another theme in the later part of the novel is the training Americans give to their persons for work, sport or good health. Side by side some are obsessed with over-eating and want to thin down their bodily girth and fat by vomiting. These practices have gone into the American blood and have become fads and fashions, men and women are chained by them. Lying on the bed Rod practices cycling with his legs—"Arun gets out of the way, quickly: one can't tell what is more dangerous in this country, the pursuit of health or of sickness" (205). The East-West encounter theme is used in Arun's reaction to the American opulence creating in him an "anxiety over spending so much, having so much" (208). The fact of basking for a tan and good health in the summer is exaggeratedly followed. While basking most of the people, even women, are almost naked. As such Arun cannot look at Mrs Patton in such appearance—"He does not even want to glance in her direction. It is like confronting his mother naked" (213). This experience of Arun throws light on the conflicing views of decorum and decency in the East and the West.

East and West seem similar in indifference to women and girls. A sort of feminist discontent against this is seen in the following words hinting at similarity between Uma and Melanie:

> Then Arun sees a resemblance to something he knows, a resemblance to the contorted face of an enraged sister who, failing to express her outrage against neglect, against misunderstanding, against inattention to her unique and singular being and its hungers, merely, spits and froths in ineffectual protest. How strange to encounter it here, Arun thinks, where so much is given, where there is both licence and plenty (213).

The comment in the last part of the paragraph has immense philosophical value which we shall discuss in detail a little later when discussing the vision of life implied by the novel. Another theme in the closing part of the novel is the hunger of those people who are apparently so much crammed with happiness and are yet in pain as Melanie. Plenty in the material sense is no plenty at all as it leads to sickness and neurosis.

A close analysis of the novels of Anita Desai always reveals paucity of external action. In most of the books internal action, that is, thought movement and feelings of individuals predominate. In the present novel also there is little physical action. What constitutes the plot in the novel is the state of a family of Papa Mama during a given period of time. Papa Mama lead an easy and comfortable life of comparative peace enjoying their breakfasts, luncheon and dinner, prepared by a good cook, served by their own young ones, particularly Uma, most of their time passes on the swing, or in markets and parks, Mama has a belated pregnancy and a son is born who is named Arun on whose education and life parents spend a good deal of money. Their prime concern regarding the daughters is to prepare them for marriage. The plot presents the story of Uma's failure to get suitably married, Arun's brilliant career and marriage and Arun's going to America for higher education. Stories of some neighbours are also narrated as neighbours, and, close as well as distant, relatives constitute the life of most Indians.

The time covered by the plot is Mama's pregnancy, birth and growth of Arun in India and his departure for U.S.A. for education. While Papa Mama family is in the centre of plot-interest, the Patton family is also introduced to cover the East-West encounter theme. The introduction of this family was a matter of great thematic necessity. The homespun domestic plot goes on a tour to America. What happens in Arun's family is his growth, and education, Aruna's and Uma's education and marriage and failure. Anamika's family is also introduced to establish verisimilitude in the plot. The introduction of Mira-masi also supplements life-likeness. The mention of various Christian families in connection with convent education also enhances the life-likeness of the book, these descriptions give the novel a wide scope and representation of Indian society.

Third-person universal observer technique of narration is employed. In most of the cases the novelist seems to identify herself with every character and gives expression to everyone's viewpoint although she always keeps herself in the background. She does not employ the traditional stream of consciousness technique but in most of the descriptions the character's viewpoints prevail. Thus there is unity of tone and structure and yet at the same time an impression of variety within unity. The narrative is straight and simple although there is running back to past in the present without complications. The book is divided into two parts, with Part I mostly describing the Indian theme and Part II dealing with the story of Arun in America. In nutshell the novel is an uneventful story of two families, one Indian and the other American.

From the viewpoint of characterisation the novel is not very significant because it is marked by a thematic predominance and similarity of life spectacle both in India and America. The plot hinges round Papa Mama whose identities are so blended that they are not shown as separate individuals. They are types and flat characters representing most of Indian middle class parents and their lives. The character of Papa is predominant, Mama yields to him most often and does everything to suit his interest and pleasure. At no stage there is a misunderstanding or skirmish, even mild in form. They are two halves of one piece as per Indian philosophy of husband-wife relationship. "Having fused into one, they had gained so much in substance, in stature, in authority, that they loomed large enough as it was, they did not need separate histories and backgrounds to make them even more immense" (6). They always present "an indecipherable face" to the world. Albeit, they have one great weakness in them, in their self-indulgence they never pay attention to the children's reaction while they are making love not very secretly. The family is overscrupulous in taking care of the food of Papa, the mother peeling segments of orange and giving them to Papa to eat. The birth of Arun makes both the father and the mother more dignified and elevated.

The character who frequently comes up for description during the action of the novel is Uma, although she does not dominate the action. She is the eldest child of the family although in physical and mental qualities she suffers from mediocrity, she is a dull student and does not succeed in the examination and seeks promotion in the class. "Uma hurled herself at Mother Agnes, threw her arms around her waist, hid her face in the starched white cotton skirts, and howled aloud" (27). She will not be permitted to continue education because of successive failures. She faints in the presence of Mother Agnes.

Uma is close to Mira-masi because both have some similarities, one is a child with retarded growth, the other is a widow. Both are allowed visits to temples together, and also a bath in the river. "An idea grew within the family that Uma and Mira-masi were partners in mischief" (44). Accompanying Mira-masi to the Ashrama makes Uma happy because here she is "more unsupervised." In the Ashrama she rolls on the floor as if in a swoon as she had done at the side of Mother Agnes. Mrs Joshi, Papa Mama's neighbour notes that Uma does not grow up with the passage of years (74). Her lack of maturity is also visible when Mrs Syal comes to see her as a bride for her son and Uma is tactless enough to reveal that the ring she was putting on was Mama's (77). Goyals also reject her. She is regarded as ill-fated and duped in marriage by a married man with children. She is considered "an idiot" and a "hysteric" (102) and often falls unconscious. Her dreams to go to Landour remain merely dreams. To her younger brother Arun she seems to be "beginning to stoop and shrink" (122). Uma's life is gloomy and full of despair. She is a pathetic and most unforgettable character.

Arun is the figure connecting the Indian and the American plot. He is a vegetarian and right as a child he was repelled by the taste of eggs. He is a sort of an introvert boy and is reluctant to go out and play even though Papa forces him to (119). He has a very strong sympathy for his elder sister Uma and feels stricken by her premature 'stoop.' He enjoys the lack of acquaintances and the anonymity in America. He does not respond to the overtures of Indian students to befriend him (171-72). He retains his introvert nature even in America and is revolted in his sensibilities by Mrs Patton basking almost naked (213). Arun is a typical youngman with a thorough-going Indian sensibility. His character is at the centre of East-West encounter: "The very idea appeals Arun, if it means the baring of flesh in public. He has never seen so much female flesh before [...]. His body shrinks and closes upon itself, affronted" (215).

Another significant character of Indian group is Mira-masi, the universal type of the Hindu widow most unwelcome in her father's as well as father-in-law's house. Mira-masi is introduced as most coveted creature to Uma though most unwelcome to Mama because she does not use the pots in her kitchen nor does she eat food prepared by the cook. She halts at Uma's house between two pilgrimages and her gossip about families was a social factor in her. The anti-social element in her is her religion (139). She takes the single vegetarian meal in a day like all widows.

She was rapidly growing old: "Her face began to look muddy and was streaked with deep lines like a river bed that has run dry, and her hair was turning thin and grey" (53). She puts on widow's white garments and is so devoted to her Lord that she carries the image with her and, when lost, does not take rest without finding it. Her devotion is so strong that she is able to get the missing image in a shop at Benaras (139).

Ramu is a minor character, a family cousin who is avoided by Papa Mama as a gutter but who is humorous and domineering and almost invincible in his ways. He is most welcome to Uma because he brings some relief to her. Mira-masi regards him as an "English-speaking, meat-eating, polluted outcast from Bombay." His clowning pleases Uma. He has the knack to take Uma out of the house and entertain her in a hotel on food, music and dance.

Bakul uncle is a smart lawyer, the brother of the sluggish Papa who is leading a humdrum life in a provincial town. Bakul's life is brilliant and successful. His daughter Anamika, although a tragic character was a total contrast to her brother Ramu with his "club-foot, his hunched back, his nearly sightless eyes" (66). Anamika's character is described in a sentence. "Wherever Anamika was, there was moderation, good sense and calm" (68). She is not only beautiful and good natured but an outstanding student and wins a scholarship to Oxford. But her marriage with an indifferent and apathetic man and her entry into a cruel family leads to her suicide. She is a tragic character in so far as so much of grace and ability has paved the way only for her doom.

Among the Christian characters Mother Agnes and others are only names and have not been individualized. The group of American characters is represented by Mr and Mrs Patton, Melanie, the daughter and Rod the son. Mr Patton is a happy, and robust American taking his son Rod for boating on a lake. He is a caring parent and cooks food for his children. He is like a minister at a congregation, but the members of the congregation are generally only two—Mrs Patton and Arun. Arun being a vegetarian does not accept the cooked meat.

In the Patton family Mrs Patton is the most liberal and hospitable. Her typical American character is represented by her obsession of bringing small cart-loads of vegetables, fruits and grocery from the market and filling the freezer with cooked food for her people to eat when they like. Her typical American character is also represented by her basking almost naked in sunlight and swimming along with Melanie with only swimming suit on. Another one of her American traits is her wrecklessly speedy car driving. She represents the general American summer consciousness and celebration and the mood of holiday connected with it. Her liberality consists in her accommodating nature and kindness in cooking vegetarian diets for Arun. Her dynamism consists in her becoming a vegetarian herself. The typical American openness of mind and quest for higher value is embodied in her becoming a practitioner of yoga. Ultimately she becomes an Indophile. Rod is the typical American young man practising, like his folk, exercise to keep bodily fit. He is healthy and robust and an outdoors man like his father. Melanie is a psychic case and her feasting is as good or bad as fasting. Balance and normal life returns to her only when she is under treatment for neurosis. She represents the excess and plenty of Americans leading to no happiness unless there is balance. She seems to be an American sister of the Indian Uma. In a certain sense they are two sides of the same coin—plight of young girls in both India and America, irrespective of difference of cultures and climates, is the same.

There is no dazzle and shine either in the plot-construction or the characterisation in the novel. The book has the balanced calm of maturity. The language, style and imagery are likewise sober and common place. They are marked by the typical simplicity of the style of Anita Desai. The words used belong to the main stream of spoken and written English all over the world. There are neither any jargons, slangs, colloquial expressions, nor untraditional words. The language is dynamic and supple and capable of expressing all sorts of ideas—simple, mundane, lurid, tense, calm or traditional.

As ideas expressed are commonplace the diction and imagery used to express them is also commonplace. Ramu has come from Bombay and is stretching himself on a chair:

> "Ramu lowers himself into a creaking basket chair and spreads out his legs and throws back his head. A mynah on the neem tree that overhangs the terrace is watching his movements and lets out a series of whistles as if in comment upon them" (46). The mynah as if like most men is angered by Ramu and his conduct and then leaves.

The language and style are powerful enough to express every shade of meaning, even the lurid fits of Uma.

> "She clenched her teeth together and bit her tongue so that the blood ran, lurid, scarlet. She began to roll on the floor, from side to side, throwing her head about and meaning [...]" (59).

Brevity, terseness, tension of situation and emotion are expressed in staccato language:

> "She filled a can with kerosene oil. She unlocked the kitchen door and went out on the veranda. Then she removed her cotton clothing. She wrapped a nylon sari about her. She knotted it at the neck and knees. Then she poured kerosene over herself. Then she struck a match. She set herself alight" (151). How tense and dramatic is the rendering of the suicide committed by Anamika. At times while describing the inner feelings of characters expressionistic style is used. Uma feels "herself drawn by an undercurrent into a secret depth, so dark that she could see nothing at all—just the darkness" (132).

The most remarkable part of the novel is its vision of life. As the title of the novel shows, fasting and feasting are equally meaningful or meaningless; they are just the same. The joy in feasting is as insignificant as the depression and sorrow in fasting. The words feasting and fasting have a symbolical connotation. On the one hand they stand for self-indulgence and self-abnegation and on the other they stand for indulgence into any sensuous experience.

There seems to be a pessimistic tinge in the description of the life and death of Anamika, who is lawyer Bakul's daughter. Anamika's physical beauty is exemplary. Her mental sharpness makes her win a British scholarship. Her manners, demeanour and conduct are so graceful. Yet destiny has in store for her apathy from husband's side, cruelty and beating by the mother-in-law resulting in abortions and her later infertility and death. Anamika's bad luck is totally undeserved. Similarly Uma's mental incapacity and lack of commonsense are a matter of inborn talent and bad luck. As such her father and mother become apathetic to her education. Uma's failure to get married, in spite of the parents' readiness with dowry is again a matter of bad luck and unimpressive features. Her ultimate marriage with a married man, having wife and children is as much a matter of her bad luck, her parents' shortsightedness as people's inhumanity in so far as money may tempt them to any sort of wickedness.

Another important idea coming from the book is that happiness is an inner matter based on balance and contentment. Aruna's marriage with Arvind is in every way happy but she is made unhappy on flimsy grounds such as wearing slippers at dinner time or a shirt with a colour not appropriate at an occasion. Happiness is based on deeper elements than sheer frivolities and whims.

A pessimistic note is again struck when Arun in America failed to befriend Rod when the latter was in a jovial mood and is despondent to get his goodwill for a second time: "life deals in singles not doubles essentially" (192). Economic plenty does not lead one to happiness. This is proved by the case of Anamika, Aruna and Melanie. It is rather dependent on a sense of balance, detachment and equanimity, regarding pleasure and pain as one. This reflects the spirit of the *Bhagwadgita.* The very title of the book *Fasting, Feasting* treating indulgence to the sense of taste, and abstaining from it as equal is also reminiscent of the spirit of the *Bhagwadgita* though no overt reference is made to it anywhere during the course of the plot by any character. But this connotation is made clear right by the title itself.

Indifference to prosperity and poverty, hunger or contentment, pain and hunger is suggested in the closing part of the chapter twenty-six wherein Melanie is seen in a pool of vomit caused by overeating from hunger and the habitual vomitting leads to pain—"[...] this is a real pain and real hunger. But what hunger does a person so satiated feel?" (224). There can be no real hunger in so much prosperity, real hunger is always felt in poverty which Mr Patton's family does not have. The question in the quotation regarding the hunger of a satiated person indicates the futility and meaninglessness of human desires and motives and the need of a sense of balance.

A fondness for the Indian way of life, culture and philosophy is indicated by the change that has come in Mrs Patton: "She dresses in skirts and long-sleeved blouses. She has voiced a tentative interest in traditional medicines, she talks of taking a course at the Leisure Activities Centre in yoga, or astrology" (227). This shows the victory of Indian culture and spirituality over the materialistic culture of America where even prosperous people aspire for happiness through Indian values and learning related to Indology.

However, the real message of the novel is an adventurous quest for the spirit of America—"the open space, that unfettered vacuum where the undiscovered America still lies" (200). The American search is the search for the millennium, for the golden dream of prosperity and affluence "the pioneer's dream of the endlessly postponed and endlessly golden America." While the Americans like Mrs Patton learn yogic and spiritual lesson from India, young and enthusiastic Arun, an Indian, learns the adventurous quest for the golden dream from America. So two sides become even, like fasting becoming even with feasting. Both India and America have to co-exist and give and take and the book throws light on the much needed interdependence and mutual co-operation and co-existence of the East and the West.

REFERENCE

1. Anita Desai, *Fasting, Feasting,* Chatto and Windus, London, 1999.

12

Cry, the Peacock: A Study in the Theme of Alienation

B.D. PANDEY

Among the post-independence Indo-English writers Anita Desai holds a prominent place not because of any inventions in style or technique or treatment of startlingly new themes that she can lay claim to, but because of the immense popularity she commands as a novelist of human predicament of anxiety, frustration and loneliness in the insensitive and inconsiderate contemporary world, and because she has given new dimension to the Indo-English novel by turning from outer to inner reality and by carrying flow of the mental experience of its characters, she has brought it in the mainstream of contemporary European and American fiction. This paper aims at tracing the theme of alienation—man's estrangement from someone or something with which he was attached or identified—his family, his group, his society and even his own self, in Desai's first novel *Cry, the Peacock* (1963).

Cry, the Peacock is Desai's maiden novel which can be considered as a trendsetting novel as it deals with the mental rather than physical aspect of its characters. It deals with the complete alienation of its protagonist Maya—a hypersensitive creature of pure instinct—from her surroundings. She is married to Gautam, an insensitive, pragmatic, and rational advocate with whom she is unable to reconcile all her life. The alienation between Maya and Gautam is because of Maya's intense involvement in her own inner world of phantasm. She is deeply attached to past, lives almost in world of memories while Gautam values the importance of action because of his rational nature.

The alienation between husband and wife is quite evident in the very beginning of the novel. The death of her pet dog Toto affects her deeply; the agony she suffers from its death is in no way similar to Gautam's reactions who adeptly manages the truck of PWD to carry the body of the dog away. Maya is shattered by a reality too hard to bear. Her imagination takes full charge of her reasoning. She sees death somewhere nearby. Death of Toto evokes a faint fear; her 'tear-hazed vision' is blurred by a horrifying sense of doom. She records the presence of shadowy something, 'that prodded me into admitting that it was not my pet's death alone that I mourn today, but another sorrow unremembered, perhaps as yet not even experienced, and filled me with this despair' (8). To mitigate her suffering she needs the assuring warmth of Gautam which at least for her he is incapable of.

One reason for Maya's present state may be injurious influence of her father. Maya being a motherless child, her father focuses all his attention on her. With his autocratic lifestyle, Maya had lived a protected life that hampers her freedom of growing as an individual. The father's over-protective love does not allow her any independence to grow, think and act as an entity. As a grown up woman now, she cannot relate herself to the realities of married life. She feels herself inferior and so there is a strong desire in her to raise herself above others. In order to establish her uniqueness and self-importance Maya builds around herself a bower of bougainvillea and jasmine buds "palpitating with living breath, open, white, virginal" (106). Anyone misfit for this world, is inferior to her. The atmosphere in Gautam's family is charged with intellectual and social discussions, it lacks the finer sensitivity of Maya. For Gautam, Maya is in unnatural situation and he attributes it to her father fixation:

> If you know Freud it would all be very straightforward and then appear as merrily inevitable to you—taking your childhood and upbringing into consideration. You have a very obvious father obsession—which is also the reason why you married me, a man so much older than

> yourself. It is a complex that, unless you mature rapidly you will not be able to deal with, to destroy (46).

Maya tries to analyze her feeling and examines her memories of the past in order to reach the source of this disturbance. She gropes for some kind of meaning and this comes to her in flashes, first during a conversation with Gautam the word 'ultimate' reminds her of a particular evening in her past and then in the stillness of the night when the moon acquires for her a demonic appearance:

> I was aware of a great, dead silence in which my eyes opened to a vision that appeared through the curtains of the years, one by one falling back till I again saw that shadow. A black and evil shadow [...]. It was, I remembered it now, fate (31-32).

In Maya's opinion, Gautam is entirely different from her father. He is cold and feeling less, preoccupied with his work, efficient but indifferent to her presence, and someone who 'saw no value in anything less than the ideas and theories born of human and, preferably male brain,' who remained 'always untouched, unscalded' (99-100). But his orderly habits are very much like Maya's father's and there must have been some basis for the friendship that had existed between the two men, no matter, how different their worldly attitudes. Her father, Raisahib, having faith in acceptance did not permit discussion whereas Gautam was interested in appealing to Maya at the level of argument. Maya, through the act of marriage has transferred her love for her father and expectations of him to Gautam, thus attempting to thrust a readymade image on him. Gautam points this out to her:

> He is the one responsible for this,—for making you believe that all that is important in the world is to possess, possess—riches, comforts, posies, dollies, loyal retainers—all the luxuries of the fairy tales. You were brought upon life is a fairy tale to you still (115).

Apart from father-obsession and incompatibility with her husband, Maya is disturbed by another phenomenon—the prophesy made by albino astrologer that one of the couple would die soon in unnatural way. She cannot get herself away with the thought of astrologer, whose eyes are pale, opaque and give him an appearance of morbidity. Regarding the impact of this prophesy upon hypersensitive Maya, Iyengar remarks:

> Over the whole narrative in *Cry, the Peacock,* which is really Maya's effort to tell her story to herself, to discover some meaning in her life, and even to justify herself, there hovers an uncanningly oppressive sense of fatality (456).

During all this nightmare of animated and induced suffering, she moves farther and farther away from reality, descending into the hideous well of loneliness and unreality where the only echoes are those of the albino's dread prophesies and of the peacocks' cries of death in the moments of love and orgasm. The imagery here of pit, corridor and well would suggest her dread, alienation and darkness, even as she unconsciously craves a cease:

> Upon this bed of hot, itching sand, I summoned up again the vision of tenebrific albino who had cast his shadow like a net across me as I had fled down the corridor of years, from the embrace of protection to embrace of love, yet catching me as surely as a giant fisherman striding through the shallows of moonlit seas, throws his fine net with one brief, expert motion and knows as it settles with a falling whisper upon the still water, that he will find in it a catch: I had not escaped. The years had caught up, and now the final, the decisive one held me in its perspiring clasp from which release seemed impossible. And now I recalled that oil-sick, sibilant tongue whispering poetry to me in the bat-tortured dark. Do you hear the peacocks call in the wilds? Are they not blood-chilling, their shrieks of pain? "Pia, pia," they cry. "Lover, Lover, Mio, mio—I die, I die." Go out into the jungles before the monsoons come—at the time when the first cloud cross the horizon, black as the kohl in your grave eyes. How they love the rain—these peacocks. They spread but their splendid tails and begin to dance, but, like Shiva's their dance of joy is the dance of death and they dance, knowing that they and their lovers are all to die, perhaps even before the monsoons come to an end (109-10).

Besides her father and Gautam, Maya has her present circle of friends. And among them there is Laila who is nursing a dying husband, resigned to her fate and also to her choice. She had married him knowing that he was a patient of tuberculosis. There is also Pom, who, after flaunting her in-laws, submits meekly to her mother-in-law where the birth of a son is concerned. Her friends, her surroundings, her father's fatalism all these lead her to fell trapped in the shadow of an astrologer and the belief that she is condemned to die. This certainly leads her to value every moment of Gautam's company; only life is so unaccommodating to her demands. In her need for comfort, Maya turns to Gautam's suggestion of detachment from the world. But detachment is difficult to attain and attachment leads to self-destruction.

The Freudian complexes are obviously the writer's concern in the novel. Maya hides her aggressive traits behind her self-effacing and self-minimizing processes. She projects herself as a helpless, suffering martyr; a childless woman, gripped by the misfortune of her pet's death. Her act of pillow beating and crying piteously enables her to see herself as a helpless child. These initial expressions lead to self-pity. Psychosomatic symptoms, like slitting headaches and fever, followed by delirium, occur. Maya becomes vindictive when finally the self alienates itself from the real centre; and self-hate takes hold—the logical outcome of a conflict between Maya's pride system and her real self.

A clear picture of Maya's psyche is provided in terms of various motifs, dreams, and hallucinations running throughout the narrative. The recurrent image of moon suggests the fast deteriorating mental state of Maya. In her acutely disturbed state, the moon appears to her as sinister and ghostly, "a demonic creature, the fierce dance [...] accompanied by a deafening roar of silent drums" (28). Later is depicted as a full bosomed woman glowing across the sky. The moon appears like:

> [...] a great multifoliate rose, waxen white, casting a light that was holy in its purity, a soft suffusing glow of its chastity, casting its reflection upon the night with a vast, tender mother love (208).

Gautam intervenes between Maya and her worshipped moon; as such she chooses to punish him to death. Symbolically, the position of the moon in the sky parallels the lucidity of the thoughts of Maya, they progress in the same degree and the moon becomes a symbol of her psyche.

Other recurring symbols, except peacocks, are those of reptiles—snakes, iguanas and lizards. Maya's terror and imaginary snake can be interpreted as the fear of the *Maya* (delusion) of the Hindu philosophy that coils round us. It is in the "Collective Unconscious" (205) of Hindus. Psychologically, reptiles stand for sexual urge. But this fear, here, is indicative of her morbidity and fast deteriorating psychic condition. Under high fever, the Kathkali dancer, the priest, rats, snakes, all become one, including her father. The forces within her react to the deteriorating process. Maya externalizes her trouble. She projects her self-hate on Gautam. Her primary instinct is self-perversion. She convinces herself that Gautam does not love life. Moreover, he has hurt her neurotic pride by rejecting her love. In order to subdue her turmoil she kills him in a vindictive rage.

The key to understanding Maya's character lies in comprehending her divided self. There is no attempt at self-analysis to apprehend her demands. The fast withering self and the receding contact with the outer world, leave the core of her integrity impaired. Her failure to find life and more of it becomes an appalling crime. She condemns Gautam for it and then, burdened with guilt, and haunted by self-contempt, self-accusation and self-hate, she drags herself into complete darkness of the world of the insane.

This hypersensitiveness of Maya is responsible for her divided or alienated self that leads to an ever widening gap in communication between her and her husband. The image of this alienation and gap is cognized by her in the position of the stars in the sky:

> [...] death linked in those spaces, the darkness spoke of distance, separation, loneliness—loneliness of such proportion that it broke the bonds of that single word and all its associations, and went spilling and spreading out and around, lapping the stars, each one isolated

> from the other by so much [...]. I cried to myself—what is the use? I am alone (22).

What she thinks of stars is true to her own life too. Both she and Gautam are alienated from each other and that space of alienation consists death—death of either of the two. She kills Gautam in order to bridge the gap. This reminds us of Edward Albee's play *The Zoo Story* (1958) where Jerry, the protagonist, in order to establish contact or bridge the gap of communication, kills himself. The difference is that by killing himself Jerry succeeds in his aim while Maya, in the present novel, does not.

In sum, *Cry, the Peacock* is a pioneering effort towards exposing the psychological problems of an alienated woman. As Meena Beliappa remarks: "the ardent introspection of Maya marks a valuable introversion in Indian fiction. It points to a line of significant development—exploration, not of the 'social' man, but 'the lone individual,'" (26) the novel is a powerful study of the experiences of a disturbed and alienated mind.

REFERENCES

1. *Cry, the Peacock* (Delhi: Orient Paperbacks, 1980).
2. K.R.S. Iyengar, *Indian Writing in English* (Delhi: Sterling Publishers, 1984).
3. C.G. Jung, "The Archetypes of Collective Unconsciousness," *Twentieth Century Criticism: The Major Trends*. Eds. William J. Handy and Max Westbrook (New Delhi: Light and Life Publishers, 1974).
4. Meena Beliappa, *Anita Desai: A Study of Her Fiction* (Calcutta: Writers' Workshop Publication, 1971).

13

SUPERSTITION AND PSYCHE IN ANITA DESAI'S *CRY, THE PEACOCK*

RAJESHWAR MITTAPALLI

Maya, the central character of Anita Desai's *Cry, the Peacock,* is obsessed almost from the beginning of the novel with the gloomy prophecy of an albino astrologer. According to the prophecy she or her husband would die during the fourth year of her marriage. Her father dismisses the prophecy as nonsense and orders that it should be forgotten. Obeying his wish Maya keeps the prophecy rigorously repressed in her unconscious until her marriage with Gautama enters the fourth year. Now triggered off by the death of her pet dog, Toto, it assumes during the course of the novel the shape of an obsessional neurosis and keeps gnawing at the core of her being like an oversized pest feeding on a tender leaf.

It is strange that Maya should so superstitiously believe in the veracity of the prophecy although she knows that Gautama and his family "hoot with derision at the mention of superstition" (75-76). In the beginning of her neurotic affliction she frequently tells herself that it was she herself who was fated to die. But she is in ardent love with life and so she soon begins to wonder whether it was not "Gautama's life that was threatened" (164). Taking this line of reasoning further fears for her life and would keep the secret for herself at any cost.

> He must not know, not even guess. Never, never, never. If he guessed, new dangers would arise like sudden fires out of the cracked earth [...]. Ah, if Gautama found out, would he, might he not put me in peril of my life? Did he not love life too [...] (151).

Not very long after she is almost convinced that Gautama is certainly fated to die and the thought makes her more and more secretive:

> I glanced at him now, slyly, for sly I had grown with such a load of secrets that had to be hidden from him, such evil and awful secrets (165).

It has been suggested in the novel and later harped on by critics that Maya is obsessed with the prophecy because of the romance involved in it. But the knowledge of depth psychology holds the promise of examining her irrational and superstitious belief from an entirely new angle. Freud attributes superstitious beliefs to suppressed hostility:

> It can be recognized most clearly in neurotics suffering from obsessional thinking [...] that superstition derives from suppressed hostile and cruel impulses. Superstition is in large part the expectation of trouble; and a person who has harboured frequent evil wishes against others, but has been brought up to be good and has therefore repressed such wishes into the unconscious, will be especially ready to expect punishment for his unconscious wickedness in the form of trouble threatening him from without (232).

Does Maya's superstition too originate in her suppressed hostile and cruel impulses? To all appearances she has been an absolutely submissive and obedient daughter, sister and wife and so it may sound outrageous to accuse her of harbouring cruel impulses. But probing into her unconscious would reveal that there is immense suppressed hostility in her unconscious against her husband and to an extent against her father (44-48, see my previous stand in notes). Being a "creature of instinct" (16) she seems to hold Gautama responsible for her unfulfilled instinctuality in the marital relationship. She is also angry with him because after four years of life together she is compelled to come to the sad conclusion that she would soon lose her already rudimentary self. She grows anxious on account of the threats to her self-preservation and neurotically perceives Gautama's death as a solution. The prophecy comes as a convenient external justification to her unconscious wish and for that reason she tenaciously clings to it. I will dwell at some length on Maya's reasons for wishing Gautama dead and then return to her superstitious belief.

Maya is extremely faithful to her instincts which, as is their nature, crave for unqualified and wild satisfaction. According to Freudian tenets normal people in her circumstances would have effected a withdrawal by influencing the instinctual urges at the psychic level. But tragically for Maya, her very life appears to be intricately woven with and highly dependent on her instincts. Given her instinctuality Maya expects some emotional and physical satisfaction in married life but both of them are denied her, one by Gautama's cold intellectuality and the other by his age. Maya's longing for the sensuous enjoyment of life is dampened by liberal doses of the *Gita* philosophy of non-attachment. Her effusive emotionality is always counterbalanced by Gautama's analytical mind. While he views "nothing subjectively, nothing with passion" (150) she is "flooded with tenderness and gratitude" (11) when he merely touches her hair, falls "into the soft, velvet well of the primordium of original instinct, of first-formed love" (11) when he draws a finger down her cheek, and takes to hating her own pretty face for failing to make any impact on him. She has to thus continually contend with unreciprocated emotionality and feels terrible on that score.

Sex is not only an intensely and intrinsically pleasurable experience but it can act as a revitalising force in an otherwise sterile life. Freud, in fact, views sex as the prototype of all pleasurable experiences of life. Maya's earth-bound nature makes her well-inclined to derive the fullest satisfaction from this intimate experience. It is difficult to conjecture what course her psyche would have taken if she were married to a much younger man and has been satisfied sexually. But because of Gautama's age and attitude to sex she remains a much disappointed woman. Even when they do make love the act is utterly devoid of passion. Several passages in the novel have been devoted to the portrayal of her disillusionment in sex. At the beginning of the novel itself Maya makes a frank admission of her sexual dissatisfaction born of Gautama's unpardonable negligence.

> Telling me to go to sleep while he worked at his papers, he did not give another thought to me, to either the soft, willing body or the lonely, wanting mind that waited near his bed (9).

Frustrated by his coldness she gives herself up to a fit of pillow-beating! As her disillusionment becomes a routine experience she increasingly sexualises her surroundings, perhaps by way of displacement. The papaya trees in the courtyard, for example, assume a new sexual significance for her.

> I contemplated that, smiling with pleasure at the thought of those long streamers of bridal flowers that flow out of the core of the female papaya tree and twine about her slim trunk, and the firm, wax-petalled blossoms that leap directly out of the solid trunk of the male [...] (92).

As her grip over herself begins to slacken she begins to experience hallucinatory visions of lizards and birds coupulating in weird settings.

> Of lizards, the lizards that come upon you, stalking you silently, upon clawed toes, slipping their clublike tongues in and out, in and out with an audible hiss [...] they have struck you to a pillar of salt which, when it is motionless they will mount and lash with their slime-dripping tongues, lash and lash again, as they grip you with curled claws, rubbing their cold bellies upon yours, rubbing and grinding, rubbing and grinding (127).

What Maya experiences here seems to be a symbolic gratification of the sexual desire which remains unfulfilled in actual life.

The image of fighting and mating peacocks, apart from being the central motif of the novel, underlines Maya's sexual frustration too. The memory of her innocent enjoyment of their call in her childhood becomes a foil to her present overcrowded mind, full of bird and animal imagery.

> But sleep was rent by the frenzied cries of peacocks pacing the rocks at night—peacocks searching for mates, peacocks tearing themselves to bleeding shreds in the act of love, peacocks screaming with agony at the death

> of love. The night sky turned to a flurry of peacocks' tails, each star a staring eye (175).

In spite of her total frustration, Maya's moral scrupulosity does not allow her to cross the bounds of marital morality. Nor is she able to sublimate this powerful biological urge in the manner of her friend Laila who selflessly serves her tuberculous husband. Her married life ends up being emotionally and socially sterile.

A continuous frustration of the body's sexual needs can be disastrous to somebody like Maya, given her fierce instinctuality. A healthy emotional and sexual life would have given her a sense of security and stopped her psyche from decaying. This view acquires validation from Freud's observation:

> experience shows [...] that women, who, as being the actual vehicles of the sexual interests of mankind, are only endowed in a small measure, with the gift of sublimating their instincts, and who [...] when they are subjected to the disillusionments of marriage, fall ill of severe neuroses which permanently darken their lives (47).

Freud attributes neurosis of women to sexual dissatisfaction resulting from the rigours of civilized sexual morality. Biologically speaking, marital unfaithfulness could be a viable cure for the ailment. However, such a thing entails perhaps the most severe indictment in the rigidly organised Indian society. Freud continues:

> the more strictly a woman has been brought up and the more sternly she has submitted to the demands of civilization, the more she is afraid of taking this way out; and in the conflict between her desires and her sense of duty, she once more seeks refuge in a neurosis. Nothing protects her virtue as securely as illness (47).

Maya too seeks a neurotic solution but only to find it inadequate. Something more drastic than neurosis needs to be considered by her psyche.

Secondly, Maya perceives that eventually she will lose herself as a result of a long experience of eventlessness. Her life appears to her as an endless tedium with nothing significant taking place at any time. She is never the centre of importance nor is she instrumental in any event. The sphere of her social activities is so severely restricted that she seems to feel suffocated within it. But by Indian standards her life situation appears to be ideal. She has a secure home, earning husband and well-defined future. These seemingly ideal external conditions are however not acceptable to her unconscious where her desire for unbridled freedom is hidden.

The novel abounds in incidents that show how her longing for outdoor life is constantly frustrated mainly by Gautama. As a child she had enjoyed the scenic beauty and cool weather of Darjeeling and now she longs to go there with Gautama. When she timidly suggests the possibility to Gautama he replies in a cold astringent tone, "Why don't you? [...] Your father would take you wherever you wanted to go. He *can*" (40). The Kathakali ballets performed at night in parts of South India, hold great attraction to Maya.

> 'I want—I want,' [...] 'to see the Kathakali dances. I have heard of the ballets they have in their villages [...]. And the dancers are all men, [...].' The masks they wear—you must have seen them? And their costumes. And the special kind of music. And it is all out in the open, at night, by starlight—and perhaps they have torches (42-43).

To her imploration to take her to the South, Gautama coolly suggests that she wait till a Kathakali troupe comes to Delhi. He apparently sees no strong reason to undertake a tiresome journey down South in the sweltering summer.

The fact of Maya's constricted life comes most vividly alive in the scene of Gautama's all male party. Charmed by the vibratingly rich Urdu poetry recited by these cultured wine-drinking gentlemen, Maya breaks an age old rule and joins them. While the other men politely, but uneasily, respond to her presence Gautama not only shatters her hope of participating in the pulsating and poetry-charged atmosphere but also subtly drives home to her the truth that she does not belong there.

> Turning his back to me, he stood talking to a friend, a

> glass in his hand, and his voice rose, in order that I might hear, when he said, 'Blissful, yes, because it is unrelated to our day, unclouded by the vulgarity of ill-educated men, or of overbearing women [...]' (104).

To add to her problems stemming from inactivity she remains childless. The birth of a child would have given her a sense of achievement and her creative urge would have got focused on a helplessly dependent human being instead of getting diffused over nature and spread outside human interest.

Three plus years of married life and the prospect of a passionless and unchallenging life for the next forty or fifty years, during which she would continue to be obedient to her husband and face neither choices nor challenges, comes as a shocking revelation to her hyperactive mind. Her repeated confession that she or Gautama will surely die, in a way, indicates that the opposite would be true—that especially Gautama will not die before her. So according to this logic if she is to live and find the happiness that is her due Gautama will have to go. And the focal point of her thought, day in and day out, becomes the albino's prophecy which appears to justify and dramatise her wish. But she allows herself considerable time before she does anything drastic. All through the novel she keeps her wish hidden in her unconscious and the prophecy itself shrouded in secrecy. This is because as a neurotic she is still aware of the moral sanctions against such wishes. Indoctrinated to be faithful to her husband, she feels her hand held back by an invisible force. The neurotic defence mechanisms such as sleep rituals, hallucinatory visions and nightmares (where her secret longings come alive to her), experience of split personality, adverse somatic symptoms and religious avoidance of violence woefully fail to blunt the edge of her unconscious wish. At most places she appears to reel under the pressure and break to pieces as a result of the struggle within. Yet she hesitates. She is aware of the unseemly consequences and she is scared of not only society but her own conscience. In order to be done with Gautama without antagonising the social imperatives and her own super-ego the only way that is still open to her is psychosis. Once a human organism is entrusted to psychosis nature takes its own course. The preservation of its physical integrity becomes more important than the protection of its social image. In fact, in psychotics the super-ego, the moral agency, becomes completely inactive. Psychosis would thus help Maya to carry out her wish without earning disapproval. She therefore progressively moves towards a psychotic solution to her struggle.

Her transition from neurosis to psychosis is powerfully underscored in the scene of the dust-storm in which she is shown as running "on and on, from room to room, laughing as maniacs laugh once the world gives them up and surrenders them to their freedom" (190). Maya's shutting herself in as a measure of protection from the raging dust-storm is symbolic of her total withdrawal from the world of purposeful action and meaningful relationships. The exact point of her plunging into the abysmal depths of psychosis, however, is her act of violence itself. Maya's pushing Gautama off the parapet of their house is not fortuitous. There are simply no accidents in psychic life. Behind Maya's final indulgence in violence there has been a prolonged psychic struggle which she has not known herself. Having done the deed and having taken recourse to psychosis she relaxes and openly declares that unlike her, Gautama has not been in love with life and so according to the prophecy he had to die.

> It had to be one of us, you see, and it was so clear that it was I who was meant to live. You see, to Gautama it didn't really matter. He didn't care, and I did (215-16).

Governed by the primary process thinking she does not camouflage her thoughts by drawing on her linguistic resources any more. Her adult life with all its responsibilities and anxieties has become a sealed book for her. She is faithful to herself and the social and moral consequences of her actions do not matter to her any more now.

Her superstitious belief thus helped her immensely in the process of unconsciously identifying her problems and their source. From a shadowy figure the albino sprang to life and has come to mean much to her during her neurotic struggle. After she embraced psychosis what the charlatan said years ago has become gospel truth to her. But for him she would not have perceived Gautama as her foremost enemy and would not have considered the possibility of violently working out her equation with him.

NOTES AND REFERENCES

1. Anita Desai, *Cry, the Peacock* (Delhi: Orient Paperbacks, 1980, rpt. 1988).
2. Sigmund Freud, "Determinism, Belief in Chance and Superstition—Some Points of View, "*The Psychopathology of Everyday Life,* tr. Alan Tyson (Harmondsworth: Penguin, 1960).
3. In an earlier article while playing down the father fixation theory I argued that Maya nursed a grouse against her father Raisahib for impeding the development of her individuality with his over-protective attitude all through her childhood and adolescence, then for throwing her into the fetters of marriage with a passionless and cold intellectual and finally for callously neglecting her thereafter. I concluded that Maya unconsciously took her revenge against him by creating a scandal which she knew he dreaded. But in psychological life things are 'over determined.' Every significant psychological event in a person's life has a multiplicity of reasons. Maya's wish to avenge herself on her father could be only one of the many reasons for her to want to kill Gautama.

   "Anita Desai's *Cry, the Peacock*: The Father's Unconscious," *Indian English Literature Since Independence.* IAES Golden Jubilee Volume, ed. Ayyappa Paniker (New Delhi: The Indian Association for English Studies, 1991).
4. Sigmund Freud, *Civilized Sexual Morality and Modern Nervous Illness,* tr. James Strachey (Harmondsworth: Penguin, 1985).

14

THE IDEOLOGY OF SPACE IN *FIRE ON THE MOUNTAIN*

RAMA KUNDU

"There is not even silence in the mountains"

—*The Waste Land*

For a period of more than two centuries space in English literature had epitomised—perhaps more sharply than any other item—the binaries of the colonial situation. Space was often perceived in imperial literature in terms of the binaries of home and frontier, centre and periphery, metropolis and the 'native,' which found their corollaries in racial and cultural binaries, with the imperial/white centre obviously holding (and upholding too) the 'correct' standards in ethics, law, art and every other aspect of social-political-cultural life. In the postcolonial era the psychocartography was ironically reinscribed from the colonized's perspective, and the binaries were reversed. But they remained binaries all the same. Only "cartography turned a cartwheel" with decolonisation" (Notes, 1). Since then the Empire has been writing back to the imperial centre not only in terms of consciousness, concepts, perceptions, but also in particular, of specific spaces. These spaces could be some lush green Caribbean island across the 'wide Sargasso Sea' (Rhys) (Notes, 2), a village by the forest in the heart of Ibo (Achebe) (Notes, 3), the lake region of Canada (Atwood) (Notes, 4), or the desert of Australia (White) (Notes, 5). Postcolonial fiction especially has often been *geografictione,* using geographical identity-marks as a device for post-colonial deprogramming of the colonizer's psycho-cartographic programming.

Again, to the diasporic perception the image of space has continued to figure as a site of intersection between the place *where* one has got lost and the place *which* one has lost; the inaccessible lost place which was home once but has now been reduced to a dot on the map, and as such, has been shifted from empirical reality to the region of nostalgic memory. Thus space epitomises for the diasporic writer a prison on the one hand, and an impossible longing for a mirror on the other, which, to use Rushdie's beautiful image, has broken, with some of its pieces being irretrievably lost.

The Indian scenario offers interesting instances of these varied phrases and trends in the discourse on space. Way back in the nineteenth century—H.D. Arnold's *Oakfield* (1863), P.M. Taylor's *Confessions of a Thug* (1838)—through the early twentieth century—Forster, Kipling, Orwell—right into the late twentieth century—Ruth Prawer Jhabvala—India as empirical space(s) has manifested to the European imagination the 'Other,' with its irresistible lure and threat, with its baffling enigma and fascination. The landscape—be it mountains or plain, desert or forest—proved to be an elusive and, not unfrequently, dangerous attraction.

During the early phase of postcolonialism one finds a self-conscious assertion in the writings of Indian authors who introduced carefully built constructs in order to epitomise the Indian space in microcosms, like 'Malgudi' or 'Kanthapura,' for example. It was their own lovable loved space despite its inadequacies. It was a proud, rather emphatic, way of inscribing one's own space. The expatriate Indian writers' tributary, nostalgic, myth-oriented poetry and prose in the post-independence decades—including Ramanujan, Parthasarathy, Ezekiel, for example—only further affirmed the same assertion that 'this is *my home* which was *your exile;* this *my centre* which was *your periphery.*'

Besides these typical postcolonial treatments of space the discourse has reached a new plateau in the last decades of the millennium in the writings of two successive generations of Indian women writers as they search for a space of 'her' own—as a woman and as an individual. This falls in pattern with the slow but steady emergence of women in various walks of life since independence. The journey has been an uphill one in the context of a society which is still largely governed by patriarchal ideologies and norms; and the women writers in the last three decades have been giving voice to their aspirations and ordeals as well as the anguish and frustration of the previous generations—their mothers and grandmothers. One of the many ways of expressing this consciousness is voicing the longing for a space of 'her' own, or the anguish at failing to find one. In the fiction of the 'Big Three' in the pre-Independence days space often served as scaffolding for social and political ideologies. The importance of 'Kanthapura' or 'Malgudi' to the affective and experiential modalities of culture was apparent. But Indian women writers since the 'seventies have inscribed the Indian landscape with new meanings, signs and signals. To quote the concluding sentence of Mary Conde's essay "Women Inscribing the Indian Landscape,"

> Lacking the titillating consciousness of writing fiction-driven fiction about an imperial possession, Indian women writers inscribe Indian landscape with moral criticism, sadness, entrapment—or simply dreariness (141).

Actually, however, it has been all this and much more. Devina, the heiress in Sujata Sabni's *Silent Whispers* (1996) 'buys' a vista; the sea.

> She loved to stand there for hours, just watching the sea, and its chameleon moods. Turbulent, calm, mischievous or mature, playful, angry, constantly changing yet always the same. This heartbreakingly beautiful vista had been the clinching factor in her decision to buy the flat (23).

Everybody is not so lucky. Thus Ammu in *The God of Small Things* has to live a cramped life both before and after her marriage and divorce; she has nowhere to go, nor does she have a space of her own to 'be' and 'become' in any of the houses of her father, husband or brother. When she rebels against this denial she is crushed. It is only in the wild garden that she gets a breather. Significantly it is a wild overgrown garden, and not the beautifully clipped and trimmed garden of *Nurjahan,* which epitomises prison and enslavement (Notes, 6). Githa Hariharan's story-tellers in *When*

Dreams Travel (1999) (Notes, 1), suffocated by the palace, which has no windows but only solid stone walls, prefer the freedom of a shanty in a desert tract, because it is open, even if dreary. In Shashi Deshpande's novels one comes across women who have been forced to spend their entire lives in a corner of an old house,—a claustrophobic space though a sprawling structure—without any privacy, any scope to indulge in creativity or thoughts of individual being and becoming.

On the other hand, in Anita Desai's *Fire on the Mountain* (1977) one finds a superb expression of the woman's dream of a space of her own. Here the author allows her protagonist the expanse of a mountain. From the very start the most noticeable aspect of the novel is its sense of geographical space. The hillstation resort of Kasauli, to which Nanda Kaul, the elegant widow of the Vice-Chancellor, retires in her old age is a real empirical space and at the same time it is apparently emblematic of Nanda's protest and assertion, the penultimate act of assertion that she has made at the fag-end of her life, regarding her need of 'a room of one's own.' It seems to be a contrast to the male spaces she had lived in in the past, which were occupied and controlled by her father or husband. Coming here "on the ridge of the mountain" she has reached "the place [...] she had wanted and prepared for all her life" (3). It gives her "a great, cool flowering of relief" (3) and she wants "no one and nothing else" (3).

Paradoxically, however, with the death of Ila at the end it appears that even this space has been abrogated by forces of violence and chauvinism. One also learns at the end that coming to the mountain was not Nanda's own choice, that this was but the appropriate closure to her inwardly barren life, though after settling down here she had persuaded herself to believe that she had at last found her real home, her goal and fulfilment.

The author's elaborate projection of the mountain as a geographic location and a fictional space consistently underscores an ambiguity,—a similar ambiguity that underlies Nanda's posture of self-assurance and her innate uncertainty, her firmness and hesitation, her withdrawal from, and reaching out to, life. The organization of the fictional space is obvious here; it operates as a structuring principle. It does not scaffold a political-social ideology, but relates to a feminine consciousness which is essentially ambiguous in its ambivalences between assertion and hesitancies, stark truth and the lure of fantasies.

The way the mountain has been made vivid with its varied sights, its wide range of sounds, its smell, its occasional dust-storms, long spells of rain, sudden flowers bursting out after a night of rain, its flora and fauna, its wind and fire is really fascinating. One can, as it were, share Nanda's cool solace in this mountain reclusion. At the same time the mountain is not envisioned as an idyllic place. The threats of disharmony cruelty, violence are also there, and cannot be ignored. The author carefully weaves a network of details to bring out this duality.

Isolation and remoteness add to the distinction of this mountain. It is necessarily not within easy reach of mundane life on the plains. One can wind up to Carignano, Nanda's house on the top, only with difficulty. It also takes long to come up from the plain as it is far far away from the big cities. Yet painful memories of the other life, spent in the big cities, remembrances of other locations where Tara suffered where Nanda had suffered, float back *en route* the protagonist's consciousness down memory lane.

The mountain is bare both literally and metaphorically. It is not a typical Indian landscape which should normally contain one temple at least. No myths are attached to it. Nor do political waves or busy commerce reach this farflung place. The only evidence of industrial operation is the medicine factory down the hills which is supposed to squeeze, crush, maul animals in order to make medicine. Neither is there a fine soothing useful river as is so common with Indian landscapes in literature, but only the ravine and the gorge receiving the factory waste.

The mountain is unambiguously clearly located. But the locationing itself sends ambiguous signals. It is a concrete, perceptible, specific place whose boundaries are drawn with care to indicate two opposite features of the naturescape. From Carignano, Nanda's home on the ridge it is an immense expanse. "In every direction there was a sweeping view—to the north of the mountains, to the south, of the plains" (4). But whereas the north-facing windows open "onto the blue waves of the Himalayas flowing out and up to the line of ice and snow sketched upon the sky" (4), the south-facing ones "looked down the plunging cliff to the plain stretching out, flat and sere, to the blurred horizon" (4). Thus, the mountain seems to suggest an aspiration towards the infinite expanse and altitude at one end, and a decline to a dull vista of the plains on the other.

Nanda prefers the knoll, the topmost point of her garden where the wind is "keenest and the view widest" (4). But there too she cannot avoid spotting the postman coming up from the plains, carrying news from the other world down there. She finds the view of the hilltop from her veranda to be "more comforting" than the other view from the back windows "of the cliff plunging seven thousand feet down to the Punjab plains" (13). This seems to be symptomatic of the ambiguity of her mental situation, her defiance and her longings, her stoic strained withdrawal, and her imaginative and wishful structuring of the past. She looks fascinated at the elusive gold and violet, (27) light and space of the peaks where "hills melted into sky, sky into snows, snows into air" (28); still she would often go round to the back of the house and gaze "down the gorge with its gashes of red earth, its rocks and gullies and sharply spiked agaves, to the Punjab plains—a silver haze in the summer heat—stretching out to a dim yellow horizon" (17). At such moments she also synchronically looks down "over all those years she had survived and borne" (17). And she sees them not bare and shining as the plains below, but "like the gorge, cluttered, choked and blackened with the heads of children and grandchildren, servants and guests, all restlessly surging, clamouring about her" (17). Here is a subtle suggestion that in spite of her apparent withdrawal from the plains and from her past life there, she still carries these other spaces within her consciousness; later she would weave her fiction,— "memory-making" (123), around these spaces.

After a rain one can get a glimpse of the extraordinary expanse of the scene. "Away in the north the rock-scarred snow range glittered. To the south many hundreds of miles of the plain were visible, streaked with streams and pitted with bright pools of rain" (87). Raka's resentment is blown away as she scrambles up to the top and sees before her "a breadth of space, a vast sweeping depth" (61). The author describes the scene as "an ancient scroll" unrolled at her feet.

> To the north, the soft, downy hills flowed, wave upon wave, gold and blue and violet and indigo, like the sea (61).

But the other end of the hill, which obsesses Raka, offers a contrast to this serene beauty:

> [...] the lip of the cliff and the sudden drop down the red, rock-spattered ravine to the plain that lay stretched out and heavy, the dusty pelt of a yellow animal panting in the sun (41).

It is also hot in contrast to the cool north. From the plains the heat comes up to assault the cool of the mountain.

> The plain below opened wide its yellow mouth and it was its oven breath that billowed up the mountainside [...] (48).

The suggestion of an ugly animal writhing in heat is appropriately accompanied by the image of a demonic creature—"a square dragon" (42) which, to Raka, "seemed to dominate the landscape" (42). It is the factory with its enormous concrete walls. It is also the "central dagger" (48) evoking the violence and disharmony of the act of 'piercing.' "The chimneys piercing the white sky, lashed about with black whips of smoke" (49). Raka sniffs the air and smells cinder, serum, chloroform, spirit,—things which are supposed to be anachronistic in an idyllic pastoral. It is the shabby, seedy assault of the industry on the mountains:

> Sharp chimneys thrust out cushions and scarves of smoke *on the milky blue of the afternoon sky* (italics mine).

Perfectly in tune with this polluting presence:

> chutes emerging from its back wall seemed built to disgorge factory waste into the ravine and immediately below them were small, squat structures that looked like brick kilns amongst the spiked, curved blades of the

> giant agaves that were, besides the pines, the only vegetation of that *blighted gorge* (42) (Italics mine).

In addition to this disturbing presence on the mountainscape the reader is also reminded that "the army is everywhere" (57), and "too many tourists" (57) scratching names and dates on trees, which stand out "as incongruous and obtrusive as the barbed wire" (57) or the "frightening" instrument up the hill that looks like an atomic reactor or "some such scientific monstrosity" (57). Nanda finds it "a shame." Nanda feels uneasy and bitter. "Too many tourists. Too much army. How they are ruining this—this quiet place [...]. It really is—is saddening" (57). An unmistakably Eliotian echo:

> There is not even silence in the mountains [...]
> There is not even solitude in the mountains.

The beauty of Dagshai and Sabathu, looking like "handful of pebbles gleaming on golden hilltops" (43) may be exquisite, but still it cannot obliterate the "daggers" or the smoke of the factory "piercing" the sky and "blighting" the ridge. Carignano, on the hilltop, may be safe, but down the hillside dangers await one. The way is full of hazards for a lonely old woman (139). At the end Ila is finished by a black shape detaching itself from the jagged pile of the rocks, "that last rock between her and the hamlet" (142) and *springing soundlessly* upon her. The mountain ceases to be a "heaven-haven" at this point and comes closer to the scene of predatory violence.

The mountain is largely barren and steep along the upper mall. The steep path makes people automatically bend forward excepting Nanda who self-consciously keeps erect (11). It is part of the Kasauli range, the author points out, whose "chief virtue" is "its barrenness," its "starkness" (4). The author carefully brings out its austere aspect. Nanda and Raka, the great grandmother and the great granddaughter walk together along "the sere, silent hillsides on which boulders seemed to have been arrested in downward motion and nothing grew on the pine-needle-spread earth but a few tangles of wild raspberries, hairy with thorn, and contorted agave" (57). Carignano, Nanda's 'own' house (the only one) at last, stands on the "bleached ridge" (5) with its "orderly austerity" (91).

Raka likes it; but she is more drawn by "the ravaged, destroyed and barren spaces in Kasauli [...] the ravine where yellow snakes slept under grey rocks and agaves growing out of the dust and rubble, the skeletal pines that rattled in the wind, the wind-levelled hilltops [...]" (91). The echoes from *The Waste Land* are too obvious to be missed:

> "What are the roots that clutch, what branches grow
> Out of this stony rubbish?"
>
> Or
>
> "The dead tree gives no shelter, the cricket no relief"
>
> and
>
> "Dead mountain mouth of carious teeth that cannot spit."

The vegetation life in the mountain is in tune with this barrenness. Pine and cicada,—again like *The Waste Land* (Notes, 8)—are the plants of this rock, and Nanda finds them appropriate and acceptable. The very opening sentence evokes the fragrance and resonance of pines and cicadas as Nanda Kaul pauses under them. They seem to throw around her a sort of protective shelter. There are some fine touches suggesting her oneness with these mournful trees. As she feels annoyed at the sight of the approaching postman who may be bringing messages from the world she wants to have no connection with, she steps backwards into the garden and "the wind suddenly billowed up and threw the pine branches about as though to curtain her" (8). Nanda fancies herself merging with the pine trees and being mistaken for one. "Grey," "tall," "thin," in her silk sari that makes "sweeping, shivering sound" (4), she is, as it were, another pine-tree, and she yearns "to be a tree, no more and no less" (4). "She would be a charred tree-trunk in the forest" (23). Here the reader is reminded of *Surfacing* the Canadian novel,—published in 1972 were Atwood's female protagonist withdraws from the city to the country, finally beyond the lake into the forest and there she attains a similar perception: "I lean against a tree. I am the tree leaning" (181).

The pines have a sort of beauty too which Nanda can perceive. As Nanda waits for Raka to arrive, the peace of her mind is "ruffled." Synchronically "on the knoll and the gate the wind *ruffled* (emphasis added) the pineneedles so that they glistened silver in the sunlight" (36).

Besides the pine and cicada there are the "thorny snatchful(s) of raspberries" (5) the truant school boy looks for; the clumps of Iris at Carignano had "finished blooming" (4). At the same time it may be noted that the chestnut tree at the foot of the hill is "leafy" (4); the signboard of Carignano is nailed onto this tree. On the northside the wall of Nanda's house is "washed by the blue shadows of the low, dense apricot trees" (5). In the deserted burnt house on the hill there are only dry pebbles. But Nanda knows better and tells Raka:

> It looks dreadful [...] but one shower of rain will bring out hundreds of flowers—lilies, dahlias that the old woman had planted (57).

By the shady veranda of Nanda's house pots of geraniums and fuchsias bloomed unimpaired by the sun (13). In the morning after the first rain Raka wakes up to find "hosts of wild zephyranthes that had come up in the night" (88). Damp lilies have also come out, though damp lilies in the milk-jug on the table look rather like Raka's mother, ill in a nursing home, under a pink blanket (89). In spite of the pervasive barrenness, starkness the hills have obviously their rare patches of colour.

As the pine is the chief plant of this mountain, the eagle is the fauna of this space which is made of light and air. Carignano has a sweeping view in every direction with an occasional eagle swimming through the clear unobstructed mass of light air (4). As Nanda waits for Raka's arrival—rather annoyed—an eagle sweeps into ken a thousand feet below, "its wings outspread, gliding on currents of air without once moving its great muscular wings which remained in repose, in control. She had wished, it occurred to her, to imitate that eagle—gliding with eyes closed" (19). Raka too feels in the same way towards the eagles. As she scrambles to the top of the Monkey Point it is for her a moment of ecstasy. She is sure "if the let go [...] she would fly, fly off the hilltop and down, down on currents of air, like the eagles that circled slowly, regally below her" (61). In the coppery light of June evenings the child watches "the eagles soar and glide soundlessly in the gorge and out over the plains" (76).

It is perhaps natural that the two freedom-loving lonely souls should seek to imitate the high-soaring eagle. But the eagle is also a predatory bird; its circling, soaring, gliding are punctuated by its hunt for prey. Similarly the vulture's circling indicates rot, dead flesh. Significantly vultures are also a common feature of this mountainscape. Raka, on her lonely prowlings on the hills, sees "in the sky, huge vultures circled lazily, *stealthily* (emphasis added), on currents of air, prowling for game" (43). Once the child is scared. As she slides down on her habitual course in the direction of the factory suddenly she sees a vulture:

> A vulture had moved its claws up a little, shrugged its massive shoulders, stretched out its rubber-hose neck and belched. The child started. Then walked backwards, away from the tree. Turning around abruptly, she dropped on all fours and came scrambling up the hill so fast [...] (73).

It does not seem to be a very safe world for the child; though she moves around unharmed there are potential threats all the time. Once on her lonely exploration of the hill Raka comes upon "a great, thick, yellow snake poured in rings upon itself, basking on the sunned top of a flat rock,"—her first view of "a loose soft sackful of snakes" (49). Even before this she had glimpses of "the tips of snakes' tails parting the cracks of rocks" and "slit eyes watching" her from shade, had heard the "slither of scales" upon the ground (49).

There are varieties of birds, animals, reptiles, insects on the mountain. It seems to be less a world of humans than of other creatures; and references to these creatures of the mountain are often disturbing, carrying suggestions of ferocity, cruelty, violence, or rot. Even smaller creatures seem to be part of the pattern. Immediately Nanda flings away an apricot, "a bright hoopoe," attracted by the flight and flash, "*struck down* at it and *tore* at its bright flesh" (4); as it feeds the nestlings their "screams were shrill and could madden" (4). Sitting in the shade of her veranda Nanda gazes at a pair of bulbuls quarrelling, falling in a flurry of feathers to the ground;

they "stirred up a small frenzy of dust, then shot off in opposite directions, scolding and abusing till a twist of a worm distracted them" (13). When apricots run out the hoopoe has to make up "by catching moths in mid-air and dragging worms out of the earth" (65). This is a compulsion on its part. A similar compulsion prompts the herd of goats in the deserted ravine, "nibbling at the sparse thorns and nettles with rubber-lipped greed and nervous avarice" (73). Not the idyllic picture of a pastoral.

However, there are a few fine strokes suggesting an idyllic pastoral peace and beauty. As Nanda, rather annoyed at the arrival of a letter, looks intently at the vast uninterrupted expanse, "a large white and yellow butterfly crossed over, disturbing her concentration" (13). Or as she leans over the gate of Carignano, her eyes resting on the hillsides mauve and violent, "cattle browsed homewards to small hidden hamlets in the valleys, all grew softer and greyer" (in tune with her graceful ageing (28). Later, during their evening walk together, Nanda watches Raka scrambling up the hill:

> Unseeing, she almost ran into a goat, then a kid, then a whole herd that came springing down, leapt over her back and flew like birds, landing at Nanda Kaul's feet and tripping nimbly homewards, the small goatsherd casually whistling and sauntering after them (60).

The "woollen hills" (65) is a fine expression evoking the scanty grassy coat as well as the coat of a sheep envisioning the mountain as a flock of sheep. The pastoral connotations of sheep and shephered hardly need to be stressed.

But there are also the "wild horde" of black-faced *langurs* who are not meek at all,—"those fierce, lithebpanthers of the monkey world, more feline than simian" (58). There are the jackals and dogs. Ram Lal confidentially tells Raka about "the ghosts of people who have died of dog-bite and snake-bite" and "roam on the hillsides" (44). The old man warns the child about the ravine. "See those chutes? They empty the bones and ashes of dead animals down into the ravine" (44). These are animals used for test and subsequently thrown away; apparently the target of the vultures. Ram Lal continues his eerie report: "Jackals come at night to chew the bones.

Then they go mad and bite the village dogs. The mad dogs run around, biting people [...]. It isn't safe, here?" (44). Inside the safety of the room Raka "met a spider that groomed its hairs in a corner, saw lizard's eyes blinking out of a dark groove" (41).

Like a living being the mountain has its own smells and sounds. Some sounds of the mountain originate from the fauna, some from the trees, and some in the wind. Humans appear redundant in the scheme. The very opening sentence evokes the "sibilance" of the pines and the "fiddling" of cicadas:

> Nanda Kaul paused under the pine trees to take in their scented sibilance and listen to the cicadas fiddling invisibly under the mesh of pine needles (3).

At once the mountain becomes vocal and vivid. This is the appropriate music of the place, and not the club music which seems incongruous and vulgar on the hills. For the lonely old woman in the old empty house "there were only the cicadas to be heard, a sound so even and so insubstantial that it seemed to emerge from the earth itself [...] a scent of pine-needles made audible" (13). They are the tireless players in a ceaseless orchestra. Raka, stealthily entering the empty clubhouse on a hot summer afternoon feels, "all Kasauli slept except for the cicadas that sawed and fiddled without stop" (43). All Nanda wants at this fag end of her life is "the sound of the cicadas and the pines" (19). The music of the withered rose-creeper is also acceptable to her, which is "an exhausted mass of grey creaks and groans" (17). Does she find an extension of herself in it? Towards the end when the two old ladies talk in the empty garden cicadas "audibly sizzled" under the sun (103). Raka seemed to move about "in a kind of dream, set to the sound of cicadas and the wind in the pines" (64). Not that the sound is sweet or pleasant; the old lady and the child stand gazing at the withering flowers under which "a cicada shrilled and whirred frenziedly" (73). Still it is the mountain's own sound, and part of its aloof, rugged grandeur, like the sound of the keen mountain wind. Just as from the hilltop the hills look like seawaves, the sound of the wind too, "rushing up through the pines and then receding was the *sound of the sea*" (61).

This is the sound of the place at its superb. But there are also other sounds—not so grand or harmonious, and sometimes even disturbing in their evocations. When the wind comes in the form of a dust storm it can be terrible, and its terror is brought out in terms of a powerful auditory image. Raka herself "a bird fallen out of its nest, a nest fallen out of a tree" (50) sees a storm-tossed bird.

> A white hen was lifted into the air and tossed past the window in a frantic, fluttery arc, its squawks snatched out of its beak and shattered like glass (53).

Jackals howl at night (44). While hiding behind the clubhall in the night of revelry Raka is scared; she remembers the painful scene of her mother being abused by her drunken father. The memory of her mother crying merges into the actual sound of a jackal howling in the ravine. The desolation, fear and pain of the shattered child is finely brought out by means of the sound.

> Ahead of her, no longer on the ground but at some distance now, her mother was crying. Then it was a jackal crying [...] (72).

As Raka scrambles uphill, she starts "small avalanches of pebbles and loud, clanking ones of empty tins. She disturbed the crickets (Notes, 9) and made them raise their voices in alarm. Like a chorus singing and singing at the back of a stage" (49). They sing in a difficult tongue she had not met before in the big cities of the world. The child is baffled and exasperated. "It was complicated, shrill, incessant and Raka shook and shook her head to get the buzz out" (50). Again, as Nanda and Raka walk homewards in the gathering darkness, the "great silence" is "*rent* (emphasis added) now and then by the clear, ringing call of some invisible bird that defied night" (62).

There are a few instances of soft sounds. For example, Nanda weaves her stories to Raka but keeps her eyes averted where the rooks "cawed" and afterwards the owls began to call softly, experimentally (99). One fine touch early in the novel seems proleptic. On the eve of Raka's arrival Nanda feels annoyed and disturbed. She remembers that she wanted to be only like the eagle, the lonely high-soaring bird.

> "Then a cuckoo called, quite close, here in her garden, very softly, very musically, but definitely calling—she recognized its domestic voice" (19). And she acquiesces.

On the other hand the sounds Raka imagines amidst an "eerie" soundlessness are disturbing. As the child looks at the distant forest fire from her window:

> Holding her ear to the cold pane closely, she thought she heard the cries of animals and birds burning in that fire. But when she removed her ear from the pane she heard only the crepitation of silence. Once, the soft hooting of an owl (75).

The soft hooting of the night-bird mingles into the eerie silence of the night instead of dispelling it.

One of the most remarkable icons of the mountain is its forest-fire which may burst out anywhere unpredictably, bring devastation in its trail and leave scars long afterwards which seem beyond healing. From the beginning through carefully accumulated suggestions the reader is prepared for the final fire-ritual. At the start it is a series of references to/reports of previous fires. Then there is an actual fire, though still seen from a distance. At the end Raka herself sets the forest on fire. Early in the novel one gets a proleptic hint. Three pine trees stand at the gate of Carignano "in their exaggerated attitudes as of *men going up in flames,* with their arms outstretched, *charred* too (emphasis added) about the trunks" (12)—a reminder of an earlier fire. Sighting Nanda, grey and faintly stirring under them, the postman "felt something ominous hover in the heavy summer light" (12).

During the dust storm Ram Lal is worried, because "this is how forest fires do start. I can't tell you how many forest fires we see each year in Kasauli" (53); the many burnt trees and houses bear evidence. Ram Lal tells Raka the story of the burnt cottage on the hilltop, where the resident "an English Mem" had gone mad after failing to rescue her cat from the fire (Notes, 10). Later a proleptic touch is added to the story as Nanda relates it to Raka:

> Up on the hill there, Raka, you will see the burnt black shell of a house. It was burnt down in a terrible forest fire [...]. An old lady lived there alone and they say she

> went mad and was put away. Poor woman, I wonder if she would not have preferred to die in the fire (57).

One may note that at the end Nanda's death is synchronised with the forest fire, started by Raka.

The images and relics of fire seem to fascinate Raka. She imagines herself to be a pine tree in flames. She stealthily visits the burnt house. Here "she raised herself onto the tips of her toes—tall, tall as a pine—stretched out her arms till the felt [...] she was alight, ablaze" (91). She climbs over the ruins and stands still in the "scorched, empty" room (90) listening to the murmuring silence and the demented birds that "beckoned Raka on to a land where there was no sound, only silence, no light, only shade, and skeletons kept in beds of ash on which the footprints of jackals flowered in grey" (90) (Notes, 11). As Raka sees her first forest fire she is excited at the scene of the silent, swift, threatening blaze; she is "obsessed" (75). The novel closes with the sound, flame and smoke of a spreading fire.

> Down in the ravine, the flames spat and crackled around the dry wood and through the dry grass, and black smoke spiralled over the mountain (146).

The reader may recall the prairie novels of Canada; there too fire is used, often with symbolic overtones as a typical natural calamity, unpredictable, uncontrollable, overpowering.

Again, when the rain comes it is also like a kind of climax after the high wind "whining" through the pine trees all afternoon and the clouds gathering like "a great polar bear crouching" and "what rain! The house shook, the roof crackled, long raindrops slanted in" (81). Nanda Kaul begins her "memory-making" stories during the rain, "raising her voice above the drumming of the rain on the roof and the booming and echoing of thunder in the hills that followed the rain like hunting horns" (86).

Carignano, Nanda's *own* house on the ridge of the mountain is a space within the space. The mountain enfolds the house with its sounds, views, smells, its storms, rain; still, being a house it retains a degree of seclusion and distinction from the rest of the landscape. Like the Mall the house too has a colonial history when it had been inhabited by a series of lonely old women. Nanda has not tried to alter it; she has allowed it to be just as it was, still she loves the place as the only house of *her own.* She has a special feeling for this house. Even when she invents stories about the houses of her father and husband "Carignano she had kept clean, true, open for the wind to blow through" (104). She also feels that Raka would be the only true inheritor of Carignano (80) (Notes, 12).

At the same time Nanda Kaul knows that Raka belonged to the mountain, the outer space, rather than the house. "Raka no more needed, or wanted, a house than a jackal did, or a cicada" (103). She perceives with perfect clarity the semblance and the difference between Raka and herself *vis-a-vis* the mountain. Both want "only one thing—to be left alone and pursue her own secret life amongst the rocks and pines of Kasauli" (48). At the same time Nanda is conscious of the difference in their respective responses to this space to which, willy-nilly, both have come for shelter.

> If Nanda Kaul was a recluse out of vengeance for a long life of duty and obligation, her great granddaughter was a recluse by nature, by instinct. She had not arrived at this condition by a long route of rejection and sacrifice—she was born to it, simply (48).

She appreciates and admires the child for being what she herself could not be.

The difference between them is the difference between two generations of women on either sides of a century regarding the outlook on a 'space' of theirs. However, it is their common attachment to the mountain that makes them true blood relations, makes the child true inheritor of her (great-grand) mother's garden in the Alice Walker sense (Notes, 13). At the same time these two lonely recluse—one women and one girl child, one rejected and ravaged by life, the other 'a bird fallen from a nest fallen from a tree,' one longing to be a pine on the hill, the other burrowing like an insect into it, enable us to grasp the meanings/suggestions of the mountain as space, and as sign, in the context of the novel.

The dream geography of a mountain stands for an idealised position in the traditional pagan, European and oriental concepts. The Greeks placed the abode of their gods on the Olympian mount. The Christian imagination founded the Paradise on a mount. The high profile gods of the Hindu pantheon are supposed to haunt the Indian mountains. To the traditional Indian imagination the mountain has been a spiritual space, especially the Himalayas which is called *Devatatma.* It is also the recluse of monks and ascetics who abandon the material world, and the route to *Mahaprasthanam,* supposedly leading to Heaven.

To the European/English romantic imagination mountain was a common image for the detachment/aloofness/sweeping view of the poet. After the war people sought the mountains as shelter or sanatoria for the 'magic' (Notes, 14) of healing. In the British colonial writings about India references to Indian mountains often measured them against English landscape which was taken as the norm. The lure and threat that epitomised India as the 'Other,' seems to acquire intensified manifestation in its hills and mountains. Forster's Marabar Hills (*A Passage to India*), for example, are the region of 'mystery'/'muddle' offering neither solace, nor peace, nor detachment. Kipling articulates a similar sense of awe at the reductive mystery of the great grey hills which make one feel dwarfed and insignificant (*The Heart of a Maid,* 1890).

In *Journey to Ithaca,* a later novel of Desai, people, including two Italians, end up at the higher regions of the Himalayas in course of their search for peace and spiritual fulfilment. But in *Fire on the Mountain* introduces an unusual mountain space with no myth or conventional adages attached to it. It is a real place of the free wind roaring, booming through the hills, of dust storm that rage and tear the rocks, of rain, thunder, of prolonged aridity and devastating forest fires, of snow-white peaks, of red-yellow gorge blighted by factory-waste. Still Desai projects it in such a way that the mountain itself becomes a trope. Though Nanda is reminded of Hopkins's "Heaven-haven" she does not mythicise her "haven"; she knows it is "a place" (58). Indeed the author gives no mythicised, or fantasised or imaginary geography as such the geographical location to the colonial past. But real geography has been made to imbibe imaginative meanings, as it is made to come alive by means of exquisite imaginative touches.

Thus, the place appears to be a parallel to Nanda's physical isolation. The fictionalised mountain emerges as a site that symbolically implies her predicament and also her dream of a world of her own. Kasauli also becomes symptomatic of the desire of women to exist without constriction/limitation. As Mary Daly observes at the beginning of her book *Gyn/Ecology* "patriarchy appears to be everywhere. Even outer space and the future have been colonised" (1). Women writers across the world today have been constructing worlds of isolation as escape from this patriarchal domination. Canadian writer Aritha Van Herk's *Places far from Ellesmere* (1990) is a typical example where she envisions an escape into a far-flung island along with Tolstoy's Anna Karenina. But whereas Van Herk's isolated island epitomises unambiguous self-assurance and assertion of the woman, the mountain of Desai seems to offer an ambiguous signal. Perhaps this ambiguity is necessarily embedded in the very nature of the space she has chosen. An island can be isolated and autonomous. But a mountain is not autonomous in that sense. The distant snowy peaks are the inaccessible utopia. At the other end the mountain slopes down into the mundane hamlets where brutal death soundlessly springs upon Ila Das from behind the dark rock. So it does not necessarily follow that the self-actualising journey of a woman reaches its goal in the mountain, though for Nanda it is the end of the road, "privacy achieved only at the very end of her life" (36), and for Raka who had always seemed to lack the ticket to social life (52) the "best" home (91).

The basic paradox highlighted by the geography of the story is that in spite of all the longings one cannot occupy a bounded or enclosed cultural space. True, the human society remains largely invisible; true, the world seems remote from here like Herk's island from where "the world exists in some enigmatic novel far beyond" (121). Still the fact remains that it is an eroded hill that has received the beatings of the weather; the purity of the hill wind is threatened by the factory; its smoke lashes the white sky; its smell of chemicals fills the air; it is haunted by violence. Even Carignano, Nanda's 'glass palace,' on the ridge is invaded by the outer world, as suggested by the postman at the beginning and by the telephone at the end.

Fire on the Mountain may be categorised as 'geografictione' to use the term coined by Aritha Van Herk, an Italian-Canadian word, to denote a species of narration which combines geography with fiction, creates its own geography as it creates its own specific narrative space. *Fire on the Mountain* represents this trend in fiction, which, instead of using place as backdrop, reinterprets it and reinscribes it with fresh meanings.

The traditional male/colonial way of seeing a place was as a "virgin" woman, a female to be conquered and possessed. Nanda and Raka do not try to possess the place. They just want to get merged like a tree or an insect.

For the perceptive reader the configuration and etching of Kasauli in Desai's novel is resonant with intertextual echoes, among which echoes from *The Waste Land* in particular—the pine and cicada, the crickets, the ruined house (even to the cawing bird on its roof), the barren rocks, the wrecked solitude—are unmistakable. But it seems significant that whereas Eliot's waste land was blessed at the end by thunder and rain, here the story finally comes to a halt at a richly ambiguous open ending with the strong forest fire quickly spreading across the mountain.

Desai's treatment of mountain as space in an emblem of her *ecriture feminine* and thus offers the possibility of fresh, varied, contrary and multiple interpretations.

NOTES

1. "Those three-hundred-odd years of European exploration, conquest colonization and empire [...] established a lasting psycho-cartography of their own, positioning Europe and the Atlantic as fount and centre, and all the rest of the vastness of creation as outlying and peripheral, and created for the purpose of serving servicing the centre [...]" (Nayantara Sahgal, "The Myth Reincarnated," *Journal of Commonwealth Literature*, XXX, i, 1995).
2. Jean Rhys in her novel *Wide Sargasso Sea* (1966) uses Sargasso as an emblem of the geographical-political-cultural-colonial divide between England and the Caribbean island.
3. Achebe, C., *Things Fall Apart.*
4. Atwood, M., *Surfacing* "I am a place" (181).
5. White, P., *Voss.*

6. "Birds in gilt cages" (26): "Little slave girls ran about" (135) (Jyoti Jafa, *Nurjahan,* New Delhi: Lotus, 1994).
7. In *When Dreams Travel* (1999) Githa Hariharan rewrites the *Arabian Nights;* new stories are narrated here by Sahrzad's sister and a slave girl.
8. "If there were the sound of water only
Not the cicada [...]
But sound of water over a rock
Where the hermit-thrush sings in the pine trees" (11.351-55).
9. "Where the dead tree gives no shelter, the cricket no relief" (*The Waste Land*).
10. Echo of *Wide Sargasso Sea*; Annette went mad after failing to rescue 'Coco,' the pet parrot, and her little son during the Coulibri fire.
11. One is struck by the resemblance between this passage and the following lines from *The Waste Land*:

    In this decayed hole among the mountains [...]
    Over the tumbled graves [...]
    There is the empty chapel, only the wind's home.
    It has no windows, and the door swings,
    Dry bones can harm no one.
    Only a cock stood on the rooftree
    Co co rico co co rico [...]. (11.385-92)
12. An echo of Forster's *Howard's End*; Mrs Wilcox wanted to bequeathe Howard's End to Margaret whom she had recognized as the true spiritual inheritor to her very special house.
13. Alice Walker in her essay, "In Search of Our Mothers' Gardens" (1983) explores the situation of women in traditional culture and celebrates the achievements and resiliency of women in history.
14. Thomas Mann, *The Magic Mountain.*

REFERENCES

1. Atwood, M., *Surfacing.* (1972) London: Virago Ltd., 1980.
2. Conde, Mary, "Women Inscribing the Indian Landscape," *The Atlantic Review,* I: 2, 2000.
3. Daly, Mary, *Gyn/Ecology.* London: The Women's Press, 1987.
4. Desai, A., *Fire on the Mountain.* London: Penguin Book, 1977.
5. Eliot, T.S., *The Waste Land* in *Collected Poems.* London: Faber & Faber, 1963.
6. Herk, Aritha Van, *Places Far From Ellesmere.* Red Deer Alberta: Red Deer College Press, 1990.
7. Sabni, Sujata, *Silent Whispers.* New Delhi: Har-Anand, 1996.

15

In Their Alien Worlds: Anita Desai's *Bye-Bye, Blackbird* and *Baumgartner's Bombay*

ASHA SUSAN JACOB

The theme of exile, immigration and alienation is common in the twentieth century literary scene. Lost, lonely, drifting characters parade before us and their mechanical march point to the absence of meaningful relationships in the era of technological development and global interaction. Political, cultural, social, economical and geographical dislocations have made each man an exile. Cultural alienation has become a universal phenomenon.

Immigration is a phenomenon as old as the history of civilization. The *Book of Genesis* tells the story of alienation and exile. Adam and Eve were alienated from the grace of God and banished from their home, the garden of Eden, to labour by the sweat of their brows. Ever since, exile, exodus and migration have been the fate of man. The motivation behind modern migration may vary from political or religious persecution to economic problems. Whatever be the reason, the impact of cultural dislocation on the individual psyche remains complex. As Viney Kirpal observes, it is not merely a physical journey from one land to another but it involves severing of "spiritual and symbiotic ties with his mother country" (Kirpal: 45).

Contemporary literature dealing with the emotional problems of the modern man reflects the injuries, frustrations and the identity crisis that an uprooted individual undergoes. A good number of Indian writers have dealt with the experience of the exile. Santha Rama Rau's *Remember the House*, Arun Joshi's *The Foreigner*, Kamala Markandaya's *The Nowhere Man*, Raja Rao's *The Serpent and the Rope*, deal with the tension ensuing from cultural and geographical displacement. Anita Desai, an expert in delineating the lacerated psyche portrays the ontological insecurity, alienation and anguish of uprooted individuals in *Bye-Bye, Blackbird* and *Baumgartner's Bombay*.

The problems consequent on alienation, immigration or expatriation can be best understood in the light of the two related yet contradictory terms 'exile' and 'home.' 'Home' is not merely the habitual abode, it is where one belongs to, that which gives one cultural and spiritual identity. It is one's native soil, mother country, and security which become part of one's self. 'Exile' is enforced or regretted absence from one's country or home. It is "literally an uprooting and often as withering in its effect on the mind and spirit which is deprived the sustenance it has drawn from native soil" (Joshi: 2). To an exile, home becomes everything one had lost: nationality, identity, culture. Estrangement reinforces the meaning of home more acutely than ever on the exile.

Postcolonial India has witnessed the migration of many an educated Indians to the lucrative abundance of the West. It can be seen as an escape from the economic and communal chaos prevalent in India. But adaptation of the alien culture has been proved very difficult. Desai depicts the gnawing sense of immigrant sensibility in *Bye-Bye, Blackbird* through three different yet related characters Dev, Adit and his English wife Sarah. Adit, comfortably employed in London, marries Sarah for something oriental in her attracts him. In order to accommodate oneself in a new environment one has to reconstruct one's self. He has to tolerate and adapt. At the initial stages of his immigration, Adit feels what every other new immigrant feels: admiration and satisfaction. He has become a "spineless imperialist lover" (*Bye-Bye, Blackbird:* 19) that when Dev visits England to pursue higher studies he is shocked to find Adit swallowing ungrudgingly the humiliations thrown at him by the erstwhile masters. He does not assert his rights for the slave mentality of the colonised. Adit tells Dev that he hardly notices the drawbacks of England and considers himself an admirer of its golden beauty. "I like the freedom a man has here: Economic freedom! Social freedom!" (18).

Even the self-satisfied expatriate gradually finds himself estranged from the new environment. A person born into a culture imbibes it as the very air he breaths; it cannot be thrust upon him. Adaptation to alien culture becomes difficult because the value systems are often different. Culture is threatened only when he confronts an alien society where he becomes aware of the disparity between his 'native culture' and the 'host culture.' Adit despite his attempts at acculturation realizes slowly that he is still a misfit. Like many other immigrants he had stowed in his subconscious mind his disenchantment with the alien sophisticated culture. All these years the conscious mind has been thrusting the subconscious under the guise of a complacent life with his English wife. But it has been proved to be the tip of the iceberg. It takes some time for this realisation to creep to the conscious level.

Adit's final visit to his in-laws disenchants him. The truth that he is an Indian and can never breathe the English air freely dawns on him. The stay with them brings in nostalgic memories of his home. He begins to see everything in a new perspective. "It was as though some black magician had placed an evil pair of spectacle on his eyes" (177) distorting and terrifying what had till been familiar and cosy.

Culture shock is a feeling of depression and frustration that overwhelms one when one realises the difference between the way of life one is familiar with and that one finds in a new environment. Despite his attempts at amalgamation, the alien culture distances Adit. Marriage does not guarantee him equal status. Adit realises this only when Sarah shuts him out "with a bang and a snap, from her childhood of one-eared pandas and large jigsaw puzzles" (176). The immigrant at such moments often retreats to his own culture and past in search of his lost identity. The distance in years as well as geography gives Adit a better perception of his country. Hatred recedes and its place is taken by nostalgia. The hypnotic charm that England had on him is over. His rootedness to the English soil is proved zero. "The ferocity of his growing nostalgia broke that stone dam that had silenced him for so long" and he tells Sarah of his "illness" and "ache" (183) and his decision to return to India though doubtful of a bright future there. But "whatever it is it will be Indian, it will be my natural condition, my true circumstance. I must go and face all that now" (204). He decides to discard the burden of his "half-English" pretence (204) and to go 'home.'

An immigrant usually passes through the phases of attraction, rejection and frustration as in the case of Adit. Through Dev, Anita Desai captures the psychic journey of an Indian immigrant. The conflict between the imaginary world created in the Indian immigrant through his colonial education and reading and the reality that confronts him is highlighted. "It is not the unfamiliarity rather it is the gap between the expected and the immediately received that keeps disturbing him" (Sharma: 71). The sight of beggars in the London streets shocks him. "One expects them in India. But here—beggars!" (62).

Dev's dilemmas emanate from his emotional and instinctive responses to the English scene, especially from an 'ex-colonised' point of view. The colonised in spite of his bitter experiences looks towards the land of his one time master as a promising land. When in reality, it does not cater to his needs he sighs incoherently as Dev does: "Willingly England had conquered his own country, then why [...] would she give nothing in return?" (120). Dev who has come with intellectual pretensions suffers from a "Caliban complex," the love-hate relationship between the coloniser and the colonised which Adit realizes in his own case only after the fatal visit to his in-laws (Sharma: 80).

To disentangle from the influence of one's own culture which has become part of his consciousness is not easy for an immigrant. One is tempted to evaluate the alien culture with the measuring rod of one's own. Hence Dev cannot understand the Western culture where "everyone is a stranger and lives in hiding" (56). Anything that goes against one's familiar way of life will create a cultural conflict. Dev fails to get accustomed to the English habit of "guarding their privacy as they guarded their tongues from speaking and their throats from catching cold" (63) because he comes to this culture of individual orientation from a milieu of group orientation. He goes through different phases of the "bewildered alien, the charmed observer, the outraged outsider and thrilled sightseer all at once and in succession" (85).

Caught between acceptance and rejection, expectation and reality he is "perfectly aware of the schizophrenia that is infecting him like a disease to which all Indians abroad, are prone" (86).

Though he feels "he can never bear to be the unwanted immigrant" (86) he is finally drawn into the magic of the land which had enchanted Adit. It is his association with nature at the home of Sarah's parents that gives a healing touch to his troubled psyche. England ceases to be "an aggressor who tried to enmesh, subjugate and victimize him with the weapons of Empire" and becomes something he can "hold and tame and even love." He no longer sees it with the eye of the "once-conquered race, or an apprehensive and short-sighted visitor, but of someone before whom vistas of love, success and joy had opened" (229). The same visit serves an eye-opener to both Adit and Dev and instills a transformation. The visitor becomes the exile and the exile retreats to his home. Desai is successful in handling the nuances of immigrant psyche as she herself has opined "I wrote it in an effort to understand the split psychology, the double loyalties of the immigrants" [Anita Desai, "The Book I Enjoyed Writing Most," *Contemporary Indian Literature* XIII, 4 (1973), 24].

It is not only Adit and Dev who share a colonial past undergo identity crisis in *Bye-Bye, Blackbird.* Even without getting transplanted physically to another culture Sarah loses her identity in her own native soil. Her situation, more poignant than that of the uprooted aliens, is not cleverly manipulated by Desai. Unlike Adit and Dev who have willingly uprooted themselves from their native soil, Sarah gets herself alienated from her society through her marriage. Her intercultural marriage does not offer her anything grand and fabulous. By marriage "she had become nameless, she had shed her name as she had shed her ancestry and identity" (31). The resultant tension, anguish and a sense of guilt withdraw her from her English society, even her parents and buries she-self inside her self-made cocoon. Fearing the contempt of her 'own' people, with typical Anglo-Saxon composure, she tries to cover her injured sensibility. Yet "her hurried rush and tough brisk of one suspicious, one on the defensive" reveals her bewilderment (30).

Her reluctance to discuss her Indian husband before her colleagues shows her identity crisis and bewilderment and invites the comment, "If she's that ashamed of having an Indian husband, why did she go and marry him" (37). Sarah feels socially alienated in her own country which creates psychological trauma in her wherein she feels herself "parading like an imposter, to make claims to a life, an identity that she did not herself feel to be her own" (37).

Marriage as a means of assimilation recurs in many immigrant writings. Sarah also tries to adjust and accommodate without showing the master-slave complex or racial superiority. Yet her culture being isomorphic she tries to build up a harmonious matrimonial relationship by keeping the past and present to two watertight compartments. Hence her life becomes mechanical keeping an emotional distance from anyone and anything. She remains an outsider in her own soil and her acquired nation. Emptiness and dissatisfaction haunt her. Her final decision to follow Adit to India is only a relief to her because in her homeland she considers herself not as a person but as roles—'Mrs Sen' and 'Sarah' and "when she was not playing them, she was nobody" (35). At least in India, she hopes, she will have only one face—Adit's wife.

Sarah has sacrificed her past to gain a new life. She has deliberately distanced even from her parents to adjust with her new identity. The fact is that Adit does not guide her efficiently in this transition because he is too preoccupied with his own problems of acculturation. He has definitely, if not knowingly, a role to play in annihilating her self, "her English self that was receding and fading and dying, in the final bargain" (221). Thus the novel captures the psychological problems of alienated individuals caught in the mesh of biculturalism or multiculturalism.

If Adit, Dev and Sarah have a choice between their native soil and their chosen homes *Baumgartner's Bombay* is the moving account of a homeless, nationless man. He has nowhere to go to regain his lost identity. He is the same in his native soil and the alien one, an outsider, a nowhere man in every sense. Unlike Adit and Dev, Baumgartner or Hugo is literally an exile driven out of Germany due to racial discrimination, to start a new life in the friendless, unfamiliar India.

Identity is a state of mind that is granted by our interaction with the fellow beings in the society and also by our acceptance in the society. But "accepting—but not accepted; that was the story of his life, the one thread that ran through it all. In Germany he had been dark—his darkness had marked him the Jew, *der Jude*. In India he was fair and that marked him the *firanghi*. In both lands the unacceptable" (*Baumgartner's Bombay:* 20).

More poignant than the other novels, *Baumgartner's Bombay* narrates the story of Hugo from his affluent childhood days in Germany to the horror of his murder in India by another German. He becomes a political exile after the anti-Jewish attitude in Germany. The political upheavals lead to financial crisis and suicide of his father. He is forced to leave Germany in search of a new future in the safe shores of India. His romantic imagination of India as the birthplace of *Gitanjali* gets shattered the moment he lands in India. The political situation in India, like the partition of India and the anti-German attitude threatens his existence and lands him in jail. As the Nazis betrayed him in Germany his Indian friends betray him in business. The war further distances him from his mother, his only sustenance.

The series of calamities—losing his home, business and finally his mother makes him mute and accepting. "Defeat was heaped on him whether he deserved it or not" (135). A man thus drilled will definitely go rudderless. When his frantic attempts to get connected to his mother fail, he withdraws into his own world, disinterested in the way of the world, in his own physical appearance, in anything except the company of his feline friends.

Hugo had learnt this attitude of resignation and acceptance right from his childhood in Germany. The ideal home often is only an 'ideal.' The atmosphere a child grows in and the relationship between his parents influences the developing mind of a child. The adult Hugo who fails to communicate is only a prolonging of the child Hugo who witnessed the estrangement between his parents. Peer group experience is essential for the proper growth of child psyche. His incomplete schooling denied Hugo this opportunity. The poignant experiences at school, being a Jew, made him feel an outsider which he still is. At the school Christmas party when his Jewish parents fail to send a present in time, he felt the agony and shame of the sense that "he did not belong to the picture-book world of the fir tree, gifts and celebration" (36). Even the experience at the school for Jewish children was not different. He first had a remark on his nose "Baumgartner's dumb, has a nose like a thumb!" (38). This unpleasant memory still makes him uncomfortable. "He felt to fingering it nervously, trying to discover the relation between his nose and his thumb, a habit that never left him" (38). Hence it is not his exile alone that makes him rootless, but his life altogether.

Social acceptance is that factor which creates in man a sense of identity. When the new milieu fails to recognise him as an individual he becomes deindividualized. Cultural uprooting, geographical displacement and failure to connect torment his psyche. Language becomes a major hindrance for establishing contact in India. Confused by the Babel of languages Hugo is uncertain which language to employ. "After fifty years, still uncertain" (6). Physical appearance enhances the distance. "His face blazed like an over-ripe tomato in the sun on which warts gathered like flies" (20) coupled with his shabby dress keeps people away.

Hugo's odd encounter with the German youth makes him plunge deep into his past. The only memories that nourish him in this lonely world are those of his mother. Her songs liberate him from agony. The absence of his only relation, his 'Mutti,' his guide and friend instill feelings of alienation and meaninglessness in his life making him feel like "an old turtle trudging through dusty Indian soil" (11). He withdraws from human company because "he had had enough of communal life in the camp to last a lifetime" (151). His friendship with Lotte, who finally identifies his dead body, comes not from her exoticism but because "she belonged to

India of his own experience" (150). Frustrated with the world, with himself, having nowhere to go, not getting recognition for his simplicity and honesty the 'pagal firanghi' is saved out of his unpleasant past and unknown future by the German youth who murders him.

Baumgartner's story is one of inherent alienation augmented by global war, colonial war and religious war. When the familiar emotional and geographical worlds are destroyed one gets deidentified. He becomes merely an object hedged in by destructive forces. While Adit, Dev and Sarah belong to someone or somewhere despite the psychic problems and frustrations, Baumgartner remains a 'firanghi' though holding an Indian passport.

Desai has brilliantly portrayed the dilemma of uprooted individuals through the two novels. The experience of exile which begins as a "condition of living" often becomes a "condition of mind" as in the case of Hugo (Prasad: 216). Cultural displacement makes them alienated and lonely in spite of their assays of adjustment.

REFERENCES

1. Desai, Anita. *Baumgartner's Bombay.* London: Penguin, 1988.
2. ——. *Bye-Bye, Blackbird.* New Delhi: Orient Paperbacks, 1985.
3. Joshi, Chandra B. *V.S. Naipaul: The Voice of Exile.* New Delhi: Sterling, 1994.
4. Kirpal, Viney. *The Third World Novel of Expatriation.* New Delhi: Sterling, 1989.
5. Prasad, Hari Mohan. "The Theme of Exile in Indo-English Novel." *Alien Voice: Perspectives on Commonwealth Literature.* Ed. Avadhesh K. Srivastava. Lucknow: Print House, 1981, 210-16.
6. Sharma, R.S. *Anita Desai.* New Delhi: Arnold Heinemann, 1981.

16

A Saga of Quests: Anita Desai's *Journey to Ithaca*

ASHA SUSAN JACOB

From the womb till the tomb mankind is on a continuous search either for worldly gains or for something indefinable. Some thrust this questing spirit deep down into the subconscious; a few others live ever realizing the futility of this world, searching for solace elsewhere. Some find it in the comprehension of their own selves while others tour the planet in search of it. It may take years of strenuous effort, which can dissuade a weak person, to reach the goal. Thus the search for Self or Truth or Wisdom or Enlightenment, as it is differently called, is omnipresent and its history is as old as human history.

The quest motif and the concomitant journey form the seminal doctrine of the prominent religions of both the West and the East. Right from his alienation from God through sin mankind has been sojourning this world to get at last united with the Lord. The *Bible* provides the most wonderful stories of search and journey. The Israelites left Egypt and took the longest and the most miraculous yet onerous course through the desert, living on heavenly manna, to reach their Promised Land. Journey has become a recurrent theme in the literary classics of both the West and the East. John Bunyan's *Pilgrim's Progress* is a master allegory on man's eternal journey to salvation overcoming the snares of flesh, intellect, the perils and deviations which hinder the soul in its quest for salvation through faith. Not only the quest for salvation but the search for one's roots have been fictionalised. In the oriental culture 'tapas' is a meditation in search of Enlightenment.

India has enchanted the West ever since its fame reached their shores, especially after colonisation not only for its alluring silks, muslins, gems and spices but also for its 'arsha samskara.' The post-war psychological unrest in the West has directed many a disturbed soul to the magic of India. The 1960's and '70's saw an exodus of them. While some sought their peace in marijuana, some others journeyed from ashram to ashram in search of a guru who could gift them a bottle of 'Shanti.' Those who seriously pursue the path of Truth are often outnumbered by those who believe they can get nirvana for a few dollars. Gita Mehta in her debut *Karma Kola* condemns the materialistic approach to spirituality. Even Indian spirituality, according to her, is entrapped in the globalisation thirst of entrepreneurs (Mehta: 18).

Anita Desai, the usherer of psychological fiction in the Indian literary arena shifts to a new subject, the mystical East, in *A Journey to Ithaca* (New Delhi: Ravi Dayal, 1996). The central preoccupation of the novel is not alienated individuals, but the quest motif and the journey undertaken to reach the goal, though in the process they get alienated from the world. The story is told from different angles using recollection and diary.

Journey to Ithaca is a saga of multiple quests made by three different personalities, at three different periods for differing intentions. Desai transports us from India to Italy, Egypt and America accompanying three foreigners—Mattoe, the Mother and Sophie. While the journey of the first two culminates in India, that of Sophie commences from India. Each of these quests is interlinked to the others and it never ends.

Born in a luxuriant Italian family Mattoe left his villa and journeyed to India in search of something beyond his understanding. Right from his childhood he had been a peculiar child defying the decency and decorum of his home. Reticent and withdrawn, he found the villa with its velvet hangings and tapestries stifling. His entire presence seemed to be made up of silence. Failure followed him to school too where he remained incommunicative and incompatible. His introduction to Herman Hesse's *The Journey to the East* by his private tutor Fabian transformed him completely. It instilled in him a desire for the mystical East. Later he admits to his wife, "It was the book that opened my eyes" (8). The dismissal of Fabian as tutor further alienated him from his family and he started running, escaping from their norms and values. This restless phase ended and the seeming normalcy only formed a prelude to the great journey he undertook to the East immediately after his marriage with Sophie.

Mattoe's journey to the East, the seed of which was sown by Hesse, began in 1975 when Mattoe and Sophie left Italy "dressed in identical blue jeans and T-shirts and sports shoes carrying identical rucksacks on their backs, as did so many of their generation in Europe" (30). In order to get a spiritual experience they also joined the other seekers who were "busily collecting saints as earlier travellers had collected gold, spices or shawls" (34).

His search "to find India, to understand India, and the mystery that is at the heart of India" (54) proved to be a difficult task. Lack of proper guidance and knowledge about India and its tradition humiliated him before other experienced seekers. The absence of a proper guru leads him astray. Shuttling from one ashram to another, meeting many a fake yogies (65) he steps on the first step of the ladder leading to spirituality in an ashram in the hills which is unique for its head is a woman. Her speech transports him to a unique experience, "an experience of unity, the unity of the spiritual with the physical, the dark with the light, the human with the natural" (94). His deeply disturbed soul finally finds solace in the Mother. Obsessed with this newly attained guru, any time spent away from the Mother seems "wasted time, empty time, dead time" (103). But to Sophie she is only a woman: "Call her what you like—the cosmic, the Absolute but she's a woman" (141). The polarity between them increases. Like many Indian Sanyasis he neglects his responsibilities to his family who now represent to him "a nightmare world of physicality" (102). Now he realizes why even the paradisaical surroundings of his home on the lake had been empty and desolate because "no one had been there to show him that they were an expression of an eternal and essential truth" (102).

Mattoe's search for spiritual wisdom or Enlightenment ends with the Mother because he does not have the will and perseverance to pursue. His quest reaches only the level of a flight from the world and its responsibilities and he does not reach the sublime though he mistakes what he gets with the Mother as real, sublimate joy or bliss. Emotional and timid, he does not realize the necessity of long years of 'tapas' or sacrifice or devotion to get enlightened. So he is torn between a kind of happiness definitely not the absolute, and a kind of ennui. Hence he gets so devastated at the death of the Mother that he cannot even eat or drink. Suddenly he decides to travel north to the mountains where the Mother received enlightenment and quits the ashram. Perhaps he will be enlightened there. His journey to Ithaca "to learn and learn from those who have knowledge" ends in defeat making his own and his family's life a mess if the vision Giacomo has in the last part of the novel is not an outcome of his imagination.

Desai also provides a more interesting and complex journey undertaken by Sophie which is closely interlinked with that of Mattoe and the Mother. While Mattoe longs for spiritual enrichment Sophie undertakes the journey to peep into the past of the Mother "to travel back, back in time, although not her own time but the Mother's" (155).

Sophie started her journey to India with no pious intention but like any other Western adventurer to explore the mountains and to enjoy the exotic East. With Mattoe she too visited many an ashram first out of curiosity and later out of compulsion. Her curiosity is soon worn off appalled at the ridiculous, blind endeavour of Mattoe. Unable to cope with the harrowing experiences her "pilgrimage through India became suffused with the rich and aromatic haze of marijuana" (55). Coming out of this stage she has nowhere else to go, but to sojourn in ashrams with Mattoe, though she proves to be a misfit. Like any other normal human being what she wants is only a decent, comfortable life, not a nomadic life scratching mosquito bites. Her ordinary, complacent-loving spirit queries, "why can we be not together again at home with the children?" (4). Even when Mattoe finds his anchor in the Mother she remains aloof and unperturbed for as far as she is concerned "they had arrived nowhere" (53). But an unexpected, dream like encounter with the Mother which reveals to her "both the mythical figure who could summon peacocks out of the wilds as she did devotees from the world over, and the aged, solitary woman" urges her to explore into the past of the "paradoxical, contradictory" woman who "looks Indian, sounds Indian, but not Indian" (125). Her queries about the Mother disturbs Mattoe but the widening gulf between them aggravates her questing spirit. The books which give only the legend do not satisfy her. She wants to "go behind that, find out who she really is, how she came here, why" (153). Montu-da's account of the Mother and the Master would have taken her to interesting directions but for the premature birth of her child. Glowing over her role of mother Sophie, for the time being, stops her search. Finally unable to cope up, Sophie leaves India with her children, first to her parents and then to the villa on the lakeside.

Once out of the ashram she realizes how she has alienated herself from the mundane world outside. She finds herself hating her association with the so-called normal people which she had longed for. Unknowingly she too was following the ways of Mattoe. Her life with him has spoilt her for life in the materialistic world. Obsessed now with knowing the truth (about the Mother) she journeys to the exotic lands where the Mother had spent her life before coming to India. Her enquiries do not go beyond the rational level but it brings into her streaks of understanding about faith, devotion etc. It dawns upon her that in her search she is abandoning her children just as Mattoe had abandoned her in his search and that "in following her she is entering an area of the chill, bleak, bitterness of renunciation" (238). Fully equipped to confront Mattoe and the Mother, when she returns she realizes the futility of her quest, for the Mother is already dead and Mattoe has left the place to pursue his search. Though the journey provides her, as she herself confesses, "nothing much" about the Mother (296) it has revealed to her "why the Mother went on that pilgrimage, why everyone goes on a pilgrimage and why she must go too" (298). For Sophie one quest ends only to begin another, a totally different one.

It is Sophie's failed assays to liberate Mattoe from the

enchanting woman that takes her to Egypt, Venice, Paris and New York to reconstruct the Mother's past. Her search unfolds another remarkable journey of a young, different and determined girl Laila, the daughter of Hamid and Alma, both intellectuals. Like Mattoe, she too was an odd, headstrong and independent child causing headache to her parents and teachers. Yearning for something different she too could not conform to the conventions of her society. Her unsurmountable urge for some sublime experience led her astray, even to a revolutionary camp. But nothing could sustain her for long: "what drew her would have been hard for anyone to tell at that stage for the truth was that she was drawn in one direction, then another, wherever she saw passion taken to its extreme, whether celebratory or ascetic" (167). Her momentous encounter with the hagdeh who professed her future "eastwards to find a temple [...] the temple of the Mother Goddess of the World" (170) propelled her disturbed soul to a new direction. But it was a poster announcing "Krishna Lila" pinned to the door of curio shop that transfigured her life. The two words Krishna and Lila, together and in separate forms caught her like a snare and precisely at that moment "she was confronted by her true self" (192).

Determined to discover her soul, she forced her entry into the oriental dance troupe. Enchanted by the mystic atmosphere she mistook the master, the dancer, as the God Krishna. Her eagerness and devotion to "meet the great sun, the great light" shut her to the reality that he was only wearing the costume of Krishna. The reality that this "Krishna had shown her only devotion to world success" when finally dawned on her she had already travelled far into the East. The diary that Sophie collects from the dance master reveals her indefatigable spirit amidst harrowing experiences in an unfriendly environment. In India temples and sanyasis failed to quench her thirsting spirit for she felt the truth must be elsewhere and pursued it.

Her strong conviction that there must be a master somewhere to show her "luminous wisdom, [...] the answer to her queries" (283) finally enabled her to find him in the North. Though at the initial stage of her journey her ignorance mistook what was only human for what is supreme and

Almighty, she was always conscious of her goal. What she "wanted of India was the outward manifestation of what already existed inside" her, what had been growing inside her like a flower since her experience at the Paris bookshop (285). On her journey to the Himalayas, with the desire to be free of this world, to escape into a better and brighter one, she had the vision of Eternal light setting her on fire: "I was on fire, the tree was on fire, light blazed and the whole sky was illuminated" (286). At the mountains her "soul too set out in quest" and her dance in prayer and joy brought the Master to her pronouncing her 'Shakti' and the 'Supreme Power.' Her earlier attempts to seek through dance the harmony between the body and the mind, thought and action, the world and the spirit had brought her only disharmony. But now her soul got satiated. Henceforth the Master and the devotee became one and she became the Supreme of the ashram after him. There ended the most turbulent phase of her quest providing her bliss, wisdom, enlightenment and her great transformation from Laila to the Mother which paved the way for many a quest.

The extract of a poem at the beginning of the novel suggests a similar quest and journey. The poet reminds us not to "hurry the voyage" but to "keep Ithaca fixed" in our minds. The Mother's journey proves to have gone through these lines. The trials and hindrances on her ways could never dissuade her thirsting soul: it only affirmed her faith. Her journey to Ithaca (for her it is India) seems to have given her "a beautiful voyage." Once there, though Ithaca "has nothing to give now" it "has not defrauded" anyone for the "great wisdom" and "experience" gleamed through the voyage. Sophie and Mattoe, though not with Laila's determination and devotion, also get this new experience and understanding which perhaps may lead to greater wisdom and knowledge. The novel seems to suggest that it is not the end or the fruit, that determines the success of the quest, but the journey itself which provides one with great illumination.

REFERENCES

1. Desai, Anita. *Journey to Ithaca.* Delhi: Ravi Dayal, 1996.
2. Mehta, Gita. *Karma Kola.* London: Minerva, 1990.

17

Staying, Leaving, Returning: The Interconnectedness of Female Identities in Anita Desai's *Clear Light of Day*

JENNI VALJENTO

In postcolonial and diasporic literature and theory a lot of attention is often devoted to the more visible phenomena of migration or exile: departure from the homeland and the reasons for it, first contact with and settling into the host society, and the varying degrees of acculturation and assimilation of different immigrant generations. These are, of course, also the processes that have utmost significance from the western viewpoint of the host societies. Less evident is the role of those who choose or are forced to stay in their homeland yet play a part in and are profoundly affected by the migration of others. The complex migrant locations in the West are paralleled by the equally complex social, economic and psychological circumstances of those who uphold the families and communities that the migrants have left behind.

In her novel *Clear Light of Day* (1980) Anita Desai explores two sisters' very different positions within the home, the family and the post-independence upper middle-class Indian society, which lead to one woman's leaving and the other woman's staying in the homeland and the domestic sphere. The female protagonist's identity development both affects and is affected by the migration and periodic return of her younger sister, someone who originally shares her familial and social circumstances but chooses to leave them behind. *Clear Light of Day* tells the story of an anglicized upper middle-class Indian family from the 1940s to the 1970s. The protagonist

Bim Das is the unmarried elder sister who as a young woman at the time of Partition must take the place of her dead parents as guardian of her siblings and custodian of the crumbling family home in Delhi. At a time when women were entering public life in an unprecedented way, she is left to take care of an autistic brother and an alcoholic aunt after her older brother Raja leaves the family to pursue a future of his own. Her younger sister Tara eventually marries a diplomat and escapes the suffocating paralysis of the family home for Europe and America. Desai describes Bim's efforts to expand her identity beyond the pseudo-motherhood she has had to take up and to come to terms with a family and society that often curb those efforts. The novel culminates in the two sisters' painful attempts to make sense of the ways in which family and home have shaped their perceptions of themselves and each other.

The protagonist of *Clear Light of Day* can be seen to occupy a position on the threshold of home in a double sense: both the private, domestic sphere and the homeland. Although she remains in Delhi, Bim's identity, the way she is constructed within her particular familial and social location, informs the processes evident in Tara of both leaving and returning. The protagonist facilitates the marriage and migration of the other woman: because the elder sister fulfils the role expected of unmarried women and maintains domestic and social continuity by accepting the responsibility of the house and those who depend on her, the younger sister is able to marry and pursue an identity outside the traumatic and restrictive childhood home. In discussing the feminization of the home, Rosemary Marangoly George sees gendering of place as "'naturaliz[ing]' the notion of 'Home'" which results in "its categorization alongside 'natural phenomena' like birth and death. [...] '[H]ome' moves from being perceived as property to become a part of the life cycle" (George: 23). What I would argue is a central ironic dilemma in *Clear Light of Day* is that, while the protagonist's identity develops in an inflexible familial and social location where, despite her efforts to the contrary, home becomes, as George says, "a natural formation" (George: 23) in her life, the process also has a crucial effect on the younger sister's leaving the home to be free to construct her own roles as a wife and mother. On the other hand, Tara's self-exclusion from, and later re-entry into, the family also severely question the fundamental motives behind Bim's self-image as the home-bound sister. The fact that Tara's distancing herself from and reconnecting with her family takes place through her relationship with Bim points not only to the elder, unmarried sister's socio-economic vulnerability at the threshold between the domestic sphere and the world outside but also to the reasons for her martyr-like claiming of home and responsibility as the defining components of her identity. In the end, the collision of the two women's different (mis)conceptions of the home and the past forces them to re-evaluate their positions in the family and society and the interconnectedness of their identities.

In examining Desai's depiction of the interconnectedness of identities Avtar Brah's discussion of experience as one way of approaching "difference" proves very useful:

> The meaning attached to a given event varies enormously from one individual to another. When we speak of the constitution of individual into subject through multiple fields of signification we are invoking *inscription* and *ascription* as simultaneous processes whereby the subject *acquires* meaning in socio-economic and cultural relations at the same moment as she ascribes meaning by making sense of these relations in everyday life. In other words, how a person perceives *or* conceives an event would vary according to how "she" is culturally constructed [...]. (Bráh: 117, original emphasis)

In contemplating the role Bim plays in Tara's identity formation, we can see how these two women acquire different meanings and positions in their social relations with their parents, aunt, brothers and also with each other as they try to make sense of these relations in everyday life. Subsequently, the difference in their construction within the family also creates different emphasis in the construction of their female identities, that is, in their perceptions and conceptions of society, marriage, motherhood and femininity in general. What interests me is the interplay of these differently constructed identities and perceptions.

The paralysis which marks the familial structure in *Clear Light of Day* stems from the parents' clinging to their comfortable, empty lifestyle in the last days of colonial India. The self-absorbed father is caught in a futile imitation of the colonial glory, even dying by falling at full speed from the open door of his chauffeured car, and remains incapable of the kind of patriarchal authority that could bring structure and security to the family. The sickly and spoiled mother is a sad caricature of the traditional Indian wife and mother: totally detached from her children, she lives for bridge and evenings at the club. Paola Splendore has approached *Clear Light of Day, Baumgartner's Bombay* and *Fire on the Mountain* as novels in which the characters experience their homes "very much like territories of exile framed by boundaries and enclosures which, while secluding them, exclude or make everybody else unwelcome" (Splendore: 449). Although this is certainly true in the case of characters like Baumgartner or *Fire on the Mountain*'s Nanda Kaul, I would, contrary to Splendore's reading, see Bim Das's identity formation as consisting of a series of efforts to break free of an *unwanted* seclusion: isolated between the pathologically unchanging home and the prospect of adopting an equally restrictive upper middle-class female identity, Bim strives to be *included* in the changing outside world. Quite unusually for a girl of her background, she finds satisfaction in excelling at school, in sports, and in testing accepted gender codes for example by trying on Raja's trousers and smoking his cigarettes. Bim responds to "the sense of dullness and hopelessness" (122) created by the parents' psychological neglect with an intellectual hunger evident in her devotion to reading and learning about the world outside their privileged circles. Her need to establish an identity that would have a function also outside the domestic sphere is evident in her admonishing of Tara for being squeamish at the sight of the sick and the poor: "'Oh, you poor little thing, you'd better get a bit tougher, hadn't you—auntie's baby? Otherwise what good will you ever be? If you can't even do this little bit for the poor, what will you ever be able to do when you grow up?'" (126). In her efforts to manipulate the established gender and class systems with her everyday choices at school and amongst her siblings at home, Bim also challenges the limits of her position within the family and society: embracing education, activity and the possibility of change constitute a total rejection of the idea of upper middle-class women as passive, compliant and conservative wives-to-be. She perceives her femininity as something that needs to be transformed, distinguished from the one advocated by her family, in order to be viable or even adequate.

However, Bim's alliance with her brother Raja, the romantic would-be poet, reveals the limits of transcending gender in Bim's particular socio-economic and familial circumstances. It is ironic that their plans of a splendid, heroic future which will distinguish them as a separate active unit within the family are inspired by, from women's point of view, rather conservative poets like Tennyson, who, according to Rajeswari Mohan, sees "women's quest for knowledge as a destructive, indeed fatal, aberration" (Mohan: 58). In fact, Bim's admiration for Raja is very reminiscent of the devotion a good Indian wife shows for her husband, a role which Bim is determined to avoid. This duality in the brother and sister's relationship is made concrete by the difference in their positions within the economic system, which in the end compromises not only their relationship but also Bim's pursuit of education and independence from the family. After both of their parents have died, Raja, who is free to work outside the home and can also expect a dowry when he marries, leaves to join their Muslim neighbours, the Hyder Alis, who have escaped Delhi, eventually marrying their daughter. In renouncing his responsibilities as the eldest son, Raja ignores Bim's economic vulnerability, binding her to the very familial system she has wanted to escape. Bim's attempts to deal with her femininity as a controllable obstacle that can be overcome through education and willpower have not changed the fundamental distribution of social and economic power which ultimately demands that she pay the price for her brother's freedom. As Rajeswari Mohan states in summarizing Bim's situation within the family, "the end of colonialism makes visible the gradual hollowing out of traditional ideologies of femininity" (Mohan: 50). Bim does not choose to change her career plans to domesticity, endurance and self-sacrifice to enhance her value as a potential wife, but they become her lot because the eldest son continues the father's disconnection from the realities of life, women's life in particular.

Although Bim's thwarted process of redefining herself as a daughter and young upper middle-class woman originates in her reactions to her parents and brother, her problematic identity development also becomes an inseparable part of her sister Tara's identity formation. Bim's efforts to gain some control over her position within family and society that have been an essential part of her character dissolve on the death of her parents into a sense of responsibility for things that are slipping beyond her control, such as Baba's autism and his need of constant care, Aunt Mira's full-blown alcoholism caused by the frustration of living her whole life as a widow, and Tara's development into the kind of woman who at a party finds herself wanting to "get away from Bim and join the women" (140). The significance of Bim's role as both a sister and a "mother" to Tara lies not only in Bim's caring for her younger sister but also in her becoming equated with what Indira Karamcheti has called the "increasing constriction, stasis, and marginalization" (Karamcheti: 142) of the family home. In the absence of their parents, Bim inherits the position of power within the family and changes from a girl trying to transform her femininity with her intellectual and social prowess into an adult head of the household with the same duties as a married man or woman but without the social status and psychological rewards of marriage; she is even described as "as dour as her father, as their house" (67). Desai contrasts Tara's tentative adventures in the social life of adults with Bim's domestic routines, her nursing of her aunt and brothers, and her embarrassed rejection of the nervy Dr Biswas. Bim is portrayed as a strict and demanding familial authority, marginalized amongst or even separate from "the women," from whom Tara must distance herself to look for a supposedly secure and acceptable identity as one of the women. Bim, who as a girl tried to avoid being defined solely by her gender, is now more or less abandoned by her sister because her unusual position as a provider and caretaker of the family marks her as disconnected from social conventions and behaviour commonly associated with women. In other words, Tara's development into a woman is very much influenced by her seeing Bim's behaviour and attitudes as a continuation of their parents' reticence and severity.

The distance between the two sisters' identities as women is also evident in Desai's juxtaposition of their marital statuses. Tara's pursuit of the economic, social and, above all, psychological protection which she sees as attainable in marriage is at the expense of Bim, the unmarried sister, who struggles with money and the family's respectability in the eyes of the community. Tara, who quite deliberately finds her way into the social circles of other, more normal upper middle class families, opts for the orderliness of married life with its traditional duties and rewards, instead of participating in the very unfeminine tasks that fall on Bim, such as having to keep the family business going or the alcoholic aunt from shaming the family. The novel dramatically contrasts Bim's quite sudden transformation from a child into a rather androgynous adult who is both a decisive and financially responsible father-figure and a nurturing, self-sacrificing mother-figure with Tara's seemingly instinctive evolution into a woman with all the conventional feminine qualities. Through this comparison Desai underlines the role which an individual's opportunities as well as obligations to respond to family's and society's expectations can play in identity formation. The difference in the feedback which Bim and Tara receive from family and society becomes clear when Tara brings home her future husband, Bakul:

> Tara smiled at her with the same small apprehensive smile the doctor's face had had, and then slipped up the steps and went towards her room, almost guiltily [...].
>
> "Bim," he [Bakul] said again with unusual suddenness, "would it add to your worries or would it lessen them if Tara married me?" [...].
>
> "Oh. Oh, I see. You want to marry Tara. Yes, I thought you did. I think she wants to marry you too."
>
> "Yes, she says she does but wanted me to speak to you first."
>
> "Oh, did she?" laughed Bim. "I'm head of the family now, am I? You think so, so I must be" (80-81).

Bim's cynicism comes from having no opportunities to act and be perceived as the kind of woman she originally wanted to be, and from a repeated obligation to be the woman others need to see her as. Hence, Bim's sacrificing of her potential at a time when Indian women were becoming involved in the Independence movement and venturing outside the home to be educated and have careers can be traced not only to her parents or her brother but also to her sister's better position in a social system which sees women first and foremost as potential wives.

Having said that, it could also be argued that Tara's more traditional femininity is so incompatible with Bim's that Tara's departure can be seen as her defence against the elder sister's encroachment upon her identity. Radha Chakravarty has described Bim and Tara's view of each other as that of "a sibling who is also an 'other'" (Chakravarty: 82). And there is in their reactions to each other's motives and choices a pattern which involves one of them centering on the very thing which the other represses. Bim's emphasis on the aspects of her identity that represent a break from the normal conventions strengthens Tara's embracing of traditional femininity as a strategy for coping in the shadow of her elder sister. While Bim is defined by her need to distinguish herself from the dismal legacy of their parents, Tara's identity development is marked by her yearning for normality, for a domestically oriented, more traditional female identity that would replace the trauma of being, in effect, motherless:

> The difference showed when they played their favourite game of questioning each other: "What will you be when you grow up?"
>
> Raja said promptly and proudly: "A hero" [...].
>
> Then Bim declared, with glistening eyes, that she would be a heroine [...].
>
> Tara looked from one to the other in incomprehension. "*I* am going to be a mother and knit for my babies," she said complacently, but the older two laughed at her so uproariously, so scornfully, that she burst into tears and ran to bury her head in her aunt's lap and complain that they made fun of her (112, original emphasis).

Bim's intellectual ambition and dismissal of traditional femininity as inadequate and even contemptible also constitute an inadvertent dismissal of her sister as a representative of that tradition. While they are growing up, Tara functions as the point at which Bim measures her distance from the kind of femininity and domesticity that she sees as passive, ineffectual and disconnected from the new social and economic possibilities within women's reach. Bim vents her frustration at being only a girl by cutting the more vain and girlish Tara's hair as a practical joke; she pushes Tara into trying dangerous things, like smoking, "driving her, forcing her through fear" (133); she avoids Tara at school, thinking of Tara's shyness and clumsiness, her "anti-social misery" (125) as contagious.

Excluded from the union of her elder brother and sister, Tara finds her female role models in Aunt Mira and their neighbours, the Misra sisters: whereas Bim seeks an entrance to the outside world through education and learning embodied by Raja the poet, Tara finds first in Mira, their desperately caring substitute mother, and then in the ordinary, dutiful Misra girls some validation of her more traditional femininity, which would usually credit her, the attractive, timid, unintellectual and domestically oriented one, as the more worthy and socially successful daughter. Although Rajeswari Mohan has regarded Tara and Raja as having "arranged their lives so that it becomes impossible for them to share Bim's responsibilities" (Mohan: 62) and "Tara's insecurity and guilt [...] as psychological defences" (Mohan: 62) for this, one could also interpret Tara's marriage and move abroad as a defence of her already limited powers of self-definition. Tara, "born to trail behind the others" (116), perceives marriage as a way of escaping her doubly marginalized position, not only as the most ordinary and timid child in the family but also as the "other" to Bim's authoritative conception of female identity.

The parts of the novel set in the present take place during one of Tara's rare visits to India. What makes this particular visit a real return in the psychological sense is the fact that the sisters become aware of each other's roles in their processes of identity development and recognize the circumstances which have produced this connection. Pushpa Naidu Parekh has stated that "[c]entered on male relatives such as Raja, Baba, or [Tara's husband] Bakul, the lives of the women and their internal struggles become peripheral; it is only by re-focusing on the women's relationships to each other and their significance for both that the dynamics of the paradigm are shifted" (Parekh: 276-77). Although in the above I have attempted to show that the women's internal struggles are anything but peripheral in the novel, it is true that on Tara's return the interconnectedness of their identities surfaces as a means of shifting the focus from the father and the elder brother as the sole reasons for these women's fates. Although the novel ends with Bim's vision of the forgiveness and all-encompassing love that she feels for her family, in a story of women's endurance in changing and at times oppressive circumstances I would regard her recognition of the similarity of Tara's experiences of helplessness and isolation with her own as more significant:

> But I think the *atmosphere* has changed—ever since you took over, Bim. The kind of atmosphere that used to fill it [the house] when father and mother were alive, always ill or playing cards or at the club, always *away*, always leaving us out, leaving us behind—and then Mira-*masi* becoming so—so strange, and Raja so ill—till it seemed that the house was ill, illness passing from one generation to the other so that anyone who lived in it was bound to become ill and the only thing to do was to get away from it, *escape* [...].
>
> Bim's eyes narrowed as she sat listening to her sister's outburst. "Did you feel that way?" she asked, coolly curious. "I didn't know. I think I was so occupied with Raja and Mira-*masi* that I didn't notice what effect it had on you. Why didn't I?" [...] (156, original emphasis).

Rid of the factors that used to render them powerless and vulnerable—negligent parents, selfish brother, ailing aunt—the sisters no longer have to see each other as "the other" with conflicting strategies of survival. In recognizing the similarities in their construction within their particular familial and social locations, they are able to assign new meanings to their experiences of femininity, marriage and mothering, and to see those experiences as parallel instead of oppositional. Parekh has called them "agents who have actualized the influence of an otherwise passive passage of time, [...] two women who come to grips with each other's individuality and the ineluctable forces of their relationship, two women who represent the diversities of complete women as well as the divided selves of a whole woman" (Parekh: 280). It is in the space between their individual female identities, in their memories, retellings and questionings, that this actualizing takes place and a clearer view of the interconnected yet different faces of femininity in their family begins to emerge. In a novel that ostensibly describes women whose personal desires are frustrated by a dysfunctional, socially and psychologically paralysed family, Desai in the end foregrounds the potential of women's joint desire to actively and productively re-examine the past.

REFERENCES

1. Brah, Avtar. *Cartographies of Diaspora: Contesting Identities*. London: Routledge, 1996.
2. Chakravarty, Radha. "Figuring the Maternal: 'Freedom' and 'Responsibility' in Anita Desai's Novels." *ARIEL* 29.2 (1998): 75-92.
3. Desai, Anita. *Clear Light of Day*. New Delhi: Penguin, 1980.
4. George, Rosemary Marangoly. *The Politics of Home: Postcolonial Relocations and Twentieth-Century Fiction*. Cambridge: Cambridge UP, 1996.
5. Karamcheti, Indira. "The Geographics of Marginality: Place and Textuality in Simone Schwarz-Bart and Anita Desai." *Reconfigured Spheres: Feminist Explorations of Literary Space*. Eds. Margaret R. Higonnet and Joan Templeton. Amherst: U of Massachusetts P, 1994: 125-46.
6. Mohan, Rajeswari. "The Forked Tongue of Lyric in Anita Desai's *Clear Light of Day*." *The Journal of Commonwealth Literature* 32.1 (1997): 47-66.
7. Parekh, Pushpa Naidu. "Redefining the Postcolonial Female Self: Women in Anita Desai's *Clear Light of Day*." *Between the Lines: South Asians and Post-Coloniality*. Eds. Deepika Bahri and Mary Vasudeva. Philadelphia: Temple UP, 1996: 270-83.
8. Splendore, Paola. "Confined Lives: Estrangement and Exile in Anita Desai's Novels." *Nationalism vs. Internationalism: (Inter) National Dimensions of Literatures in English*. Eds. Wolfgang Zach and Ken Goodwin. Tübingen: Stauffenberg, 1996: 449-53.

18

Anita Desai's *Where Shall We Go This Summer?* A Critique on Existentialism

HARIOM PRASAD

On the literary map of Indian women writing Anita Desai appears to be a leading luminary. In the critical circles, she is rightly considered to be 'an Indian Jane Austen and Virginia Woolf.' Her short stories and novels have earned for her fame of a serious and skilful author of world stature. In Indian writing she has established herself with her remarkable contribution to the development of art and ethos of novel writing technique. Her novels create clonal effects on our mind and heart for the varying Indian social values and present the microcosmic study of man-woman relationship in the changed atmosphere of the modern times. Among other things, her novels deal with urban life in contrast with Nature and the socio-psycho attitudes of man caught in the crucible of tradition and change. She achieves a cohesive design of content and form in her psychological novels and imposes harmony over different streams of feeling and sensibility, found in different strata of human society. In her novels, we find a fine match between '*what is life*' and '*how it has to be lived*' with the natural make-up. In many places, she delves deep into the inner world of her characters and brings out many truths of psychological interest. In most of her novels she tries to mark a distinct break from the traditional themes and techniques used by the earlier Indo-English novelists. She is not concerned with the social, political or moral problems that beset the characters in the early Indo-English fiction. She chooses new themes and characters. For her "The inner climate, the climate of sensibility that lures or cleares or rumbles like thunder on suddenly blazes forth like lightning, is more compelling than the outer weather, the physical geography or the visible action."[1] In her novels, she creates a rich galaxy of characters, both male and female although she articulates especially the feminine psyche—from childhood to old age. She does not create the dumb characters, whose problems are concerned with food, clothes and shelter. Instead, most of her protagonists feel alienated from the world, from society, from families, from parents or other relations and even from their own selves because they are not ordinary people but individuals made to stand against the general current of life and who fight that current and struggle against it for the realization of an imagined world.

With her novel *Cry, the Peacock* she entered the field of novel-writing and was shot to fame immediately. *Where Shall We Go This Summer* (1975) is her fourth novel which depicts the inner-outer world of its protagonist Sita and her fatigue for life. The novel tells the story of the middle-aged Sita, who is fed up with the mundane routine of a meaningless existence. She feels suffocated in her well-ordered, posh flat in Bombay and struggles hard to break away from it all. She wants to go back to the island Manori where she had spent many golden days of childhood with her family to seek peace, pleasure and a great pause in her life. This novel is shorter in size but deeper in meaning. The structural pattern of the novel is strikingly similar to that of Virginia Woolf's *To The Lighthouse*. The concrete form, the befitting style, and the economy of detail make the work a curious *tour de force*. Similar to Woolf's novel, it has three parts: Part one, Monsoon '67; Part two, Winter '47; Part three, Monsoon '67; each section of the novel is concerned with a particular season, time and space. The beginning section assimilates us on the island Manori and manifests the present time of Sita's life. The second section connects us with the events of her past life and the concluding section evinces what she has accepted as her fortune of future life. In the first section Anita Desai has dealt with the entry of Sita into the island after living a life of "dull tedium of hopeless disappointment."[2] The island has been portrayed by the novelist as a heaven for Sita which wonderfully holds the master key to her final liberation from the existential anxiety, hopelessness and suffering. She feels, on the island, all of her problems will be magically solved and she will be calm and comfortable being relieved of her physical and mental anxiety. The psychological cosmos of Sita's life moves around the island and her father's fantasy. Before coming to Bombay she had enjoyed the memorable company of Rekha, Jeevan and her mystic father who had always been surrounded by his disciples and had a glorious lifestyle on the island. In the mental make up of Sita, Manori is imbued with miracles and mysteries. In the core of her heart, she believes that the magic of the island will wipe out the evil spell and her unborn child will remain within her womb for ever. She is so badly sensitive and afflicted with the prevalence of violence and terror around that she wishes to check the delivery of her child. She does not dare to bring it out to face the cruelties of life, rather she hopes against hope. Her tragedy is palpably due to her "constitutional inability to accept the values and the attitude of society—and her irreconcilable temperament."[3]

Her concern to save the small bird from the ferocious crows shows her tender heart full of boundless compassion. She is furious at the cruel crows and tries her best to drive them away and to save the life of the wounded eagle knowing that the bird has really no hope of survival against the attack of crows. In this event she identifies herself as the wounded eagle. Through this symbolism the novelist has very skilfully suggested the tragic mental world of her protagonist.

Sita is a bit abnormal and introvert. She wants to escape from the brutal realities and harsh facts of human life. She forgets that life in one part is full of violence, suffering and pain. Treasons, betrayals and treacheries are mixed up with pleasure, joy and happiness to colour it. She does not feel ease in the city life of Bombay so she wishes to relinquish the sweat and turmoil of the urban atmosphere of Bombay where she and her husband Raman live with their four children in a bourgeoise neighbourhood. The humdrum life of urban area bores her to the very roots of her existence.

Sita wants to exercise her full freedom in the bosom of nature. So she decides to go to Manori in search of the aspired world. She wants to keep herself aloof from "duties and responsibilities, from order and routine, from life and the city [...]. She had refused to give birth to a child in a world not fit to receive the child" (139).

She does not want her child to be trapped in the pathetic, violent and painful conditions of human life in which she finds herself suffocated and tortured from all sides. She constantly dangles between self-realization and self-delusion, natural and the unnatural wishes and above all, consciousness and anguish of life. She finds herself to be a mere, helpless object.

She completely fails to find joy and happiness in her conjugal life as well as with her children. Her husband Raman is a successful business man and he loves her as a responsible husband. But at this stage of life when she is over forty and her fifth child is on the way, she feels a strange loneliness, restlessness and boredom in her existence. She also thinks that no one cares for her as she was cared before as an individual. She becomes defiant in her words and deeds in a fit of depression and ultimately she takes the decision to leave the house and her husband and to go to Manori. Raman tries to enlighten her mind about the 'contraries' in life, saying "other people put up with it—it's not so—so insufferable" (143). But she lacks courage, practical knowledge and wisdom which make others believe that "life must be continued, and all its business" (138).

Manori is more a symbol than a place in the novel. Forming the central image, it plays very vital role in connecting the life and thought of Sita from past to future. It also affects the present predicament of Sita. It primarily exists in her mind and heart. She retreats into it as one would into a womb, with the desire to recapture once again her childhood fancies, full of innocence and purity. Manori provides a symbolic solace to her suffering soul and projects her inner psyche beautifully. Further, surrounded as it is by the sea, waves, sky and the rugged, rustic characters, symbolises Time—its flux and fixity, in a broader sense. Thus, Manori fuses into one the Time-span of present, past and future and the Life-span of childhood, youth, and old age. When she remembers Manori she goes back to her buried memories and experiences of her inchoate childhood. She gets relief when she thinks of the island, amidst her present suffering. She always tries to soothe her feelings and thoughts with the enjoyment of the natural scenery on the Island and the adolescent bewilderment about the strange relationship between her father and her sister Rekha and her dead and forgotten mother. Like Shakespeare's Prospero, Sita's father presided over the island with his supposed magical spells and enjoyed a great esteem there. But Sita does not judge whether he was a charlatan or a genuine mystic. But her father had cast an illusion as a fisherman casts a net. Sita does not know much about her mother who had escaped into the dark depth of the ocean.

Now she wants to live in her small heaven of fantasy on the island, totally cut-off from social responsibilities, mental tortures and physical problems. In this state of mind she desires to take refuge on the island knowing that it lacks in even the basic amenities. She seeks relief, freedom and peace in life. "Ordinary life, the everyday world had grown so insufferable to her" (72).

She prefers servitude to unbearable anguish, and submission to freedom. Her own frustration appals her to such an extent that she is unwilling to bring forth her fifth child into this cruel world. She does not approve of childbirth and begins "to fear if as yet one more act of violence and murder in a world that had more of them in it than she could take" (38). She has already born four children before this one, "with pride, with pleasure with all the placid serenity that supposedly goes with pregnancy" (32). But her crisis and suffering start from the fifth, the unborn child. Her husband Raman is puzzled over her behaviour and thinking at this stage. He tries to understand her but fails utterly. Now Sita feels forlorn and neglected. She has begun to think of the meaninglessness of life. She has confronted the seamy side of life. She does not share her husband's acceptance of life's ordinariness. All friends, acquaintances, relatives and business associates of her husband are for her no better than animals, "nothing but appetite and sex. Only food, sex and money matter" (31-32). She calls them "animals" who are neither pet, nor wild beasts but "pariahs [...] hanging about drains and dustbins, waiting to pounce and bill and eat" (32).

Sita is certainly not an average woman. She thinks that children are a source of anxiety, concern, and pessimism. She does not derive happiness, love, and affection from them. The only thing she gets from them is "sentimentality." Her mental age does not correspond with her chronological age and she becomes a pure combination of the real and the unreal, the ideal and the trivial, the beautiful and the ugly. Her ideas and activities are determined more by the past events than the actualities of the present and the probable course of future events. She wants to live in the continuum of suspended time disobeying its inevitable flux, development and destruction. In some cases, the grown up Sita has the unrealistic mental attitudes of a child or at best an adolescent. She fails to live and cope with the age and time of her present condition. She does not try her best to face the basic problems of life with patience. Instead she wants an escape, like a coward, from the battlefield.

Her daughter Menaka presents a contrast to her in many respects. For Sita past is important and not the future. But Menaka gives greater value to the future. Sita is less intelligent than her daughter. When Sita is caught in the difficult condition of mental agony on the island, it is Menaka who convinces her and redeems her. On many occasions Menaka shows her wisdom to solve Sita's problems. It is Menaka who reminds her father to come urgently and to take them all from the island. Sita is well aware of her limitations to accommodate herself to the social imperatives as well as her obligations towards her husband and children. She accepts the turbulence which has crept into her life and confesses her incapability to cope with the gloomy realities of life. When her decision making power comes to a standstill on Manori island, she feels herself to be falling into a deep chasm. And she recognizes her failure and she also approves of the many sided talent and worth of her daughter Menaka. She praises her interest in art and the effortless way she sketches and paints. She is under the impression that Menaka possesses talent for music and many other fine arts.

Anita Desai has projected the character of Sita in a fascinating manner which arrests the critical urge of the readers and the critics as well. Even as a child Sita differs from other children of her age-group. She bears no resemblance whatsoever to her younger brother Jeevan or sister Rekha whom Jeevan regards as their stepsister. Sita feels helpless and ill-informed before her clever young brother Jeevan and she accepts the worth of her sister Rekha as the sweet singer of bhajans (religious songs). Other contrasts in the novel are also sharply pointed out. Her husband Raman and their children obviously stand for the prosaic side of life, conformity and sanity while she is all sensitivity, feverish imagination and vague romanticism. Her home in Bombay presents a set of values that she is unable to accept while Manori island represents past glory, romance and fancy which have been less valuable in the practical world of today.

Her philosophy of life is punctured by her over sensitivity and ill-judgment. She has brought her children, Karan and Menaka to the island to feel happy and secure but she gets the whips of forlornness, boredom and helplessness. She does not feel fully secured here. Everyone around her winces at her harshness and wildness. Many a times she becomes vexed and perturbed with her own judgment. The betrayal of her husband, his family, her children, friends and acquaintances violently tears her apart. When Raman comes to the island she thinks he has come for her while he has come there at his daughter Menaka's instance, to take her away to the mainland and to get her admitted to the Medical college. Raman stares at Sita with distaste, neglect and indifference when he meets her on the island.

Sita escapes to the island in order to "stay whole," "to maintain her freedom," and "to keep the child unborn." But Raman interprets "her escape" as "desertion." She does not accept Raman's plea and is pained much over his opinion for her. She seeks justification for her action saying:

> "No, no,—desertion, that's cowardly. I wasn't doing anything cowardly," she begged him to see, with a turbulence of pride. "I was saying No, but positively, positively, saying No. There must be some who say No, Raman! [...] Perhaps I never ran away at all. Perhaps I am only like the jellyfish washed up by the waves, stranded there on the sand-bar. I was just stranded here by the sea, that's all. I hadn't much to do with it at all" (108).

Raman listens to her carefully and ridicules saying:

> "So you're no more than a jellyfish," he said bitterly. "You call yourself a helpless jellyfish. Yet see what you have done to yourself, to all of us."
>
> "All of you," she vaguely asked. "But you have nothing to do with it. Nothing. There's just the sea—it drowns us or strands us on the sand-bar and there's the island. That's all (108).

Raman's retort makes her helpless and she starts feeling bad about her doings. Here, she becomes "inauthentic" and "object-like." She unknowingly tries to behave like Hugo, the Sartrean hero in *Dirty Hands* who does not accept that he has murdered Hoederer. He says:

> Did I ever do it? It was not I who billed—it was chance [...] chance fired three shots [...]. But me? Me? Where does that put in the things? It was an assassination without an assassin.[4]

Thus, Sita becomes the content of her cold cruelty and cries in vain when Raman criticises her for wrong doings. He tries to draw her attention to the trauma and tension she has caused her family. Then, Sita comes to realise her mistakes. She herself becomes a prey to rejustification of her past deeds. So, when Raman prepares to leave for the mainland she mends her ways and follows the footprints of Raman that he had laid out for her:

> She lowered her head and searched out his footprints so that she could place her feet in them, as a kind of game to make walking back easier and so her footprints mingled with his (150).

This gesture of Sita reveals her existential predicament, of the values of society around her and her return to conformity. Now she has come to accept the prosaic nature of life which runs through difficult human situations in different ways. The happy ending harmonises all hues of human life which forms the blood and bone of the novel. Sita finds the courage to face life, in the end, with all its ups and downs. Speaking about the conclusion of the novel, Suresh Kohli rightly points out that as compared to the earlier works, there is one distinct change:

> Sita neither dies in the end nor kills anyone nor does she become mad. She simply compromises with her destiny.[5]

In all her novels Anita Desai seems to be under the spell of existentialism. All her protagonists champion the cause of existential philosophy. In this novel too the central character Sita is a free but isolated individual who is solely responsible for her own actions and reactions. This way, *Where Shall We Go This Summer?* deals with the facts and paraphernalia of the existential theory enunciated by Kierkegaard and Sartre.

REFERENCES

1. K.R. Srinivasa Iyengar, *Indian Writing in English* (New Delhi: Sterling, 1994) 464.
2. Anita Desai, *Where Shall We Go this Summer?* (New Delhi: Vikash, 1975) 58.
3. B. Ramchandra Rao, *The Novels of Anita Desai* (Kalyani, 1977) 49-50.
4. Jean Paul Sartre, *Dirty Hands* (New York: Vintage, 1971) 240.
5. Suresh Kohli, "The Fiction of Anita Desai," *The Statesman* 6 Nov. 1977: 3.

19

THE DIALECTICS OF MARITAL POLARISATION IN ANITA DESAI'S *CRY, THE PEACOCK*

S.P. SWAIN

Maya in *Cry, the Peacock* is a delicate housewife unable to cope with the apathy of the in-laws and the dehumanized and depersonalised urban milieu. But she is not a "haunted protagonist" (Raizada 1984: 17) who flees from reality. She is an individual involved in the drama of life and death, in existential predilections and predicaments. Morbidity qualifies her suffering as a housewife. Grappling with the morose shadows of the past, she is overwhelmed by a staggering sense of ontological insecurity. But she puts up a single-handed struggle against her phantasmal and morose past—something that she cannot comprehend, something that never rests—a nothingness that preys upon her disconsolate marital self. Her problem is to adjust herself to the hostile urban milieu which uproots her from her instinctive emotional moorings, which keep her at bay. Promilla Kapur observes:

> In the impersonal and de-individualised atmosphere of the big urban centres, one is liable to feel alienated as well as neglected and almost starved for genuine love and affection *(Love, Marriage and Sex* 1973: 244).

Anita Desai believed that "literature should deal with the most enduring matters" (Desai 1978: 2). What matters is the psychic and the existential reality of the characters. Their obsessions, eccentricities, tremors and traumas. "The enduring human condition" (Heinemann 1953: 178) and "the emotional life" (Macquarrie, 1977: 1) of the women characters hailing from an urban milieu are her chief concerns. Moving on the plane of subjective existence, *Cry, the Peacock* reveals her remarkable ability to focus on the interior landscape of the alienated self.

The novel opens with Maya's morbid obsession with death. Toto the family dog is dead. The dog, so dear to her heart, is dead:

> No, she cried and fled to the bedroom to fling herself on to the bed and lie there, thinking of the small, still body stiffened into the panic-stricken posture of the moment of death (7).

Maya and her husband Gautama react differently to Toto's death. One emotionally, the other intellectually. While Maya sheds tears, Gautama sips tea. The passing away of Toto symbolises Maya's psychic death for he was a child-surrogate to her. What has a childless wife to live for after his (Toto's) death?

Something inscrutable distresses her. Inscrutable but real, very real. She wants to dodge it, but cannot, reluctantly encounters it, but ends in despair (8).

There remained a certain unease, hesitation in the air, which kept the tears swimming in my eyes, and prevented their release. I was not allowed the healing passion of a fit of crying that would have left me exhausted, sleep washed and becalmed. Something slipped into my tear-hazed vision, a shadowy something [...] and filled me with this despair (8).

She attempts to shrink from the fear of it, but fails. She tries to escape but finds no way. She struggles to come to terms with a reality imposed upon her, but it rebels against her ethical self. She wants to make love to Gautama, but Gautama stands apart. And now Toto's death has created a spiritual vacuum in her. The death of the dog distances her from the animal. It distance her from Gautama. The husband and wife do not share anything between them, not even the sensibility that can differentiate between the "half-sweet," "half-sad fragrance of petunias" and "some astringent smell of lemon" (19). "He was not on my side at all," exclaims Maya, while Gautama is sitting beside her, "but across a river, across a mountain, and would always remain so" (114). She is repelled by Gautama's "dispassionate objectivism" (78). Her wish for contact and companionship with Gautama remains a need unfulfilled. This alienation between Maya and Gautama is the result of polar motivations. Maya looks for the uncanny and the romantic, Gautama for the pragmatic and the practical in life.

Desai uses the death of the dog to point out their warm and cold responses to the world about them and within them. Maya loves the way of the flesh, Gautama the world of the spirit. Maya is sensitive and emotional, Gautama is rational and logical. Gautama preaches the non-attachment of the *Gita,* Maya practises attachment. She struggles to escape from the mundane realities of life but her physical self holds her back. It turns all her efforts for a psychic release into a cry in the wilderness, a peacock's cry. The husband-wife alienation brought about by temperamental discord—one of the major existentialist themes in Anita Desai that repeats itself more conspicuously in her fourth novel, *Where Shall We Go This Summer?*—forms the focus of this novel.

Maya abhors the cooing doves, since she fails to find in them a cogent correlative for her moods. She fails to reckon in them her identity. In other words, she fails to 'connect.' It is her failure to 'connect' and 'correlate' that makes her exasperated to see the doves mate. The cries of the ornithopes caught in the rut of love are like frantic warnings to her ears. Her inner tumoil gains momentum:

> Something, similar heaved inside me [...] a longing, a dread, a search for solution, despair and my head throbbed and spun as I lay flat on my back through the long afternoons, under the fan that turned, turned relentlessly (35).

The fate of Maya is indeed the fate of the anguished self craving for companionship and harmony in an emotionally chaotic milieu. It is the fate of the hysterical mind of an Indian housewife. Prediction and fatalism is a fact to Maya. The mournful cry of the brain-fever bird, with the advent of Spring, is, to Maya, the peacock's cry. It is a cry of intellectual sickness and uneasiness born of emotional and spiritual atrophy. The spiritual crisis in Maya issues from her struggle between desire and recognition of loss. She yearns for love and affection:

> Without strong ties with her husband, she feels lost and isolated: What has driven Maya towards insanity? The reason could easily be seen as the impending death, but the real reason is perhaps the unfulfilled desire and the perpetual longing for Gautama's love and affection (Singh 1995: 40).

Maya's marriage with Gautama was imposed from outside and hence, neither true nor lasting. Gautama's family had innumerable subjects to speak on, and they spoke incessantly. But they never spoke of love, far less of affection. Maya and Gautama had different family-backgrounds. This accounts for Maya's state of *de trap* existence in Gautama's family: "I knew I was one of those outsiders who could be used for this purpose and were, therefore, necessary, though not necessarily loved [...]" (49). She is their "pretty plaything" (49), one of those doomed, forsaken individuals who find no security and repose in a harsh, bitter, pitiless world. Gautama's temperamental apathy is hereditary and biological. He has inherited the dry, callous nature of his father and the rational, calculative and mathematical mind of his mother. "Gautama," says Maya, "was very far away from any world of mine" (201). And between them is the "unpassable desert" that isolates them. Meena Beliappa observes:

> It is against a background of frustrated married life that the haunting sense of death obsesses her. The fatal distance between Gautama and Maya [...] is basis to the theme of psychic disintegration (Beliappa, 1971: 10).

Isolation in the novel operates at two levels—physical and mental. Moments of anguish were, to Maya, moments of reckoning. The image of her father keeps intruding in the flux of her consciousness bringing about the "desired lull" (this may be a reference to her temporary psychic tranquillity achieved through her recollections of her childhood attachment to her father). The father in the unconscious disturbs her marital life. She fails to integrate herself to Gautama's intellectual make-up. Maya's innate and instinctive impulses drive her to hysterical feats of psychic trauma. Her love for her father is an obsession like her infantile love for her Toto, and it is this divided love which accounts for her distance from Gautama. Like other modern women, Maya "exists in man's world on his terms. She is either the Other, for man or she is untaught" (Tong, 1993, 224). And this "Otherness" of women—of being excluded, shunned, rejected, dislocated and marginalised—is a major theme in deconstruction. But Maya represents the negative side of 'Otherness,' often given to dark and dismal thoughts of death and annihilation.

Maya lives incommunicado. The child in her craves for the filial touch of that 'vanished hand' (a reference to the dead Toto or the love of her father), whereas the adult in her longs for the husband:

> "No one, no one else," I sobbed into my pillow, "loves me as my father does" (46).

Maya's memory of the happy days with her father serves as a foil to the unfulfilled loveless life with her husband. Drowned in silent bitterness, her marital world had pushed her into extreme state of fragility often labelled as madness. As a married woman she exists almost solely within her emotions, and is excluded from certain kinds of marital experiences which are vital to creativity.

Maya's reminiscential excursions into the past are an effort to seek harmony in a deformed and deranged socio-psychic world. During her odyssey, she stumbles on two temperamentally opposite pedestrians, Leila, a believer in fate and Pom, a non-believer. She lives both mentally and physically in a world of contrasts, a world teeming with variety. *Maya,* the very incarnation of illusion, finds herself at odds with the world of reality. The past, which streams into her consciousness as a chiaroscuro is at once attractive and repulsive. The remembrance of Laila and Pom fascinates her imagination and, at the same time, mystifies and stupefies her by the creation of horrific dim shadows for which she has an abhorrence and shadows, from which she wants to flee, since they rejuvenate the latent image of the cadaverous albino. Life is flooded with shadows. She has to encounter them. The mountain waters, the ferns and nights full of stars are no longer an anchor to her torpid and solitary self. They beguile her longing for quietude and companionship. Her desire for communication fails. The remembrances do not alleviate her anguish but only create tenebrous shadows that remind her of the albino astrologer, who casts oneirodynic and fulgurant nightmare on the placid tenor of her life. The albino figures as a perilous obsession in her conscious self, a persistent and obtrusive intrusion in her stream of consciousness. She is unable to get over the repulsive sight of the albino. It pursues her:

> Wherever I laid myself, I could think only of the albino, the magician, his dull opaque eyes, the hand twitching the fold of cloth between the swallowing thighs (64).

Maya's marriage with Gautama was imposed from outside and hence, neither true nor lasting:

> Coming slowly up on his bicycle, in the evening it was my father Gautama used to come to call upon, and had it not been for the quickening passion with which I met half-way, my father's proposal that I marry this tall, stooped and knowledgeable friend of his, one might have said that our marriage was grounded upon the friendship of the two men and the mutual respect in which they held each other, rather than upon anything else (40).

Maya is morbidly involved in the trivialities of life: a pregnant woman, a grub house, a dull urchin. Is it due to her craving for companionship or to her desire for self-identification and self-assertion? Fate, astrology, palmistry form a part of Maya's life, a nightmare that stirs her subconscious self with tremulous cadence. At the restaurant, she turns into a prim lady with the question, "Do you, too, believe in palmistry?" Maya's lacerated self pines for order and poise through contact and communication in an emotionally ruffled milieu. The clash between the two worlds, Gautama and Maya, reality and illusion, splits her from within. She can identify herself neither with the world of Gautama nor with her own visionary world. The encounter with the Sikh and his forebodings and deliberations about palmistry remind her of the pale albino. The Sikh is a perverted and distorted projection of the shadow of the albino. The cabaret dance which she witnesses at the club becomes a sordid reality, an image of exploitation and perversion. It becomes a dance of liberation, symbolising the cabaret girl's desire to annihilate the anguish of her despair and estrangement from a psycho moral world. Maya's inner world of fantasy is fused with the outer world of perceptual experience by the juxtaposition of the bear dance and the cabaret. The dance of the cabaret-girls is not simply vulgar and debasing. It is the symbol of Maya's tormented self struggling for liberation from an inescapable fatality, her thanatophobia which appears to have been "built in the very structure of the story" (Singh: 231).

The indulgent smile of Gautama is to Maya a barrier, the limbo that had separated them. The lack of emotional rapport between them is evident when she says, "Were I to force him to follow me, he would follow unseeing [...]" (91). Gautama is the father substitute. She wants to touch him, feel his flesh and hair, and then tighten her hold on him:

> "Is there anything?" she asks him, "is there nothing in you that would be touched, ever so slightly, if I told you I live my life for you?" (114).

Gautama's indifference convinces Maya of the need for emotional, and not physical communion in the fulfilment of her sexual life. She yearns for contact that goes deeper than flesh. As a woman, Maya has neither Essence nor Existence. She has no part in ontological reality. She is "Not," she is "Nothing." A fragment of an empirical reality, she has no soul, no individuality. Without an independent Will, she is excluded from a higher metaphysical existence. "Maya of all Desai's women characters," says Jasbir Jain, "is the one most aware of her body" (Jain 1987: 117). Hence her sensuality clashes with the image of the father in her psyche resulting in her neurosis.

In alienation between Gautama and Maya, there is a perpetual see-saw movement between factual reality and transcendence. Polarization causes this movement. The citation from the *Gita* shows Gautama's commitment to transcendental love. Maya's attachment is only physical. The facts of life and the fiction of imagination are at war in her splintered self. Gautama is physically attached but emotionally aloof. He is with her and without her. Maya "is repelled by her husband's surgeon like responses as he performs the last rites for Toto" (Jamkhandi, 1981: 38). But has Maya gained from her marriage?

Nothing but the ossification of her sense of "Otherness" in discharging her role as a motherless wife. What she gains from marriage is "gilded mediocrity lacking ambition and passion, aimless days indefinitely repeated, life that slips away gently toward death without questioning its purpose" (Beauvoir, 1974: 500).

Maya's anguish reaches its climax with the heart-rending, wistful vail of the peacocks. In a way, she symbolises the panting and heaving peacocks:

> I felt their thirst as they gazed at the rain-clouds, their passion, as they hunted for their mates. With them, I trembled and panted and paced the burning rocks [...] (46).

Gone are the childhood days when the cry of the peacocks inspired in her awe and wonder. With the advent of the albino into her life, the phantasy of her childhood days sluggishly crystallises into awful clarities, and she finds a mirror reflection of her split self in the mortal agony of the peacocks. Maya's existentialist predicament is akin to the plight of the love-lorn peacocks whose shrieks in the stillness of the night penetrate her heart and leave it palpitating. She reckons her identity in them: "Now that I understand their call, I wept for them, and wept for myself, knowing their words to be mine" (97). The discovery of such kinship stifles her sensibility:

> Am I gone insane? Father! Brother! Husband ! who is my saviour? I am in need of one. I am dying, and I am in love with living. I am in love and I am dying. God, let me sleep, forget, rest. But no, I will never sleep again. There is no rest any more—only death and waiting (98).

Such a psychic state is not despair but madness. It is an animate death whose horror is its inability to escape from itself:

> Already we belonged to separate worlds, and this seemed the earth that I loved, so scented with jasmine, coloured with liquor resounding with poetry and warmed by amiability. It was mine that was hell. Torture, guilt, dread, imprisonment, these were the four walls of my private

> hell, one that no one could survive long. Death was certain (102).

A woman's role as a wife blocks her freedom. Beauvoir believed that the institution of marriage has marred the spontaneity of feelings, between the husband and wife (marital lovers) by "transforming! freely given feelings into mandatory duties and shrilly asserted rights" (Tong, 1993: 207).

A woman is more than her body. She is not only a Being-in-itself but also a Being-for-itself. Maya wanted sexual union, not mere physical contact: "It was not only for his presence, his love that I longed, but mainly for the life that would permit me to hold and then tighten my hold on him" (102). Maya's alienation under the rubrics of sexuality is on account of Gautama's cold intellectuality. All the pulsating and throbbing world around Gautama serves to deepen her own dull and dreary existence. Her infatuated and hysterical obsession with the idea of death makes her passive to the passions and charms of the world around her. The shadowy and vague augury of the albino astrologer shatters her identity as a housewife and as an individual. Desperately, she longs for self-abnegation and the renunciation of her morbid feminine self: "Full personal freedom for a woman consists in her ability to renounce her false feminine self in favour of her true self (Long, 1993: 4). Her pessimistic and saturnine attitude towards life, her disgust and rancour with the milieu intensifies her anguish and estrangement. Her striving towards equanimity through detachment and renunciation is an act of sheer futility. Instead of giving her psychic equipoise and stability, it only disturbs and dissociates her identity. R.S. Pathak talks of "total lack of communication on the part of Gautama" (Pathak, 1971: 21), but Gautama at times consoles Maya, he converses with her. This participation, this communication is, however, only physical:

> How little he knew of my misery or of how to comfort me [...]. Telling me to go to sleep while he worked at his papers, he did not give another thought to me, to either the soft, willing body, or the lonely, wanting mind that waited near his bed (9).

How can there be sexual union without sexual communion?

Is cohabitation merely the gratification of the flesh? Is it only a biological necessity? Maya's contact with Gautama must go deeper than skin: "There was no bond, no love, hardly any love. And I could not bear to think of that" (108). She is unable to satiate her sexual urge because of Gautama's aloofness, his "dispassionate objectivism" (78). For Gautama, Maya is a mere object, not a reality; an appearance only to be looked at. To be watched. Thus she becomes "an object of vision: a sight" (Berger, 1972: 47). "To be a woman," observes Bejamin "is to be excluded from rational individualism, to be either an object of it or a threat to it" (1980: 47). Maya's desire to have Gautama sexually is to want him as mere flesh, but no sooner does she appropriate the desired body as mere flesh than she discovers that it is not flesh that she desired but a body, a psychic object in the midst of the world. The ancient strains on a learner's Sitar from the neighbouring house mingle with her life, her fate. The rhythm of its music becomes a symbolic projection of the rhythm of her life.

"Because when you are away from me," says Maya to Gautama "I want you" (113). Maya sees nothing real in life but only delusions that ruin her discriminative faculty. She exists and yet does not exist. Life and Gautam have equally betrayed her, made her a neurotic. She is restricted to the cribbed confines of her home and denied free access to society. Ann Foreman considers women's alienation profoundly disturbing because women experience themselves as fulfilment of other people's needs:

> Man exists in the social world [...]. For the woman, however, her place is within the home [...] the effect of alienation on the lives and consciousness of women takes on even more oppressive form. Men seek relief from their alienation through their relations with women; for women there is no relief. For these intimate relations are the very ones that are the essential structures of her oppression (1977: 101-02).

Maya lives in a dream world, where fancy reigns supreme. Therefore, when Gautama quotes excerpts from *The Gita* to make her realise the value of existence, she turns away: "I am different from all of you" (117). Maya is different. She is a fractured self striving for re-affirmation and re-discovery of her identity. Maya does not participate in the intellectual life of Gautama. Yet her temperamental discord with Gautama fails to engender an abhorrence for life. For her, the world is still full. Herself intact, she gropes for socio-psychic and psycho-emotional values in a physical and moral world. Her quest for meaning is material, not chimerical. Her identity crisis is more of socio-psychic than of a psycho-ethic nature. Deprived of the sanctions of a harmonious conjugal life, she is out of touch with society—a "tortoise with its limbs withdrawn" (119).

Maya's memory statements made on various occasions carry with them the conviction of her own identity. Her transition from the objective to the subjective and *vice versa* "get short-circuited into self-conscious attitudinising" (Beliappa, 1971: 23). "Only a dream, an illusion. Maya—my very name means nothing, is nothing but an illusion" (172). She is a bird caged, an animal ensnared. So when Nila and her mother want to leave her, she implores them to stay on: "Stay another week. There will be dust storm, it will be cooler [...]" (163).

The image of the dust storm is a significant extension of the dance image. It suggests the infidel storm raging in Maya's subconscious. The raging storm sweeps everything, obliterates and annihilates all vision. It relieves her. It gives her a sense of flying, of being lifted off the earth and into the sunset, release from bondage, release from fate, from death and dreariness and unwanted dreams:

> Here was turmoil, a wild chiaroscuro of oven-hot colours that churned over and over in a heat-swelled bubble around me, it was mine, this life was mine (188).

The storm brings her relief. It gives her the hope of a new life, of survival. The albino's smothering prediction begins to die. Black and bizzare thoughts that bedimmed her vision of life slowly vanish. The dust-storm reveals the true nature of Gautama. It is a pattern she must accept.

Nila, Gautama's sister serves as a foil to Maya. Unlike Maya, Nila falls a prey to marital discord and temperamental incompatibility. She seeks divorce from her husband. Unlike Nila, Maya is emotionally isolated from Gautama but is physically in touch with him. Her neurotic sensibility makes her hysterically aware of the past. The vision of the time trees is enough to make her nostalgically insane. They remind her of Toto. They remind her of Gautama's loneliness which insulates him from her hallucinatory and psycho-neurotic world. Loneliness that produces anguish in Maya provides intellectual and spiritual repose to Gautama. Gautama was "a figure of granite," a repertoire of "books that smelt faintly of mouldy rice and wisdom" (201). Maya recounts her past with regret—deep, hopeless regret. Maya, the domestic outcast and alien housewife wants from Gautama love and passion but what she gets is logic and philosophy and cold sensation. Thus Maya is unable to satisfy her basic human instinct, her biological need. Unable to participate in the world of reality, she seeks in alternative form of gratification by "regression to the phantasies that constructed the psychic reality of the unconscious" (Sayers, 1985: 79). Further Maya's hysterical symptom serves to "recapitulate this form of gratification in somatic form—in a form that is termed 'hysterical' because its basis was not real and organic, but unreal and phantastical" (Sayers, 1985: 79).

Engrossed in a metaphysical world of abstractions, Gautama fails to discern the 'pied beauty' of the world:

> Poor Gautama. Not to be able to notice the odour of limes, not to hear the melancholy voice singing somewhere behind the plantains, not to have time to count the stars as they come out one by one—poor Gautama, my poor, poor husband (206).

Gautama is unable to share a common understanding with Maya whose world is 'full.' Maya's appetite for the real, the close, and the living is insatiable but contrarily Gautama fails to grasp the pulsating richness of life. Maya's obsessive love for the splendid, the colourful, the sensuous and the picturesque in life stands in sharp contrast to Gautama's prosaic aloofness. The outer world serves as an apt objective correlative to Maya's fleeting moods and changing identities. Gautama often talks of the 'basics of life' but fails to apply them to a successful man-woman affinity. "Poor Gautama, poor dear Gautama who was so intense and yet had never lived and never would" (208). Maya and Gautama cherish different interests, ideas and values. What they share is pity and sympathy for one another, though neither shows it. Desai posits this psychic compulsion through the inner mind, the second tract. The temperamental discord between Maya and Gautama symbolises their struggle for survival in a world of competing egos, each defining its own interests. Maya says: "The man had no contact with the world, or with me [...] what would it matter to him? It was I, I who screamed in mute horror" (175). Sunaina Singh observes:

> A young wife left alone the whole day, ignored in the evening and worse, not even allowed to speak, to open herself, and reveal her agony of alienation and isolation: all this leaves Maya agitated, disturbed (1995: 41).

Talking, gesturing, Gautama comes between Maya and the moon, his figure "an ugly, crooked, grey shadow" (208), an extension of the maniac albino, an object of abhorrence for Maya. Her neurosis rises. Her conjugal identity fades. She becomes a liberated self symbolising the dancing Shiva, eager to destroy everything, annihilating everything. Coming in the way of Maya's odysseys, Gautama violates the basic principle of life and love. This violation of the love of life and love of freedom ultimately prompts her to murder her husband in a fit of frenzied fury. Maya is an unstable, self-pitying, spoilt woman who cannot save herself, cannot spare others. After hurling Gautama to death from the edge of the roof, she becomes mentally deranged. Maya is too attached. But she is not involved in life, love and Gautama. She is attached to the fantasy of dreams and delusions, and death. She projects her self-hate onto Gautama. She must live and Gautama must die for he is "so uninvolved with life that he does not savour it—he merely exists" (Sujata, 1993: 48). But hatred is futile. It lives in our mind and haunts us for ever. Logically we may hate a person and annihilate him but memory of him would continue to live on for ever in our mind and become an inalienable part of our thinking self. Hence Maya's killing of Gautama out of sheer hatred fails to bear any fruit as Sartre observes:

> Hate does not enable us to get out of the circle. It simply represents the final attempt, the attempt of despair.

> After the failure of this attempt nothing remains for itself except to re-enter the circle and allow itself to be infinitely tossed (1956: 412).

The murder of Gautama is, in a way, Maya's self-fulfilment and wish-fulfilment. It is the culmination of her psycho-neurosis. Maya is not ready for death. Gautama is. He with his detachment has reached a state of staticity. Maya tries to enter his world, but Gautama is too absorbed in his work to realise that she had "entered the room, had spoken, had left. Could death disturb him then?" (166). The prophecy of the "tenebrific albino or her circumstances are in themselves not a sufficient reason for her to push Gautama off the roof [...] the root of this tragic action lies within her" (20). Like Som Bhaskar, in Arun Joshi's *The Last Labyrinth,* Maya is haunted by death-neurosis. But unlike him, Maya has the fear of death ingrained in her nature. Thus the killing of Gautama is the manifestation of her latent psycho-neurotic urges and compulsions. One remembers Rhoda in Virginia Woolf's *The Waves.* Maya loses her grip over life. She scrambles towards love and attachment to find herself. But fails, since her object of love becomes wooden to her emotional participations and promptings. The self-world relationship is lost. She is frustrated as subject because she is unable to (or she is not allowed to) fulfil herself through her objectives, her desires, and because she fails to involve herself in self-defining activities.

Maya's alienation is human. It is caused by her intermittent psychic confrontations with death and the albino's weird prophecy, and not just by Gautama's apathy and callousness. Her quest for identity is concerned with her mental journeys in the world of reality and in the world of illusion. The albino figures in her world of illusion, Gautama in the world of reality. The clash between Maya and Gautama is a clash between illusion and reality. Their psychic confrontations are attempts at identity assertions, each trying to decipher his or her own identity in the other, the other identity. In dealing with the elements of fantasy and illusion, incertitude and insecurity, *Cry, the Peacock* becomes 'metaphysically evocative' and not 'metaphysically speculative' like Raja Rao's *The Serpent and the Rope.*

Anita Desai depicts in her fiction the dissolution and disintegration of the feminine sensibility in marriage. Marriage, which denotes union of two hearts, simultaneously connotes the split of the feminine self and the consequent alienation of the wife from her husband. Gautama and Maya end up as two facets of the same coin.

Maya's quest for linkage and affiliation becomes intricate on account of two forces at work on her psyche—the strict and orderly world of her father and his blind love for her. Maya does not wholly belong to either of them. Her love for her father is, in due course, transferred to Gautama. In the transaction, she loses her real self. Self-alienation leads to the loss of identity. These "injurious influences," believes Karen Homey, prevent a child from arriving at a just self-estimation. Father's love hampers her growth "from a corn into oak tree" (Homey, 1965: 18). The father in the unconscious restricts her growth into adulthood, and thus alienates her from her real ideal self. "Maya is the sacrifice offered at the altar of his image" (Jain, 1987: 117). Thus, attachment of the father was unreal and affected. Maya's inability to bring about a rapprochement between her childhood world of fantasies and the adult world of realities leads to her socio-psychic disintegration. Her alienation from Gautama remains a feeling, a sensation but not a reality. She is not wholly alienated. She thinks her loneliness is of Gautama's making, but is it so? No, certainly not. Gautama does care. He himself attends to Toto and together, they lift him. Gautama is aware that Maya is unhappy and seared. He is not insensitive to her sorrow. He wipes away her tears and philosophises with her on the merits of emotional intensity. He senses her tension and helps her relax. Their alienation is fragmentary and unenduring. Besides, Gautama in Maya's eyes is a "harmless and guileless being who walked the fresh grass and did not know he touched it" (169). Yet why was there so much tension? R.S. Sharma and Madhusudan Prasad attribute the absence of mutual love and attachment to their marital alienation. Gautama's dry concern makes him blind to Maya's feelings. He lives inside himself. Whereas Maya's love is a powerful ideal, which, despite its illusions and fantasies enlivens our understanding of others. Her love is an emotion, capable of expanding consciousness, enlightening our vision of life. Through Maya, Anita Desai demonstrates how even the noblest impulses like love when pursued and pushed to the extreme can be disastrous and catastrophic. But, as already stated, it is not the lack of love but love itself that tears them apart:

> [...] there were countless nights when I had been tortured by a humiliating sense of neglect or of loneliness, of desperation that would never have existed had I not loved him so much [...] (201).

Maya's compulsive fear and obsessive death-wish manifests in her suicide. They bring about discord in her marital life. Her identity as a housewife is disturbed. Maya's quest for identity is an eternal quest for meaning and value, freedom and truth, in this sad, bad, mad world. It denotes a collective neurosis which shatters the identity of women in our male-dominated patriarchal society where women longing for love and security are driven mad or forced into suicide. Maya's quest thus assumes a universal dimension. It is the alienated self's frantic and frenetic struggle for a socio-psychic release from the drab reality of existence in order to find a voice and a vision, a theme that runs into Desai's second novel, *Voices in the City.*

REFERENCES

1. Beliappa, Meena. *Anita Desai, A Study of Her Fiction.* Calcutta: Writers Workshop, 1971.
2. Benjamin, Jessica. "The Bonds of Love: Rational Violence and Erotic Domination." Ed. Hester Einstein and Jardine. *The Future of Difference.* Boston: Mass, 1980.
3. Beauvoir, Simone de. *The Second Sex.* Ed. and trans. H.M. Parshley. New York: Vintage Books, 1974.
4. Desai, Anita. *Cry, the Peacock.* New Delhi: Orient Paperbacks, 1980. All citations from the text are from this edition of the novel and are followed by page numbers in parentheses.
5. Desai, Anita. "Replies to the Questionnaire." *Kakatiya Journal of English Studies.*
6. Foreman, Ann. "Feminity as Alienation: Women and the Family." *Marxism and Psychoanalysis.* 1977; rpt. London: Pluto Press, 1978 (3.1).
7. Heinemann, F.H. *Existentialism and the Modern Predicament.* London: Adam & Charles Black, 1953.
8. Horney, Karen. *Neurosis and Human Growth.* London: Routledge & Kegan Paul.

9. Jain, Jasbir. *Stairs to the Attic: The Novels of Anita Desai.* 1965; rpt. Jaipur: Printwell, 1987.
10. Jamkhandi, S.R. "The Artistic Effects of the Shifts in Points of View in Anita Desai's *Cry, the Peacock.*" *The Journal of Indian Writing in English,* 9.1 (Jan. 1981).
11. Kapur, Promilla. *Love, Marriage and Sex.* Delhi: Vikas, 1973.
12. Macquarrie, John. *Existentialism.* London: Penguin Books, 1977.
13. Pathak, R.S. "The Alienated Self in the Novels of Anita Desai." Ed. R.K. Dhawan. *The Fiction of Anita Desai.* New Delhi: Bahri, 1971.
14. Raizada, Harish. "The Haunted Protagonists of Anita Desai." Ed. R.K. Srivastava. *Perspectives on Anita Desai.* Ghaziabad: Vimal, 1984.
15. Sartre, Jean Paul. *Being and Nothingness.* (Trans.) Hazel E. Barnes. New York: Philosophical Library, 1956.
16. Sayers, Janet. "Sexual Contradiction: on Freud, Psychoanalysis and Feminism." *Free Associations,* I, 1985.
17. Singh, C.P. "The Visitor and the Exile: A Study in Anita Desai's *Bye-Bye, Blackbird.*" Ed. H.M. Prasad. *Response.* Bareilly: Prakash, 1983.
18. Singh, Sunaina. "The 'Crazy' Ones in Anita Desai and Margaret Atwood." Ed. R.K. Dhawan. *Indian Woman Novelists,* Set-3, Vol. 2. New Delhi: Prestige, 1995.
19. Sujatha, S. "The Theme of Disintegration: A Comparative Study of Anita Desai's *Cry, the Peacock* and Bharati Mukherjee's *Wife.*" *The Commonwealth Review,* 4.2 (1993-94).
20. Tong, Rosemarie. *Feminist Thought.* London: Routledge, 1993.

20

Indian Life and Sensibility in the Short Stories of Margaret Chatterjee and Anita Desai: A Comparative Study

R.K. MATHUR

Margaret Chatterjee and Anita Desai are two well-known Indian writers in English who have also written short stories. Both are women and both are endowed with poetic imagination. While Margaret Chatterjee is an English woman who married an Indian and settled down in India, Anita Desai, though by birth an Indian, is in fact only half Indian and half foreigner by blood, for her father was an Indian, her mother a German. The object of this paper is, therefore, to make a study of the short stories of this interesting pair of writers with a view to assessing their Indianness, that is, how much of Indian life they are able to depict and how much Indian sensibility they reveal, and comparing their achievements and limitations.

Before embarking upon a discussion of these two writers, it will be proper to define the term "sensibility." M.H. Abrams defines it thus: "When a modern critic talks of a poet's sensibility, he refers to his characteristic way of responding, in sensation, thought and feeling, to experience' (173). If, therefore, a writer's characteristic way of responding to experience is that of a typical Indian, he may be regarded as possessing Indian sensibility, and the possession of Indian sensibility presupposes not only full familiarity, but also empathy, with Indian thought and culture. In short, the ethos of a writer with Indian sensibility is Indian. In a literary work, Indian sensibility of a writer in English manifests itself in Indian themes, characterization, settings, mythological allusions, values and philosophical stances, and even in words and phrases.

Margaret Chatterjee is essentially a poet who has written short stories as well. Before publishing her collection of short stories in 1973, Mrs Chatterjee had already published her three anthologies of poetry, *The Spring and the Spectacle* (1967), *Towards the Sun* (1970) and *The Sandal-wood Tree* (1972). These poems reveal her increasing love for India culminating in her complete identification with her, calling her "my land," "my India" (23). A very large portion of the corpus of her poetry is about India—her life and culture, religion and philosophy, seasons and natural environment. And her treatment of Indian life is marked by love and sympathy. So deeply is she imbued with the spirit of India that she categorically declares in an interview to O.P. Mathur: "I am completely assimilated in India and feel unhappy if anyone considers me a foreigner." This is no exaggeration, for its truth is amply borne out by her poetry.

Unlike the short stories of most other Indian writers in English, those of Mrs Chatterjee are a by-product of her poetry-workshop, as is evident from the fact that all of her stories, except one ('Kalidasa and City Lights'), were written between the early sixties and 1973, when she also published her three anthologies of poetry. In her, the poet and the short story writer are inseparable, for the same Indian sensibility as that which is revealed in her poetry is revealed in her short stories also. Moreover, her poetic imagination is at work in her short stories as well. She herself is fully aware of their interrelationship: "[...] there are many links between my poetry and short stories. Poems could be written on some situations contained in my short stories and the themes and characters of some of my poems could have been developed in short stories. In both my poetry and my stories I have tried to make my style condensed and distilled and not diffuse."

Unlike Margaret Chatterjee, Anita Desai is essentially a novelist who has written short stories also. Before publishing her collection of short stories in 1978, she had to her credit the publication of five novels, *Cry, the Peacock* (1963), *Voices in the City* (1965), *Bye-Bye, Blackbird* (1971), *Where Shall We*

Go This Summer? (1975) and *Fire on the Mountain* (1977). As a novelist she is more concerned with the inner world of the individuals than with the outer world of society or nation they are part of. That is, instead of focusing on social or political problems, she mostly prefers to present psychologically delineated characters. In this respect she contrasts sharply with her contemporary woman novelist, Nayantara Sahgal, who is primarily a political novelist.

Though Mrs Desai as she tells Jasbir Jain, finds the short story form "much less satisfying" than the novel, she began to write short stories as early as her college days. And the interest in psychological study of characters which distinguishes her novels, also characterizes her short stories, though they do not offer scope for full-length psychographs as the novels do. Consequently, the short stories contain miniature portraits, the largest being that of Pat, the American woman, in her story "Scholar and Gypsy." Her Novels and short stories are also interrelated through the presence of similar ideas or scenes in both of them. For example, the scene of very tender and intense, almost divine, love between an extremely beautiful, young, fatally anaemic, or fatally tubercular, *"borkha"* clad, Muslim woman and a very old man that Suno the protagonist in the story "Studies in the Park" (30-31) sees and which revolutionizes his emotionally-starved life occurs also in the novel, *Where Shall We Go This Summer*? and is seen by its heroine, Sita, who is also emotionally starved, and is in dire need of such love (145-47).

Both Mrs Chatterjee and Mrs Desai portray in their short stories typically Indian middle-class families living in the traditional manner. Mrs Chatterjee's stories, "The Lantern," "A Happy New Year," "Tapan's Mother," "All Men Are Mortal" and "Keys," contain good descriptions of middle-class families. "The Lantern" presents an old women's reminiscences of her childhood days who feels a nostalgia for the vanishing of the joint-family system, a system which has been an integral part of Indian culture. It also refers to a wife's devotion to her husband, who would lay meals for him and fan him while he ate. "A Happy New Year" is a humorous dramatization of a domestic scene.

Through natural witty dialogues of the characters, it depicts a typically Indian family with a large number of members—Grandmother, Father, Mother, Uncle, and a number of children, and all respectful and obedient to the eldest member of the family, *Thakurma*, whose decision is peremptory. "In Tapan's Mother" again it is through the reminiscences of a character that the life of a middle-class family is depicted. In "All Men are Mortal," the description of the daily chores of Grandmother is that of the daily chores of a typical elderly woman of an Indian household who always remains busy with domestic work, thinking that she is indispensable, that without her the whole domestic establishment will collapse. Again, the feast which the protagonist of the story gives is in the traditional Indian style, that is, the guests take off their sandals, wash their hands, and sit on the floor, and food is served to them in *thalis.* "Keys" focuses on the symbolic value of keys in the life of a married woman. The swinging of a bunch of keys tied to the corner of her sari thrown over her shoulder symbolizes that the wearer of the sari has been handed over full control of the household by her mother-in-law. This is a typically Indian custom.

Mrs Desai's stories, "Private Tuition by Mr Bose," "Studies in the Park," "Surface Textures," "Sale," "A Devoted Son," and "Pigeons at Daybreak," depict the life of Indian middle-class families. "Private Tuition" portrays in a humorous vein the domestic life of a middle-class Indian, Mr Bose, who earns his living by giving private tuition. It depicts the love and consideration of Mr and Mrs Bose for each other. At the same time it also presents a "scene of domestic anarchy" once created by Mrs Bose's jealousy. But it is soon replaced by a scene of domestic happiness. The reconciliation is brought about by Mrs Bose's frying hot *purees* for Mr Bose and coaxing him to eat more, one more, as though the extra *puree* were a peace-offering following her rebellion of half-an-hour ago, and the reciprocation of the gesture by him by coaxing her to take one more *puree,* just one more. In "Studies" the attitude of the protagonist's father to the education of his son is that of a typical middle-class Indian who educates his son with a view to enabling him to get a good job: "You must get a first, Suno, [...] must get a first, or else you won't get a job [...].

Must get a job, Suno [...]" (28). In "Surface Textures," the protagonist's wife reveals in her frugality, in her consciousness of avoiding to buy what is expensive, an attitude characteristic of an Indian middle-class housewife. Her use of *kum-kum* that daily 'cuts' a gash of red colour "from one end of her scalp to the other" (37) is also something uniquely Indian. In "Sale," the description of the poor artist's wife kneading dough in a brass bowl, with her head bowed and her long hair brooding down to her shoulders, and her child sitting beside her playing with a spoon, is a slice of middle-class life in India. "A Devoted Son" portrays a model of filial piety which is not uncommon in middle-class families. The protagonist, Rakesh, when he learns of his success in the examination, touches his father's feet, as is the Indian custom. "Pigeons at Daybreak" depicts the devotion of a true Indian wife to her valetudinarian husband. Despite the fact that her husband "seemed to her" "foolish and unreasonable" (102) in his sickness, she looked after him sincerely.

But while Mrs Chatterjee confines herself to the portrayal of the traditional middle-class families, Mrs Desai has a wider range and portrays also the upper-class Indian families living in a highly westernized manner, though her attitude to this type of life is that of disapproval. The lack of human sympathy, artificiality, and snobbery of the upper-class have been brought into sharp focus by her, in the story "The Farewell Party," by juxtaposing the two sessions of a party given by Mr Raman on his transfer. The first session is characterized by a demonstration of superficial and perfunctory emotions by the guests at his transfer, and its atmosphere is marked by boisterous revelry and lack of inhibition, children playing the Western music, the new Beatles record, and "making themselves tipsy on Fanta and Coca-Cola, the girls giggling [...] and the boys swaggering around the record-player (90). In sharp contrast to it, the atmosphere in the second is marked by more human sympathy, intimacy, and sobriety. Music is again there—but not of the Western "Beatles" or "Chubby Checkers" record! This time it is the sweetest and saddest songs, Indian songs, of Tagore, sung in heart-broken tones by an Indian. The Westernized and artificial life of the rich is again condemned in her story "Scholar and Gypsy," but in this case through an American woman, Pat, who regards them as "not civilized" (110).

Mrs Desai's range is wider also in the sense that it is not limited to a portrayal of outward life, but includes a psychological study of the characters. Her short stories such as "Games at Twilight," "Pineapple Cake," and "Studies in the Park" are studies in child psychology. Moreover, she delineates characters not only of normal human beings but also of abnormal ones, such as that of Harish, in "Surface Textures," who has a mania for gazing at and feeling surface textures of things. She also portrays the eccentricities of old age in "The Devoted Son."

The characters and settings of the stories of both the writers are Indian. But both of them have introduced in some of their stories foreign characters as well. In Mrs Chatterjee's story "Encounter," the Indian-English encounter is not a confrontation but an opportunity of mutual understanding and sympathy producing the feeling of oneness between persons of two different nations, and thus refuting Kipling's dictum about their immiscibility: "Oh, East is East and West is West, and never the twain shall meet." And in her story entitled "Pahari Story," the English woman, Katharine, identifies herself with the hill people so completely that it is impossible for her to return to England and, therefore, she tells her servant: "There will be no packing tomorrow, Abdul, Miss Sahib will not be going, she too is a Pahari, don't forget" (18). Again an Indian's encounter with a Frenchman in her story "The Excursion" also shows great intimacy and love between an Indian woman, Gita, and a French priest, Paul. They playfully tease each other—Paul calling her his Krishna (guiding him as Lord Krishna did Arjuna), and she imitating a French guide. Paul says he would not go back from India if he were only "permitted to stay" (56). Commenting on their emotional relationship, the author suggestively observes, "A priest cannot love more, because he has to give his love to many. But so many men love less" (56). However, the Indian-American encounter is in a different key as it reveals their difference and misunderstanding. For example, in her story "The Last Book," the American regards not only India but the whole of East as "mysterious," a notion frowned upon by the young Indian woman. The treatment of Indian-American encounter by Mrs Desai also emphasizes the difference between the two nations, but at the same time it indicates that India has something to offer an American who is disillusioned with her present life. In her story "Scholar and Gypsy," the American woman, Pat, leaves her husband to become a hippie, and ultimately a Buddhist, and to live in a commune in Manali in India.

Besides urban life, Mrs Chatterjee gives a vivid picture of rural life. Her story, "Chokra," contains a graphic description of life in an Indian village. Mrs Desai, whose stories deal essentially with urban life, too gives in her story, "Surface Textures," a glimpse of the credulous and superstitious nature of Indian villagers who have great faith in the spiritual power of sannyasis and worship them blindly.

Both Mrs Chatterjee and Mrs Desai refer to Indian religion and mythology in their stories. Mrs Chatterjee makes a reference to "Vyasa the sage [...] dictating the *Mahabharata* to Ganesh" (29) in the story "A Happy New Year"; to Krishna and Arjuna in "The Excursion," and to the pilgrimage to the holy shrine of Badrinath in "Who Are We to Judge?" Though these references show her familiarity with Hindu mythology, she does not deal with any religious theme in detail in her stories. On the other hand, Mrs Desai not only refers to Hindu gods and ancient Buddhist texts such as the *Dhammapada* but also shows the deep impact of Buddhism on the life of one of her major characters, as has already been mentioned above.

According to Venugopal, thanks to the pioneering work of Mulk Raj Anand and Raja Rao, the Indian short-story writer in English has achieved considerable success in evolving an idiom that can "communicate the Indian scene fully and faithfully," (115) "convey nuances of Indian thought and culture" (56) adequately. Some of the important devices used for this purpose by the pioneers are (1) "literal translations of typical Indian expressions" (56) and (2) "Interpolation of [...] vernacular words" (57). Both Mrs Chatterjee and Mrs Desai use Indian words in their stories to evoke local colour. But Mrs Desai uses them more sparingly than Mrs Chatterjee. Moreover, Mrs Desai neither uses Indian phrases nor literally translates Indian expressions into English. Her use of Indian words is restricted mostly to nouns—names of Indian dishes, dresses, musical instruments, games, and certain other things which cannot be expressed with precision by using their English equivalents. She relies more on the technique of paying attention to details to achieve realism and to create the necessary atmosphere in her stories. On the other hand, Mrs Chatterjee, besides paying attention to details, exploits fully both the devices mentioned above for evoking local colour and suggesting the cultural backgrounds of her characters. She frequently resorts to the use of dialogue in place of narration to depict Indian environment more vididly. A good example of this is her short story, "A Happy New Year." Consequently, her short stories, especially those depicting domestic life of Indian middle-class families, are more deeply steeped in Indian sensibility than those of Mrs Desai.

As Mrs Chatterjee is a poet, her short stories abound in poetic descriptions: who but a poet would think of identifying herself with the "flickering life of a flame in the lantern" (20), or of comparing the tapered carved legs of a *charpoy* to the "waists of the sculptured dancing figures outside the temple" (6). And Mrs Desai, though not a poet, is gifted with poetic imagination. The following passage from her story "Games at Twilight" is a fine specimen of her poetic description of a typically Indian summer afternoon, and deserves to be quoted *in extenso:*

> It was too hot. Too bright. The white walls of the veranda glared stridently in the sun. The bougainvillea hung about it, purple and magenta, in livid balloons. The garden outside was like a tray made of beaten brass, flattened out on the red gravel and the stony soil in all shades of metal—aluminium, tin, copper and brass. No life stirred at this arid time of day the birds still dropped, like dead fruit, in the papery—tents of the trees; some squirrels lay limp on the wet earth under the garden tap. The outdoor dog lay stretched as if dead on the veranda mat, his paws and ears and tail all reaching out like dying travellers in search of water. He rolled his eyes at the children—two white marbles rolling in purple sockets, begging for sympathy—and attempted to

> lift his tail in a wag but could not. It only twitched and lay still (1-2).

To sum up, the study reveals that the short stories of both the writers reflect their Indian sensibility in themes, characterization, settings and language. Both are upholders of Indian values. For example, the characters in Margaret Chatterjee's stories believe in non-violence, as Torubala Devi in "At the Homeopath's; in the joint family system; as *Thakurma* in "The Lantern"; and the efficacy of a pilgrimage to a holy shrine, as Kalicharan's mother in "Who Are We to Judge?" And those in Anita Desai's stories are critical of Westernized life and culture of the upper-class Indians. But while the stories of Mrs Desai have a wider range of themes as well as of characters, those of Mrs Chatterjee are more deeply steeped in Indian sensibility. Her characters are more authentic as they are based on real persons, for instance, she herself is the prototype of Katharine in her story "Pahari Story." On the other hand, Mrs Desai herself says in Jain's interview that though "the minor and incidental characters" she has "picked from real life," "I don't think any of the major characters in my books are taken from real life. They are entirely imaginary or an amalgamation of several different characters." Both Mrs Chatterjee and Mrs Desai use Indian words in their stories to evoke local colour, but the former uses them more lavishly than the latter. Furthermore, Mrs Chatterjee literally translates Indian expressions into English, a practice which not only makes her descriptions more vivid and realistic but also reveals how deeply she has imbibed Indian spirit and culture. What a contrast both of them offer to their contemporary woman short story writer Ruth Prawer Jhabvala, a foreigner who married an Indian! Iyengar reports that she lived in India for some years, but always like a foreigner, and ultimately left this country of "heat and dust" in sheer disgust, declaring frankly: "My husband is Indian, and so are my children. I am not, and less so every year" (742).

REFERENCES

1. Abrahams, M.H. *A Glossary of Literary Terms,* 4th ed. (1981; rpt. New York: Holt-Saunders Japan, 1984).
2. Chatterjee, Margaret. *At the Homeopath's* and *Other Stories* (Calcutta: Writers' Workshop, 1973).

3. Chatterjee, Margaret. *Towards the Sun* (Calcutta: Writers' Workshop. 1970).
4. Quoted in O.P. Mathur, "An Interview with Margaret Chatterjee," *The Journal of Indian Writing in English,* II, No. 2 (July 1983).
5. "Kalidasa and the City Lights," Indian Literature, No. 112 (Mar.-Apr. 1986), 100-02.
6. Quoted in O.P. Mathur, "The Short Stories of Margaret Chatterjee: An Interview" (December 1987), *The Modern Indian English Fiction* (New Delhi: Abhinav Publications, 1993).
7. Desai, Anita. *Games at Twilight and Other Stories* (Bombay: Allied Publishers Private Limited, 1978).
8. Quoted in Jasbir Jain's Interview with Anita Desai on 16th November 1979. Jasbir Jain, *Stairs to the Attic: The Novels of Anita Desai* (Jaipur: Printwell Publishers, 1987), 13.
9. Desai, Anita. *Where Shall We Go This* Summer? (1975; rpt. Delhi: Orient Paperbacks, 1982).
10. C.V. Venugopal. *The Indian Short Story in English* (A Survey) (Bareilly: Prakash Book Depot, 1976).
11. London Magazine, Sept. 1970. Quoted in K.R. Srinivasa Iyengar, *Indian Writing in English,* 5th ed. (1985; rpt. New Delhi: Sterling Publishers Private Limited, 1990).